D1564376

Person and Polis

Political Theory: Contemporary Issues
John G. Gunnell, Editor

Person and Polis:

Max Scheler's Personalism as Political Theory

Stephen Frederick Schneck

State University of New York Press • Albany

Published by
State University of New York Press, Albany

© 1987   State University of New York

For information, address State University of New York
Press, State University Plaza, Albany, N.Y., 12246

Library of Congress Cataloging in Publication Data

Schneck, Stephen Frederick, 1953-
    Person and polis.

    (SUNY series in political theory.   Contemporary issues)
    Bibliography: p.
    Includes index.
    1. Scheler, Max, 1874–1928--Contributions in political
science.   2. Political science--Philosophy.   3. Political
psychology.   4. Personalism.   I. Title.   II. Series.
JC263.S252S36   1987   302'.01   86-23014
ISBN 0-88706-340-3
ISBN 0-88706-339-X (pbk.)

10   9   8   7   6   5   4   3   2   1

Contents

"The supreme despair," wrote Kierkegaard, "is not to feel desperate."

One can no longer tell what man is, and as we watch him today undergoing such astonishing transformations, some think there is no such thing as human nature. For some people this idea becomes translated into "everything is *possible* for man," and in that they find some hope; for others, "everything is *permissible* to man," and with that they abandon all restraint; for others, finally, "everything is *permissible against* man," and with that we have arrived at Buchenwald. All the games that might divert us from our disarray have lost their savor, or have been indulged in to satiety. . . . The religious lunacy which worships the God of philosophers and bankers would indeed justify us in proclaiming that God is dead, if indeed that idol were he. Could we only have a little respite from the wars, to carry on with our technical miracles, then, glutted with comfort, we should then be able to declare that happiness was dead. Another fourteenth century, as it were, crumbling away before our eyes: the time for "a second Renaissance" is at hand.

Emmanuel Mounier
Personalism

Acknowledgements and Dedication

AX SCHELER insightfully revealed that the person as an individual emerges only within a circle of other persons in sociality. This is a keen insight. Although the limitations of the following study are entirely mine, what if any credit it deserves must be shared among many. The Office of Advanced Studies of the University of Notre Dame and the Deutscher Akademischer Austauschdienst provided the vital financial support necessary for completing this study's research at the Scheler Archive of the Bayerische Staatsbibliothek in Munich. Professor Manfred Frings of De Paul University, editor of Scheler's *Nachlass*, kindly offered permission to examine portions of the archive and on more than one occasion has clarified key points of Scheler's thought. Special thanks are due the three anonymous reviewers whose careful reading of this study for the State University of New York Press proved so valuable for its final form.

More personally, I am deeply indebted and grateful to Fred R. Dallmayr, Dee Professor of Government of the University of Notre Dame. This work plainly owes much of its inspiration to Professor Dallmayr's own penetrating studies of the character of the political subject and political intersubjectivity. I thank my wife, Patricia. Sharing my failures and rejoicing in each modest triumph, she has fully borne the burdens which accompanied the completion of this research. Finally, I thank my parents whose hands I ever see behind my own.

In 1955, with the birth of my brother, my father was forced to forego the completion of his own education in order to support us. This book is dedicated to him in thankfulness for that sacrifice.

S.F.S.

Introduction

RAWING UPON THE WORKS of Continental philosophy and social theory from the present century, a growing number of political theorists are rejecting the still predominant understandings of politics as either being the interplay of autonomous agents or the result of a confluence of various contingent factors. An almost classical sense of politics as "praxis" is achieving increasing acceptance. The practical character of politics is emerging as the shared touchstone, the point of consensus among these otherwise diverse thinkers. Praxis is the meeting ground of the way things are and the way things could be, the junction of being and becoming, inescapably structured by both, which is somehow closely identified with being human. It is defined as an "acting within the world."[1] Avoiding the illusion of standing apart from the world of everyday existence, and avoiding the delusion of being utterly submerged in the world of everyday existence, praxis is acting, with acceptance and awareness, as part of the context of such existence.

Attempting to sketch an outline of a political theory based on Max Scheler's understanding of the "person," the following research, it is hoped, may add to or sharpen certain aspects of the contemporary turn toward praxis. Scheler stands in the vanguard of those philosophers and social thinkers whose combined influence has led political theorists in the direction of greater sensitivity for the eminently "practical" character of politics. For a variety of reasons, however, enormously insightful and suggestive elements of his thinking have lain dormant since his 1928 death in Weimar Germany. Yet, it is the contention of this study that the *Person*, as understood in Scheler's personalism, suggests a new ground on which to understand the political subject and the political community so as to outline a politics and political theory which transform the ego-based politics

1

of modern liberalism and Marxism. This is personalism as political theory.

In the most basic sense, personalism as political theory finds the be-all and end-all of politics to be the "person." Yet, it is not the legacy of Descartes which here is celebrated. Personalism is not a mere restatement of the *cogito*, an absolutization of the subject. Its stress is not on the individual ego, not on the thinking or willing subject. Scheler's person is a transcendental unity of *acts within the world*. Beyond understanding in terms of simply "subject," in the Cartesian or even Husserlian sense, the person is inseparable from the context of the world and others.[2] All this is reminiscent of current interpretations of many of the oldest traditions of political thought. Aristotle refers to man as a political animal, as a *zoon politikon*. In the *Nicomachean Ethics* and the *Politics*, he presents politics as a practical affair of persons within the polis, persons who thereby share a common perception and a common sphere of experience. Persons are full persons only in light of this shared perspective and in light of their embeddedness in the practical, political world. The practice of politics enables the development, the "becoming," of the person and the polis itself. Beyond the embrace of this practical realm, the person is an impossibility. Beyond the polis, as Aristotle states, there could exist only beasts or gods. Although profoundly different in other regards, the personalism of Max Scheler, *as political theory*, reveals a similar sensitivity for politics as praxis. Neither god nor beast, the person is seen neither as standing above the context of everyday existence nor as wholly identified with this context. The person is manifestly a practical being of the practical world.

If personalism as political theory, however, is reminiscent of politics as praxis in the classical sense, it is more than merely a reinterpretation of the ancient theories. The classical conception is vastly and qualitatively altered in Scheler's personalism in at least two very basic regards. *First*, although the person is never considered in terms of the individual ego, the concept nevertheless incorporates certain emphases on the person as developed in the Judeo-Christian and Western humanist traditions. *Second*, the person in Scheler's thought must be perceived as essentially and existentially a historical being. While somewhat evidenced in classical thought, the consideration given these points in Scheler's philosophy is such that his understanding of the person is substantially different. In the first is revealed what Scheler would refer to as the inherent dignity of the person. In the second, the person's individual and social development in history is lent a radically deeper existential context than the political *animal* of Aristotle, while being at the same time less than the full *political* agent Aristotle portrayed. More deeply incarnate within the context of the existential and historical world than the ancients believed, in Scheler's estimation the person is also possessed of a dignity derived from *extra*-political sources.

Where the ancients' understanding is radically antithetical to modern paradigm of politics, personalism as political theory only intensifies the antitheses. In the personalist and the classical conception, politics and persons are reciprocally "grounded." More than symbiotically interrelated, person and polity attain their respective full realities only as aspects of a process of becoming in which both partake. A truly political life is thus a communion of persons, and persons emerge only within the practices and discourses of political life. In losing sight, therefore, of either the person or the truly political life, what passes for either—is neither. This is precisely the charge which Scheler raises against political thought of the modern era; more implicitly, this is also the charge inherent in the nature of classical political thought and the contemporary turn toward praxis. If Aristotle is correct, the loss of polity and person leaves only beasts and "gods."

The dominant varieties of modern political theory do little to disconfirm the implications drawn from Aristotle. Politics and persons in modern political theories, as if following the division between the thinking subject and the extended world elaborated during the transition to modern thought, are denied grounds for the fundamental linkage which is vital in the understanding of the ancients, in Schelerian philosophy, and in the turn toward praxis. As a result, modern political thought preponderantly presents both politics and persons either in isolation from the context of existence or in complete submergence within this context. The political theories of the rationalists, voluntarists and romanticists picture the political actor and his actions as endowed with almost godlike freedom from contingent constraints on reason, or will, or history. Whether the actor in such visions is possessed of a reasoning able to transcend the limits of the body and its situation in time and place or of a will similarly accoutered, it is agreed here that man is somehow, in some part, greater than history, greater than nature and greater than the demands of the here and now. In like fashion, naturalism, historicism and nihilism are construed in political theories where the "praxis" sense of politics is lost in a morass of differing contingencies and causalities, where the political actor and his actions are undifferentiated from the rhythms of the surrounding world—natural, historical or ontological. Naturalism, thus, reduces the actor and his actions to the interactions of hormones or enzymes, ecosystem stimuli or genetics. Historicism finds the actor and his actions to be particular manifestations resultant from the experiences of individual psychological development, or group standings and traditions, or more indistinct features of social and individual history. Nihilism, the ultimate reduction, effectively erases the significance of both actor and action by equating both with nothingness. It seems, therefore, as interpreted in political theories, the general currents in modern conceptions of human activity have been a series of rejections of the practical character of politics; their effect has been a blinding to the reality of politics as an acting within the world.

More currently, the cutting edge of research in the investigation and appraisal of the sphere of human activity lies in what is variously called "post-structuralism," "deconstruction," and, generally, "anti-humanism." Scheler's deep and pervasive concern with the person, with life and spirit, would surely find a suspicious reception among such writers. Charged with the all-important task of charting a responsible course between the Scylla of subjectivity and the Charybdis of objectivity, the quaint Schelerian concern with comprehending the problematic which is man in the contemporary age may be lost upon such writers whose ever-narrower and more mundane visions of ontology leave scant room for "man's place in the cosmos." Scheler, however, is deserving of genuine attention. To be sure, he takes his first and final bearings from what is human and personal, and he admits that a *"conclusion* as to the true attributes of the *ultimate source* of all things can only be drawn by *starting from* the picture of the essence of man."[3] Perhaps in so doing he steers too closely to the maelstrom of subjectivity. However, there is none of Narcissus' vanity in Scheler's approach; he seeks to reveal man in the full range of his existence and promise. Terming his philosophy the *"open hand,"* a veiled allusion perhaps to Nietzsche's closed one, Scheler painstakingly endeavors to clarify and continually reclarify the image of man in his totality.[4] At the very least, Scheler's is a quiet reminder to those charged with the all-important task of our times that there remain *two* whirlpools—subjectivism and objectivism. He holds out the possibility of a mode of inquiry and concern regarding man and man's condition which could be more than a system of cloaked and furtive manipulation. In an era held hostage to the all-too-human threat of an end to man and history, Scheler gently shakes us from any bemused fascination with notions that our responsibilities are somehow other than *our* responsibilities.

These sentiments underscore the purpose of this study, a purpose which aspires to more than Schelerian scholarship. The subtitle of the study, ''Max Scheler's Personalism as Political Theory,'' captures the primary focus of its research, but it does not well convey the interpretive quality of the work. The study is not a review of the ideological positions taken by Scheler in his few political essays, nor a representation of his political philosophy, such as it is. Rather, it is an attempt to take his ''personalism'' as a basis for a contemporary theory of politics—one which stands at some distance from modern liberalism, conservativism and Marxism, both in their bourgeois and Enlightenment varieties.

This personalism, moreover, does not easily find a place with the philosophies which the history of philosophy has lumped under the rubric of that label. It is very much unlike the personalism of medieval scholasticism and, despite intriguing affinities, unlike the existentialist personalism of Mounier, Marcel, Camus and the like. Scheler's personalism has its roots in that same, rich admixture of life philosophy and phenomenology which gave rise to Martin Heidegger's early philosophy. It is a philosophical anthropology founded on Scheler's own realist phenomenology, sociology of knowledge and non-formal ethics. In this study, the attempt has been made to interpret Scheler's concept of *Person*—a concept akin to Heidegger's *Dasein* and Nietzsche's ''will to power''—as the cornerstone for a fresh understanding of political subject and object, the polis and the theory and practice of politics. Its conclusion posits the possibility of a ''post-modern'' politics which turns on the inestimable value and non-objectifiable dignity of the human person.

Although the study finds in personalism as political theory at some odds with specific political positions taken by Max Scheler, it nonetheless adheres tightly to his philosophy in spirit and method. Scheler's thinking comes at a crucial turning point in Western intellectual history and its impact, as a result, has been far-reaching. Among social and political theorists his influence extends to writers as diverse as Dietrich von Hildebrand, Maurice Merleau-Ponty, Karol Wojtyla, Jürgen Habermas and Ernst Block. Martin Heidegger acclaimed him as one of the foremost philosophers of the age, a most potent philosophical force, and an intellect of the first magnitude.[5] Hannah Arendt, Eric Voegelin, Hans-Georg Gadamer, Carl Friedrich, Herbert Marcuse and Alfred Schutz all testify to the lasting value Scheler's thought has offered their own work and to the profound impact he wielded upon that marvelous generation of thinkers which germinated between the wars in German universities. In an indirect manner, this study joins an emerging renaissance of interest in Scheler's work, a renaissance evident from the rebirth of political theory in Poland, to the turn to language and philosophical anthropology among critical theorists, to the renewed interest of social scientists in phenomenology and the sociology of knowledge.

Yet, the intent of this research is not so much to reintroduce political theory to the insights of Max Scheler's thought as it is to suggest the fundamentals of a new political theory. Indeed, in so doing, certain limitations to Scheler's personalism become evident. Troubling ambiguities are uncovered which raise vexing difficulties for personalism as "political" theory. The study concludes by addressing these ambiguities, reconsidering troubling aspects of Scheler's personalism and briefly outlining grounds for possible resolution. Still, the core of this personalist theory—the inestimable value, intersubjective character and non-objectifiability of the human person—remains regarded as a worthy and even requisite starting point for a new politics and political vision.

Perhaps Scheler ought not be approached, therefore, as a curious specimen in a bottle. That is, he ought not be labelled phenomenologist, or *Lebensphilosoph*, or proto-existentialist, or philosophical anthropologist, and locked into the appropriate shelf in the cabinet of the history of ideas. Rather, the best of Scheler's farseeing thought ought to be taken-up, critically considered and thereby reanimated in the discourse of present day political theory. This, at least, is the author's hope. Yet, it seems that Martin Heidegger was more prophetic than any would have believed when, in a memorial lecture within days of Scheler's untimely death in 1928, he spoke: "Max Scheler is dead. We bow our heads before his destiny. Yet again, a way of philosophy falls into darkness."[6] The presience of Heidegger's eulogy is incontestable in retrospect. Sadly, although many would concur with Heidegger's remarks which designated Scheler as "the most potent philosophical power in present day Germany—nay, in present day Europe—even in all of contemporary philosophy," his works fell into the darkness of the ensuing years.[7] Jewish on his mother's side, the election and capturing of power by the National Socialists saw Scheler's works placed under censor and saw scholarship on Scheler research prohibited. Scheler's library, correspondence, and many of his unpublished manuscripts were destroyed by the British aerial bombardment of Cologne in 1944.[8] Although the world more then ever confirmed his suspicions regarding the failure of modern societies and politics, Scheler's own penetrating insights into these matters have been only slowly rediscovered.[9]

In part, too, perhaps the slow rediscovery of Scheler's thought reflects the historical tenor of his works. Pre-eminently a philosopher and intellectual of *engagement*, he is embroiled in the turbulence of the Weimar years. Born near Munich in 1874, his mother was Jewish and closely related with the most prominent Munich Jewish families of the period.[10] His father, a Protestant from an agricultural background who had previously managed a Hungarian estate belonging to Bavarian royalty, had—by the time the young Scheler knew him—experienced severe financial setbacks and was living out his days in a cloud of resigned despondency. Scheler, as a result, was apparently raised as a Jew by his doting mother in the Munich home of her brother. Somewhat undisciplined in school, during his *Gymnasium* years Scheler attended various special institutions which had reputations for working with the spoiled and lazy.

His university education was begun at Munich with the study of psychology and philosophy. Within the first year of his studies he switched to the field of medicine. Ostensibly to continue his medical studies, Scheler transferred to Berlin in 1895, though it now seems apparent that romantic interests played a large part in this decision. Curiously, (and fortunately for philosophy and political theory) it was not the pursuit of medical knowledge, but philosophy and sociology that became the focus of his studies at this time. Although Berlin during this period was gradually becoming more than a Prussian capital and was beginning to acquire the cosmopolitan ambience of an important international metropolis, it was at the same time increasingly acquiring the more gloomy aspects of modernity. The stark contrast between the Berlin of 1900 and Scheler's Munich must certainly have made a strong impression on his appraisal of his era, formal ''Prussianisms'' coupled with the brightest and darkest of the industrial revolution versus *Gemütlichkeit* and tradition. At the university, the air was laden with the intoxication of intellectual ferment, although such ferment seems to have only partly permeated the institute of philosophy. While the lectures of Dilthey and Simmel appear to have made a lifelong impression on the young Scheler,

Wilhelm Stern and others have reported that the driest of logical analysis and Machian-style positivism dominated the philosophical atmosphere of Berlin at this period.[11] It is little surprising, therefore, when after three years in Berlin Scheler transferred to the small university town of Jena, where under the life philosopher, Rudolf Eucken, he completed his studies. The study of philosophy in Jena at this period was vaguely divided and inter-mixed with Eucken's spiritual life philosophy on one hand and Otto Liebman's "back to Kant" Kantianism on the other. Additionally, Rudolf Steiner and his mysticism were also some small part of the Jena intellectual atmosphere, as were the legacies of Goethe and Hegel. Eucken's influence on the development of Scheler's thought is unmistakeable, although Scheler hesitated but a few years before breaking with many of the transcendental aspects of his teacher's thought.

Scheler's doctoral thesis under Eucken, *Beiträge zur Festellung der Beziehungen zwischen den logischen und ethischen Prinzipien*, primarily contends that although logic and ethics are correlative and parallel in direction, they are nonetheless not interdependent, but mutually independent.[12] While this position is later rejected by Scheler, his understanding of the "extra-rational" intuition of values which is fundamental in his subsequently developed ethical theory is embryonically evident in even this early work. Following completion of his doctoral thesis at Jena, Scheler studied for a year at Heidelberg, working on his *Habilitationschrift* and gaining a close acquaintance with Max Weber's cultural studies. Evidencing Weber's influence, Scheler's first published work, "Arbeit und Ethik," also demonstrates the direction in which his thought was traveling—i.e., toward understanding cognition and rational evaluation amidst a context of concrete human practices.[13] Although less borne out in his *Habilitationschrift*, the publishing of which allowed Scheler to return to Jena in 1899 as a teacher under Eucken, even with this work it is evident that Scheler is gradually distancing himself from more Kantian elements incorporated in Eucken's own philosophy.[14] Entitled *Die transzendentale und die psychologische Methode*, the work demonstrates the growing rejection of psychologism common among a number of philosophers of this period, but it also reveals a modest retrenchment from Eucken's concept of man's transcendental freedom from any measure of psychic determination. The important year 1899 also marks a short-lived conversion to Catholicism and a subsequent marriage in Munich to the older, divorced woman with whom he had been romantically involved in his earlier move to Berlin.

Scheler's turn in the direction of understanding man within the context of man's practices was greatly intensified in 1901 with his meeting Edmund Husserl at a Kant Society gathering hosted by Hans Vaihinger in Halle. Here begins his phenomenology. Although the similarities and differences between Scheler and Husserl will be considered in substantial detail in later pages, the phenomenological sense of "intentionality" and the general focus "on the things themselves" obviously augmented and supplemented Scheler's growing inclinations. In fact, Scheler claims to have moved toward phenomenology independently of and prior to his acquaintance with Husserl's phenomenology.[15] Regardless, it was with the recommendation of Husserl in 1907 that Scheler was offered and accepted a position in philosophy at the university in Munich. Here he joined a circle of young scholars under the auspices of Theodor Lipps, including Alexander Pfänder, Moritz Geiger and Theodor Conrad, who were attempting to "do" philosophy along the lines of Husserl's early works. Dietrich von Hildebrand, who with Hedwig Conrad-Martius and Herbert Leyendecker shuttled between Husserl in Göttingen and the Munich circle, notes of this period that Scheler moved like an enchanter among the group, entrancing the younger scholars and older students with his extemporaneous brilliance and spellbinding lectures while antagonizing his superiors with his lack of discipline and undiplomatic university behavior.[16] Scheler's career at Munich was ended abruptly when various scandals in his private life prompted the staid and religious university to revoke his tenure on the grounds of immorality.[17]

Following his dismissal, Scheler went first to Husserl's circle at Göttingen and then back again to Berlin. The years in association with the phenomenological circle at Göttingen and the literary and political communities in Berlin were among the most productive and creative of his life. Including von Hildebrand, Adolf Reinach, Roman Ingarden, Alexandre Koyre, Rudolf Clemens and Edith Stein, it was in conjunction with his association with the young Göttingen phenomenologists of this period that the major themes of his philosophy and much of his social and political theory began to take shape. Even after moving to Berlin, taking a position with an intellectual journal, he continued to return periodically to the Göttingen group. At the same time, Scheler's life in Berlin brought him in contact with the rising political intelligentsia of the period, establishing acquaintance with Walther Rathenau, Werner Sombart and a number of center and left-liberal figures. In large part his experiences in Berlin before the outbreak of the First World War set the stage for his sociological and anthropological philosophy during the Weimar years.

Scheler's productivity during these years at Berlin and Göttingen was unflagging. Coupled with his free-lance work with various journals and his now often overlooked co-editorship of the *Jahrbuch für Phänomenologie und phänomenologische Forschung* the sheer output is staggering. Three particular works are especially worthy of consideration: *Ressentiment, The Nature of Sympathy,* and *Formalism in Ethics and Non-Formal Ethics of Values;* they represent the great range of Scheler's interests.[18] The first, *Ressentiment,* stands at the threshold of his more phenomenological subsequent works. Still under the influence of Dilthey, Eucken and the life philosophies, Scheler seems to combine such analyses with Werner Sombart's and, to some extent, Friedrich Nietzsche's pathological investigations of the phenomena of modernity. Although phenomenology (and the phenomenological method) pervades the work, it remains very much in the background or is utilized as *a posteriori* justification for other insights. *The Nature of Sympathy,* the second major work of this period, marks a high point in Scheler's phenomenology. Here, in thorough and rigorous fashion, Scheler considers the phenomenon of sympathy, reviews various interpretations of the phenomenon, and concludes that sympathy itself is insufficient grounds for ethics and (implicitly) politics. In the process, it is revealed that sympathy rests ontologically and epistemologically upon something deeper, which he terms "love." Perhaps his most widely known work, *Formalism in Ethics and Non-Formal Ethics of Values,* represents Scheler's efforts phenomenologically to explore values and their order. On the basis of this exploration, Scheler is able to demonstrate the deficiencies of all formal (i.e., Kantian) ethics and reveal the possibility of an ethics based on objective, perceived values.

The outbreak of the first world war brought Scheler's thoughts to a wider popular audience, initially as a strong apologist for the German war effort. Rejected for active military service due to his age and eyesight, he worked as a reserve with an artillery unit and later took a position as a propagandist with the diplomatic corps with which he served in Geneva and The Hague. *Der Genius der Krieg und der Deutsche Krieg,* a militaristic and chauvanistic pastiche of anti-bourgeois, anti-English and anti-"West" ruminations, represents what is clearly the lowest point of Scheler's intellectual life.[19] In publishing the work, Scheler, moreover, alienated a pacifist circle of acquaintances in Berlin, including Martin Buber and Max Brod. It cannot be said, unfortunately, that this work is without some loose linkages to his earlier works. In passages similar to many of Nietzsche's, he lauds the vitality and authenticity of the warrior as against the manipulations and rancorous vindictiveness of the shopkeeper. The war is praised as a purifying struggle to rid Europe of bourgeois, especially English, pleonexie. By 1915, as evidenced in *Krieg und Aufbau*, a turning point was reached in Scheler's consideration of the war.[20] No longer does he portray the struggle as some sort of dialectical process through which the German spirit would emerge victorious over the bourgeois decadence of Britain or suffocating orthodoxy of Russia. Rather, he finds the war to be a tragic result of the moral and spiritual bankruptcy of Western man. The only glimmer of hope to be found in the horror of this war, may be in the opportunity revealed for the reconstruction of Western culture. For Scheler this opportunity was the chance for a renewed European unity, mirroring the unity of pre-reformation and pre-bourgeois Europe under the solidarity of Christianity.

Although such thinking pervades Scheler's work, at this time it seems likely to have been influenced by his rapprochement with his subsequent re-conversion to Catholicism at the Benedictine abbey of Beuron in 1916. This begins the "Catholic" period of his thought, which saw his return to academia, accepting the directorship of the Institute for the Social Sciences and a professorship in sociology and philosophy at Cologne in 1918. His works of this period endorse much of Catholic dogma and theology—albeit more Augustinian than Thomistic—and appeal for Christian unity as the basis for a transformation of the European spirit. Politically, such themes were manifested in his endorsement of the youth movements and in his theoretical forays into intriguing concepts such as Christian socialism and democracy. His major theological work, *On the Eternal in Man*, appears roughly at the middle of this period.[21] Although the major portion of the work elaborates the concept of the person in theological terms—i.e., man's person and God's person, it also treats the sociological question of religion, and contains key essays into the nature of philosophy and into the possibility of European spiritual rebirth. His thinking of this period, however, soon chafed under the strictures of Catholic teachings. Led by his most penetrating efforts to comprehend the character of persons within the context of the social and material world, he grew more and more critical of what he perceived as the Catholic doctrine of the suffiency and efficacy of man's soul or spirit. Formally breaking with the religion in 1923, friends and acquaintances report the profound agonizing and emotional turmoil preceding Scheler's carefully considered decision.[22]

As in Berlin, Scheler's tenure in Cologne saw him engaged in the general intellectual life of the city and its university. He established close relationships there with the theologians Paul Tillich and Romano Guardini, and with the literateur Ernst Robert Curtius. Scheler's circle at the university included the phenomenologist and metaphysician, Peter Wust, and academics such as von Weise and Driesch. In the cafes and nightclubs, chain-smoking cigarette after cigarette despite his physician's orders to the contrary, he frequented the company of artists and literati, from Otto Dix who painted his well-known portrait to Rainer Maria Rilke and Romain Rolland.[23] His thought began to branch more systematically into cultural, political, sociological and anthropological questions. Searching for the ontological and metaphysical foundations of man he strained against the confines of mere epistemology and, hence, against borders of—at least Husserlian—phenomenology. The year 1925 saw the publication of *Die Wissenformen und die Gesellschaft*, which incorporated an analysis of the real and ideal structures of society in history with a powerful revelation of the existential grounds for cognition and reason.[24] The thrust of his inquiry into these topics culminated in his uncompleted philosophical anthropology. Aware of his declining health, the philosophical anthropology of his last years was his effort to draw together the whole of his intellectual endeavors under the rubric of what he termed on occation "meta-anthropology." Sharply aware of a continuing erosion of the grounds of metaphysics and philosophy in the currents of intellectual inquiry, and of the erosion of the privileged place of the human subject, Scheler's work was intended to outline the indisputable ground upon which men could always and universally rely—the certitude of man's own reality within the reality of the world. Hence, although himself changing the title of his last published work from *Die Sonderstellung des Menschen im Kosmos* (*The "Special" Place of Man in the Cosmos*) to *Die Stellung des Menschen im Kosmos* (*The Place of Man in the Cosmos*), he holds out the possibility of a meta-anthropology for the metaphysics which he perceived as so necessary for our times.[25]

In 1928, shortly after being called to a new chair at the university in Frankfurt, Scheler died of heart disease at the age of 54. He was interred without his brain, which was saved for scientific study of human genius.

Chapter One
Phenomenology and Ontology

I N ACCORDANCE WITH HIS contention that ideas are mere fancies without their embodiment within real forces in life and history, Max Scheler's thought needs to be seen from the perspective of its situation in its time.[26] For the height of Scheler's life and work, this situation in Weimar Germany: a heady, intoxicating melange of cultural and intellectual renaissance, restoration and radicalness. From the vantage of the history of ideas the scant decade and a half between the conclusion of the hostilities of the First World War and the first steps toward the second is a period of incredible creative activity. It represents both the high point of the "turn toward man," an understanding which itself begins in a similar epoch of intellectual tumult some four centuries previously, and a turning point away from at least the excesses of this same man-centered understanding. Weimar thus marks a watershed for mankind's understanding of itself, the cosmos and man's place within it. Whereas in that earlier epoch an understanding of reality in terms of divine providence is gradually transformed into a different vision which saw the human subject as its foundation, so too beginning with Weimar a turning point is reached for this same vision, which would seem to be unleashing a new understanding. Foreshadowed in Hegel and the absolute spirit, in Marx's material dialectic, in Nietzsche's overman, in pragmatism and historicism, it is in Weimar Germany most clearly evident that the man-centered understanding reaches its critical mass and at which point some new perception begins to everge in its own right. The human subject, as God in the previous epoch, is gradually shaken from its privileged role as the ultimate and indubitable foundation for knowing, doing and being.

The resultant confusion only serves to underscore the pervasive experience of "alienation" and "homelessness" which characterizes

13

not only Weimar Germany, but which has become the central, even
unifying, experience of the ''post-modern'' period. Shaken from his
privileged place, where now is man, what is his purpose, who, indeed, is he? Capturing so well this contemporary problematic in his
oft-quoted remark, Scheler exclaims that ''we are the first age in
which man has become utterly and unconditionally 'problematic' to
himself, in which he no longer knows who he is, but at the same time
knows that he does not know.''[27]

Sketching the place of Max Scheler and his thought in this jumble
of old and new, certitude and uncertainty, is no easy task. Over the
span of his life, his thinking must be seen as a growing and reflective
exercise, not as a static, dogmatic system. His thinking in regard to a
number of fundamental points undergoes subtle changes of emphasis
and outright reversal.[28] In the turbulent intellectual storms of the era,
however, one cannot simply perceive Scheler's philosophy and social
theory as kites buffeted to and fro in the prevailing breezes as some
have suggested.[29] Rather he epitomizes his time and betrays an un-
canny knack for being ever at the locus of greatest uncertainty, at the
frictious border between the old and new visions of reality. Always at
the center of the maelstrom, Scheler and his thought defy assignation
within either the old or the as yet shrouded and uncharted new
understanding. Stumbling on occasion, he walks the perilous ridge
between Nietzsche's celebrated ''last men'' and being the ''first man
of genius, the Adam of the new Paradise'' as Ortega y Gasset
designates him.[30]

Among the many influences in Scheler's intellectual development, three roughly grouped currents appear to be most dominant:
Lebensphilosophie (philosophy of life), phenomenology and the so-
called ''revival of metaphysics.'' To some extent the progression of
his thought might be divided—if only conceptually—along these lines
into periods where various combinations of these elements mark the
prevailing character of his work. The period prior to his transfer to
Munich, his early period, can be seen as predominantly concerned
with the agenda of the life philosophies, and to a lesser extent with
Eucken's metaphysics. His middle period, following his exposure to
phenomenology and his acquaintance with the Munich circle, could
be similarly seen as one dominated by phenomenology and the use of
the phenomenological method. As the works of this period indicates,
however, there remains a vital concern with the certain metaphysical
questions even at the peak of his interest in phenomenology. Finally,
in the sociology of knowledge and philosophical anthropology of his

last period, Scheler somehow incorporates all three elements rather uniquely and evenly in his thinking: life philosophy, phenomenology and metaphysics. All three elements are at the minimum nascently present in each period of his intellectual development. Even in regard to phenomenology, there is evidence supporting Scheler's claim that he was reaching out in the direction of phenomenology prior to his meeting with Husserl.[31] Obviously as well, these three intellectual currents can hardly be conceived as "schools" or distilled into canonical cores of precepts and tenets. More properly, life philosophy, phenomenology and the rivival of metaphysics appear as *ad hoc* constellations of thinkers grouped around common concerns. Furthermore, there are no unbridgeable fault lines between these different movements, even in the minds of their respective adherents. Ambiguous borders admit various personalities to be identified with two or all of the movements. Scheler, thus, is far from alone in acknowledging an ambiguous standing within each of the currents.

LEBENSPHILOSOPHIE

The philosophy of life is perhaps the most nebulous and least focused of the movements. Under its elastic canopy, writers as diverse as Friedrich Nietzsche, Henri Bergson, Wilhelm Dilthey and Rudolf Eucken can be grouped—each of whom are profoundly influential in the development and background of Scheler's thought.[32] Broadly, life philosophy, as illustrated in the works of these thinkers, affirms the fundamental role of "lived experience" in contrast to the formalism of pure reason and the passivity of rational knowing. It emphasizes the life-based concepts of growth, development, evolution and dynamism. Reality is pictured in what can only be called an "organic" manner, undergoing a developmental process. To some extent this reflects an often unacknowledged Hegelian influence; or, as Hans-Georg Gadamer remarks in specific reference to Dilthey and Nietzsche, it reveals that the life philosophers came "to see Hegel's concept of mind [*Geist*] as a genuine living historical concept."[33] In its more vitalistic versions, as in Bergson's celebrated *elan vital*, room is granted in reality for a powerful, often impulse-like, life principle which in a growing process struggles to overcome or vivify non-life. Rejecting the mind-body dualism of Descartes as well as Kant's noumena-phenomena dichotomy, life philosophy strives toward achieving a reconciliation of all such divisions in the unity and reality of the process of life.[34] Scheler being closely familiar with the works and thought of each of the mentioned figures, a consideration of their thought draws out the legacy of life philosophy in his own work.

Nietzsche

Called by Ernst Troeltsch "the Catholic Nietzsche" (about the time of his conversion), Scheler admits to having studied Nietzsche's aphoristic works as early as his *Gymnasium* days.[35] From his doctoral dissertation where he briefly wrestles with Nietzsche's critique of the rational subject, to the "Man in History" essay written in the last year of his life wherein he explores Nietzsche's insight into the ideology of the European idea of truth which is seen as needing to be overcome by the understanding of truth as "will to power," Scheler draws on Nietzsche for the themes, directions and points of departure for his own works.[36] *Ressentiment*, the major work of the transition from his early to middle period, is a prime example of the utilization Scheler makes of Nietzschean analysis for his own ends.[37] Here Scheler takes the Nietzschean conception of resentment, the bitter self-poisoning but repressed hatred of the lesser man for the greater which Nietzsche sees as the rotten foundation for all Western and especially Christian morality, and he revises Nietzsche's argument to convincingly illustrate that resentment-based morality does not emerge with Christianity and the West, but with the appearance of modernity and the bourgeois, and ultimately triumphs with the rise of mass society. In the more apparent stream of the life philosophies, he concurs with Nietzsche that it is in resentment that the general thrust of modern thought finds its emotional roots, arguing that "a secret *ressentiment* underlies every way of thinking which attributes creative power to mere *negation* and criticism."[38]

Although Scheler discusses Nietzsche's creativity and insight with praise throughout his works, in the final analysis he remains at some distance from central elements of Nietzsche's thought. In the rejection of modernity, Scheler contends that Nietzsche yet remains covertly dependent on the methodology and metaphysics of modernity. As Scheler understands him, the failure of Nietzsche lies in his reduction of the person and the sphere of the person to the status of objects or epiphenomena of the natural world. In so doing, it is implied that the perverse one-sidedness of modernity's stress on the transcendental subject is transformed into its mirror image—i.e., transformed into a perverse one-sidedness which stresses the objectivism of the empirical subject.[39] Both Nietzsche and modern thought, moreover, are criticized for remaining locked into an individualism which perceives the person, whether as subject or object, solely as ego. For Scheler, this too is one-sided. Mimicking the terminology of other life philosophers, it is contended that the individual is not a primal, isolated, unit of life; the individual is *ab origine* equally a facet or manifestation of its community, species and the process of life as a whole. Despite these fundamental reservations, Scheler finds in Nietzsche, in concepts like the overman, the transvaluation of values, the analysis of resentment and so forth, the turning point in thought from which he interprets his own philosophical "mission." In regard particularly to the concept of life and its status in reality (which transformed into personalism and philosophical anthropology becomes the central focus of his own thinking) Scheler acknowledges his far-reaching indebtedness to Nietzsche's vision. In words with which Scheler might as well be describing his own position, Scheler says of Nietzsche in an early essay...

> "Life"—this becomes for Nietzsche, in both the least and the greatest forms, somewhat like a daring undertaking, a metaphysical "adventure," a brave thrust into the possibility of being which will, in success, first form itself into a being [*die sich erst im Gelingen zu einem Sein gestalten (wird)*]—by which all possible "knowing" [*Wissen*] is perceived. Life—this is the place standing before existence, within which existence and nonexistence are ascertained. Making use of the inexpressible, he loves with ancient friends, with Heraclitus, the image of the flame, the flickering of which decides the form which is offered to the watcher. Like Heraclitus, Nietzsche's last word is also "becoming," and truly life is a becoming life— or better, life is wholly becoming.[40]

Bergson

Henri Bergson plays a similar, if less pervasive role in the background of life philosophy within Scheler's thought. In many ways, as contemporaries, it seems that the many affinities between their respective philosophies reflect more commonality of interests rather than anything like "causal" influence. Yet, clearly, Scheler is closely acquainted and impressed with the work of Bergson.[41] Key aspects of Bergson's thought appear in various degress of reinterpretation in the works of Scheler. Among these, Bergson's investigations into matter and spirit, his so-called *élan vital*, his critique of reason and subsequent elaboration of the concept of intuition, are perhaps the foremost in their affinity with themes in Scheler's writings.

Generally critical of Bergson's concepts and never fully accepting his analyses, Scheler reacts most sharply to Bergson's critique of reason and to his turn toward mystical intuition. This is indicative of Scheler's overall ambiguous relationship with much of *Lebensphilosophie*. Bergson contends that human reason is anthropologically directed toward the exterior world of things. It developed in the species as a function by which man was able to gain mastery over objects in the world in order that he might secure his continued existence. Unlike instincts, which establish a static pattern of reaction to stimuli, reason lends an organism a measure of flexibility in responding to the demands and opportunities of the exterior world. Based on the character of this evolutionary development, Bergson contends that reason is inherently directed outward toward the world as an assemblage of objects which must be mastered in order for reasoning life to succeed in living. Reason seeks to inform the action of an organism by drawing knowledge from what is perceived in the exterior world, as opposed to instinct which informs the action of an organism by relaying the knowledge which inheres in life itself. Reason is an active acquiring effort, not a passive transmission of knowledge. Because reason is ever looking outward, however, it is unable to in any way transcend or become independent of its intentional relationship to objects. Instinct, on the other hand, being merely a conduit of genetic knowledge, is likewise unable to transcend and reflect upon itself. Thus, Bergson contends that there exists a third function, "intuition," which transcends the intentionality and exteriority of reason and the interiority and immediacy of instinct. Intuition somehow informs human actions with immediate critical insight into the fullness of experienced reality, joining exterior usefulness with interior purpose.[42]

For Scheler, curiously, Bergson's error is perceived as being one of naturalistic reduction, on one hand, and one of supernatural realism, on the other. Like Bergson, as will be explored in another section, Scheler too sees an intimacy between knowing and living. He contends, however, that Bergson is unable to shake the positivist conception of mechanical causation which is shared by the British evolutionists to whom Bergson was indebted; and, he mistakenly focuses too narrowly on the phenomenon of life. Bergson appears to be claiming that reason is utterly and solely reducible to the process of life and life's material demands. This is a naturalistic reductionism in Scheler's appraisal, prompting him to write of Bergson, that "the 'intelligence' of man is only a development from man being 'homo faber' to him."[43] This is an absolutizing of the life concept, a failure to see the rich variety of factors in which reason, intelligence and logic emerge. History, the objects of reason, nature and the values of the subject *all* play a fundamental part in the process of reason and its development. Scheler objects to Bergson's reduction of reality to the metaphysical monism which is termed "life." Moreover, cognition, a Schelerian theme to be examined subsequently, is itself not uniform but comprised of three essential modes only one of which, [*Herrschaftswissen*] the knowing which aims at domination, is contained in Bergson's notion of "intelligence." Finally, Scheler rejects the mystical overtones which pervade Bergson's works. Forced to resort to a mystical "intuition" to overcome the instrumental rationality of reason, Bergson, in Scheler's estimation, succumbs to a supernational realism which cannot be verified either phenomenologically or empirically. Indeed, inasmuch as intuition is an outgrowth itself of the process of life, it is "not only mysticism, but quite *questionable psychologistic mysticism,* in addition."[44] What knowledge might be given in Bergson's intuition would be incapable of rising above its origins in the psychological life processes of the human organism. Bergson, Scheler contends, errs by taking life as an improbable unity of both supernatural and empirical character, and by seeking to comprehend the totality of man from the perspective of the single factor "life." He argues that all is not contained, explained or understood in terms of life; the values of life are neither the basis for all others, nor the most sublime.

Dilthey

Wilhelm Dilthey more directly shapes the background of Scheler's thinking. Studying under him at Berlin, Scheler incorporates key Diltheyan concepts rather directly into his own philosophy, sociology and political theory. Of such concepts, three are especially relevant for present concerns: the conception of experiences [*Erlebnisse*] and its relationship to knowledge and action, the understanding of history and culture in world-views, and the conception of resistance as the most primal experience of reality. Less overtly, Scheler's appraisal of the character of the natural sciences, the cultural sciences and philosophy also would appear to owe much to the overall tenor of Dilthey's investigations in the same areas. He is forthright in his acknowledgment of the genius of Dilthey, and of the profound influence exercised by Dilthey's research on his own thought. Noting, time and again, the strong similarity between his own *Wesensanschauung* (insight into essence) and Dilthey's renowned Weltanschauung (insight into a world), Scheler at one point refers to "the pioneering genius of Wilhelm Dilthey and his school" as attempting to reveal by means of a "phenomenological doctrine of world-views," phenomenologically clarified "structures of lived experience relative to a particular epoch" which would serve as the genuine basis for the cultural sciences.[45]

The gist of Dilthey's thought can be inferred from the shared concern both thinkers evidence in regard to the cultural sciences. He sees man as a living being which on the basis of the possession of spirit [*Geist*] is no longer able to exist prereflectively within the unity of nature. Man's "nature" is, therefore, the world of his culture and history. By means of this bifurcation between the natural world and his "nature," man twists and turns the objects of the natural world toward the service of his needs and desires, both biological and cultural. According to Dilthey this division is the original, essential difference between the natural and the cultural sciences. Like Bergson, he rejects the monocular, natural science vision of reality, where reality is perceived only in terms of objects to be explained and utilized. Unlike Bergson, however, Dilthey does not himself propose a counter monocular vision which reinterprets reality as simply organic life. For Dilthey, while man is admittedly part of natural life, he remains somehow alien to natural life. Man does not live prereflectively in nature, but in some manner he *does* so live in culture and history. Where man must gain knowledge of nature by *hypothetical explanation* (the "knowing" of the natural sciences necessary because man is not wholly immersed in nature), man *understands* history and culture through reflection upon his own personal experiences, which is the 'knowing' of the cultural sciences. Replacing the single vision of the natural sciences, therefore, Dilthey argues that both explanation and understanding are necessary in order to comprehend the *objects* of physical reality and the *objects* of historical reality.[46]

The alienation between man and nature is also the origin of man's experience of reality. Reality becomes real for man when he experiences the resistance the world raises against his spirit. It is at this primal level that the reality of the world is affirmed. Not directly intuited, as was the case in Bergson, for Dilthey the awareness of the "reality" of reality arises when consciousness compares it intensions with the actual performance achieved in acts. From this experience of resistance, true egological self-consciousness and cognition are made possible. This understanding is closely paralleled in Dilthey's presentation of the genesis of any particular weltanschauung in history. The basic experience of a people in history leads to a relative individuation of their respective framework for apprehending the world; i.e., leads to their unique weltanschauung. The relativity of such world-views, their individuation, is not *a priori*, but rather reflects the shared universal structures common to all peoples in all times. Inasmuch as man is "naturally" a historical being, therefore, the task of the human sciences is to bring such structures to transparency.[47] Hence, the point of Dilthey's teachings on the idea of weltanschauung is not to propound the relativity of being and knowing, but to found a science on the theory of weltanschauung by which the structures of history can be revealed in order that more responsibly informed and more rationally based actions might be made possible.

Although Scheler acknowledges the significance and influence which these and similar themes in Dilthey's thought exercise on his own works, only little of this is accepted uncritically or without qualification. In particular, Scheler is quite apprehensive of what he perceives to be Kantian legacies, in Dilthey's project. For example, the question of knowledge and existence, as treated by Dilthey, is seen to raise a dilemma concerning the status of reality in regard to the human subject. As noted, ostensibly being is *directly* and *essentially* perceived for Dilthey via the primal experience of resistance—a position which would appear to reject the Kantian premise of reality being unknowable in its essence. Scheler argues, however, that Dilthey's understanding of "experience" is not in fact a penetration to things in themselves. The key to his argument is his claim that Dilthey portrays the primal experience of reality through resistance as appearing immediately in the conscious mind, pre-egological or not. Thus, foreshadowing the error Scheler finds in Husserl's phenomenology, he contends that, in almost Kant-like fashion, Dilthey fails to pierce through to the ontological level of reality and remains at the level of the constitution of the phenomena of reality in consciousness. Elaborating somewhat further on this theme in a late essay, he claims that "Dilthey does not notice that the experience of reality is above all an ecstatic one [pre-conscious and prior to the subject-object distinction by which comparison is grounded], and not an ecstatic 'knowledge of' but an ecstatic 'having of' reality."[48] Like Dilthey, Scheler takes the experience of resistance as the bedrock of his philosophy, but where Dilthey's concept is what would now be termed "phenomenological," his is ontological.

This ontological concern in his thinking makes more understandable the various reinterpretations which many of Dilthey's concepts undergo in Scheler's thought. Dilthey's remaining at the level of subjective consciousness permits him only to consider the *objective* character of history, culture and the sphere of the person in general.[49] Deeply concerned, as he is, with community and intersubjectivity, Scheler recoils from what appears to be a requisite objectification of other person in this approach. Scheler stresses strongly the ability to participate directly in the subjective intentions and experiences of others. His own conception of weltanschauung, stemming from this, reveals an attempt to join together the material and spiritual factors and the objective and subjective structures of history into a unified inquiry.[50] It can further be assumed that his own understanding of the cultural sciences would be similarly patterned.

Eucken

Scheler's professor at Jena, Rudolf Eucken, has been largely overlooked and his significance underestimated by contemporary appraisals of late nineteenth and early twentieth century philosophy. Without question, however, few thinkers enjoyed the popular acclaim in their day which was accorded Eucken. Having not only a wide following in Germany, but in English-speaking and Scandanavian countries as well, in 1908 he receive the Nobel Prize in literature as recognition for his philosophy. Himself a student of the neo-Aristotelian Adolf Trendelenburg (who terms his Aristotelian philosophy an "organic world-view"), Eucken accepts with all the life philosophers that reality of spirit and the reality of life. He presents the two as organic stages in a process of development, where life is able to attain a state of being-with-itself which is "spirit," and the sphere of spirit. His term for this broad concept of spirit is "spiritual life." All spirit, not only thought, can be seen as an organ of life, which is the perspective of naturalism. However, naturalism fails to perceive the transcendent quality of spirit and the primacy of spirit over life. Despite its character, spiritual life cannot escape its roots in the life process. Philosophy and all theorizing depend upon a basis in the actions and experiences of human life. As with other life philosophies, Eucken demands that living, doing and experiencing come prior to and ground all operations of mind. Hence, though he posits a realm of pure being to which pure truth corresponds, he contends that such pure being is only gradually uncovered in history. Man's lived actions drive this uncovering process, and pure truth remains only the ultimate end to be achieved in the total revelation of being. Actions, in similar fashion, are the movement of reality toward the full actualization of spirit in this end. The self-conscious manifestation of life, man is, it would seem, the disclosing and discerning agent through which life reveals the truth of pure being and by which spiritual life achieves total actualization. Calling to mind the idealism of Hegel and Fichte, Eucken terms this philosophy "activism." As Scheler states, he endeavors to ground the "idealism of spiritual life" on Johann Fichte's act-idealism.[51]

Not a systematic philosopher, Eucken's notions do not fit comfortably within even the indistinct boundaries of life philosophy. Like Dilthey, Eucken too inserts certain critical aspects into his philosophy which are derived from Kantian or neo-Kantian sources: a so-called "noological method" and transcendental, individual subjectivity. Utilizing the noological method in his own habilitation thesis, Scheler describes Eucken's approach as an attempt to unite the methods of transcendental philosophy and transcendental psychology, methods which in Kant are somewhat dichotomous and contradictory.[52] The purpose of the noological method is two-fold. First, it endeavors to endow the processes of the mind with the capacity to perform transcendental inquiry. In so doing, second, it makes possible a linkage between the developing world of action (which Scheler calls the *Arbeitswelt* at this point) and the world of objects of transcendental inquiry—the realm of pure being. Against psychologism, on one hand, which reduces spiritual activity to mental processes, and against pure transcendentalism, on the other hand, which would insulate spiritual activity from the development of life and history, Eucken struggles to bridge life and spirit, phenomena and noumena. The embodiment of this bridge being the human person, however, Eucken is required, more than other life philosophers, to posit a transcendental character within the human subject. Regardless of his origin in life and the developing world, man must in Eucken's view possess a capacity to transcend both.

The influence of Eucken's thinking on his, varies over the span of Scheler's intellectual work. In Scheler's early period, Eucken's life philosophy forms the medium through which his concerns with ethics, religion, emotions and culture are joined. Yet, about the time of his meeting with Husserl in 1901 Scheler turns sharply away from the notion of the transcendental subject and Eucken's noological method. Adopting phenomenology's turn toward the constitution of things in consciousness (Husserl's "intentionality") augments his growing criticism of the proximity of Eucken's understanding to Kant's regarding man's ability to transcend the contents of consciousness. Reminiscent of his teacher, however, toward the end of his life Scheler elaborates his own cosmology of spirit and life where both engage dialectically in the person, ending in the spiritualizing of life and the vivifying of spirit. Although greatly reworked, other Euckenian themes also reappear, including the concepts of act and person upon which Scheler founds the larger structure of his whole philosophy. Scheler's development of these concepts, however, which are only sketchily treated by Eucken, ought to be reckoned among the more original and important theoretical enterprises of the present century.

PHENOMENOLOGY: HUSSERL'S IDEALISM AND SCHELER'S REALISM

The phenomenological movement is only marginally less fragmented than the life philosophies. Yet there remains a unity to the movement which goes beyond sharing topics of concern or confronting common dilemmas. Well illustrated in the rallying cry of the early phenomenological movement, "to the things themselves," phenomenology attempts to break free from the traditional conceptual constructs and ideological modes of analysis through which reality is typically approached. What is sought, is the revelation of things themsleves as they appear *originally* to man, before any judgement of hypothesis. Rationalist, empiricist, positivist and even pragmatist philosophies consider phenomena only in light of certain criteria by which they are screened for validity and acceptability. They approach phenomena, in other words, with certain pre-conditions in hand. Phenomenology strives to overcome such pre-conditions, strives to accept the "givenness" of things with a naive openness, allowing the things speak for themselves. As Husserl, Scheler and the other co-editors of the *Jahrbuch für Philosophie und phänomenologische Forschung* explain in 1913:

> It is not a system that the editors share. What unites them is the common conviction that it is only by return to primary

sources of direction intuition and to insights into essential structures derived from them that we shall be able to put to use the great traditions of philosophy with their concepts and problems; only thus shall we be in a position to clarify such concepts intuitively, to restate the problems on an intuitive basis, and therefore eventually solve them—at least in principle.[53]

The statement "return to primary sources of direct intuition and to insights into essential sturctures derived from them" reveals a *second* aim of phenomenology. Not only does phenomenology in radically empirical fashion seek to return to the things themselves, i.e., to primary sources of direct insight, but it also seeks to perceive the essential structures derived. In other words, phenomenology goes beyond detailed and unprejudiced description of things as they are "given;" *it attempts to derive the essence of what is so given*. This derivation is accomplished by way of what is sometimes termed "the phenomenological reduction." Variously understood by phenomenologists themselves, all generally concur that the reduction distinguishes the essence of phenomena from their existence in some manner suspending the existential so that the essential stands forth —or is "intuited." Such intuiting is not a recourse to the semimystical understanding of intuition as is presented in Bergson's life philosophy. Rather, intuition for phenomenology refers to a self-evidential insight into the character of something given. While phenomenologists would deny any innate knowledge or categories of the mind, they contend that mind has the capacity to recognize or "intuit" a general or universal notion such as equality—not by means of manipulative analysis, but through perceiving the essence of equality directly in experience. *Finally,* presumed in the discussion of phenomena as given, is the phenomenological notion of "intentionality." Again attracting various specific formulations, the concept demonstrates the unique position which phenomenology, especially Scheler's phenomenology, holds in the foreground of the Weimar watershed regarding the place of the human subject in reality. As typically interpreted, a given phenomenon is present to the "subject" only as an "object" in an intentional relationship. Using the words subject and object very loosely in this context, both are considered possible only within the framework of "intentionality." To speak of either subject or object implicitly begs the acknowledgement of their connectedness. Subjectivity, thus, does not escape from experience and experience is inexplicable apart from subjectivity. Not independent things in themselves, subject and object have no effective status apart from their intentional relationship. Neither is prior or posterior to the other: both are co-original aspects of intentionality.

Husserl's Phenomenology

A consideration of Edmund Husserl, founder of the movement, lends detail to much of the foregoing overview and highlights areas of contrast against which Scheler's own phenomenology can be advantageously compared. The background of Husserl's development of phenomenology begins with his turn from an early training in mathematics itself toward inquiring into the epistemological and psychological roots of mathematics and logic—first from the stance of a radical psychologism. Arising out of British empiricism and widely popular among German academics before the turn of the century, psychologism not only undercut ethics—Eucken's concern—but equally called to question the foundations of even mathematics and and logic. Argued by philosophers like Theodor Lipps, the psychologistic explanation of mathematics and logic contends that even fundamental concepts such as number, identity, equality and so forth, have no objective reality and are but reflections of certain psychological processes and psychic experiences. Husserl gradually came to reject these contentions, as had Gottlob Frege and as would the early Bertrand Russell. Husserl's rejection, however, greatly differs from Frege's, Russell's and most of the others involved in this general reaction to psychologism, for where the others in a sense turned toward something approximating metaphysical realism (numbers, for example, being objectively real and knowable) he does not entirely make a parallel move. His hesitation is not so much owing to doubts concerning the reality of mathematics and logic, rather it is centered on the manner in which such things are knowable. He takes, as it were, a middle course between psychologism and these various metaphysical realisms, affirming that principles of logic and mathematics are discovered in experience, but only within the context of a very special type of experience—a *phenomenologically clarified* experience wherein all concerns with the particularities of the experienced given are disregarded. Like the psychologists, Husserl focuses on individual psychic experience, on consciousness. Unlike them he disregards (at this time) all links to a reality outside or exterior to these experiences; or, better, he focuses on only what is given to consciousness. In like fashion his move ignores any bridge between consciousness and any objectively real metaphysics.[54]

At this point is revealed the underlying trust of Husserl's phenomenology, for experiencing becomes being *consciousness of* some "thing". Just as the "known" and the "knower" are not independent and sufficient in themselves, representing only terminal ends of a "knowing," so some "thing" is that which one is "conscious of" and consciousness is always consciousness of some thing. This is the basic sense of Husserl's intentionality. In a sense, Husserl borrows from the thesis of the empiricitsts, whereby all experience is reduced to pure data and where all theorizing and conceptual manipulation of such raw data is (supposedly) eliminated. Yet, phenomenology acquires even greater comprehensiveness in its rejection of *a priori* theorizing, for Husserl starkly criticizes the empiricist positon because it is not sufficiently radical. Empiricism errs in its haste to overcome pre-judgement by failing to see its own implicit pre-judgement by which all experiences of universals are rejected out of hand. Husserl seeks the pure and primary experience, regardless of whether its character is particular or universal. Moreover, as all experiencing is a "being conscious of something," he is led to conclude that intentionality is the sufficient criterion of reality and truth. In making this move he avoids the subject-object duality of metaphysical realism and avoids the relativity inherent in psychologism's reduction of mind to the determinations of psychological experiences. He overcomes the problem of correspondence between ideas *in mente* and objects in reality (which so bedeviled the idealists) by suspending judgement on both the subject and object apart from their interdependency in intentionality. With this, intentionality becomes not an attribute of subject, but consciousness itself, not a reflection of reality, but what must pass for reality itself. In simplest words, without recourse to an existence of subsistent subject there can be no subjectivism without recourse to an existent or subsistent object, there can be no objectivism.

Tidy as Husserl's theory is in response to many of modernity's epistemological puzzles, it might yet be wondered how his interpretation of intentionality solves the initial problems of the universal and certain character of logical or mathematical principles? Or, looking beyond his narrow original query, how is it possible for anything to be known with universal certitude when it appears that any degree of universality has been lost in the shattering of knowing into a seemingly endless number of intentional relationships? Possibly from similar concerns, Husserl's phenomenology develops through a series of insights which are in some way a response to these questions. In the early Husserl, the Husserl who had so deeply impressed

Scheler in their 1901 encounter, the response hinged on the derivation of intentionality. Husserl had adopted the notion from his teacher, Franz Brentano, for whom intentionality referenced the sphere of meanings. Reflecting this sense, Husserl very thoroughly and carefully demonstrates that logic operates in regard to what is meant or what is intended. Its concern is not with the stream of *real* psychic acts which the subject is performing, but with meant or *intended* objects of consciousness.[55] Inasmuch as intentionality refers to such intended objects of consciousness, each act of intention, each act of meaning, points toward *an ideal unity of meaning*. The endless number of intentional relationships are, then, individually unique and relative in themselves, but they point in the direction of certain unities or generalities, some of which (including logical principles) are universal in character.[56] For Husserl at this juncture, the process by which these unities are discerned is a means of abstraction called "ideation" [*Wesensschau*]. Ideation is a special "intuitive" apprehension of a given thing in consciousness that reaches behind the given's particularities toward its essence. It must be clear, however, that concepts such as ideation, essence, ideal and universal do not evidence any sort of metaphysical realism in the understanding of the early Husserl. Essences and universals are not Platonic forms in the sense of being higher or more perfect than particulars, or in the sense of being eternal and unchanging. Moreover, their status vis-a-vis any reality beyond intentionality, as discussed above, is dismissed as irresolvable by Husserl. His position is much less ambitious, much more mundane. Essences, universals and ideals are only conditions for the possibility of objective, general knowledge. Hence, during these years, the universality of logic and the certitude possible for any knowledge in general is a determination based in the ideation process wherein special intuitive insights are given in the appearance of a thing in consciousness.

That Husserl himself was unsatisfied with the comprehensiveness of his position at this point, which is demonstrated by his subsequent modifications, leaves open the door to question the satisfaction his early theory lends to the question of epistemological certitude. How, for example, are his universals or essences experienced in or given to consciousness? Where precisely does certitude lie in his process of ideation—in the essences, in the process itself or in something entirely different? Spurred by similar questions Husserl begins a gradual shift in his phenomenology. Although not acknowledged by Husserl himself until very late in his life, the term "transcendental phenomenology" has become widely accepted as a description for this turn in his thought. Four themes drawn from Husserl's thinking following his change serve to illustrate its conceptual direction: the transcendental-phenomenological reduction, *noesis-noema* intentionality, the phenomenological ego and phenomenological idealism. Some would also include Husserl's concept of the life-world in this turn. Yet, it seems likely that Husserl borrowed the term from Scheler. Moreover, the notion of the life-world is not easily congruent with the general trend of Husserl's turn here.

The transcendental-phenomenological reduction to a great extent modifies Husserl's earlier understanding of ideation as a special intuitive process of abstraction. He finds the ideation notion, which is now discussed as eidetic reduction, to be insufficient for the achievement of certitude because it remains at the level of what is termed the "natural standpoint."[57] From the perspective of the natural standpoint, which comprises the sole stance of his earlier phenomenology, Husserl contends that the world is present to one as *simply there*, naively, immediately and intuitively experienced as a menagerie of realities. Via eidetic reduction other standpoints can be obtained from the natural standpoint, from the perspective of which general essences can be grasped amidst the variety of particular realities. Logic and mathematics, for example, are grounded on standpoints which, though differentiated from the natural world, do not reject the natural standpoint but are annexed to it. Here the central motivating problematic behind Husserl's enterprise is uncovered, for from the natural standpoint nothing is finally revealed but the natural world. And, while a modest phenomenology is valid and worthwhile for the intuiting of essences at this natural level, such a phenomenology cannot be the process by which absolute epistemological certitude is obtainable. Husserl would seem to be arguing that from the natural standpoint phenomenology is itself not radical enough in its search for pure phenomena (the things themselves) because it tacitly and unreflectively accepts the reality of the world. Pure consciousness, directed toward pure phenomena, must be sought. The phenomenological reduction is the method by which this is to be achieved.[58]

Starting point for this reduction is what Husserl terms the "phenomenological *epoche*," through which belief in the existence and reality of the natural world is suspended. Vaguely resembling Descartes' universal doubt, the epoche substantially differs from Cartesian doubt in that its aim is not the discovery of a locus for sure and certain being (viz., I think that I *am*, God *is*, etc.) but aims instead at locating an arena where knowing and being are absolutely correlated so that *epistemological* certitude might be obtained. Indeed, so radical is Husserl's epoche, that even the bedrock of the Cartesian reality, the *substantive cogito*, is suspended in its existence. In striving to reduce all existentiality to pure phenomena, Husserl is engaged in what he himself refers to as "pure phenomenology." Yet, behind the epoche, and in fact revealed as a residue of its very operation, remains a reality which is impervious to all efforts to suspend its existence and which is made transparent to itself by these operations. Phenomena do not subsist in themselves, clearly, they are constituted in *consciousness*. Demonstrated again, therefore, is Husserl's purpose, for he seeks to establish what is "given" with the certitude of necessity. What was but groundlessly a fact from the natural standpoint becomes constituted in consciousness and rendered certain. The constitution of phenomena within the certitude of consciousness forms the basis upon which Husserl is able to consider phenomenology the rigorous science of essences upon which all other sciences must depend.

This conception of consciousness and its phenomena is a significant reinterpretation of Husserl's earlier presentation of intentionality. Not a reversal of his position, or even a modification; instead Husserl here sharpens the earlier notion so that it is construed in a very specific fashion. Unlike the ambiguous sense of intentionality as simply "consciousness of something," Husserl now very narrowly redefines intentionality as the unity of cogitating (designated as *noesis*) directed toward that which is cogitated (designated as *noema*). Deeper reaching than the previous understanding, the noesis-noema intentionality is presented as the sufficient ground for knowing and being. Thus, it is the reality of "consciousness of phenomena," the noesis-noema relationship, which forms the field in which all questions of being and knowing can be resolved.[59] And, as the absolute correlation of being and knowing, of pure phenomena within pure consciousness, it is in the noesis-noema relationship that certitude is achieved.

As before, however, Husserl is left with a further dilemma. If certitude is obtained only in the fleeting pluralities of the noesis-noema relationships, is it then to be assumed that the ontological status of this "certitude" is equally transitory and relative? In other words, without a measure of "subsistence" of either "knower" or "known" which is constant and transcendental to each particular intentionality, it would seem that certitude itself is not constant, enduring or subsistent. Wrestling with this dilemma Husserl moves in directions which continue to provoke controversy among phenomenologists and which drew sharp criticism from Scheler. He turns toward a transcendental, phenomenological ego—a concept which requires him to accept phenomenological or, better, "transcendental" idealism. Doing so returns Husserl's philosophy much nearer to the subject-object duality of modernity from which he had originally labored hard to distance himself. But, it also allows him to postulate a unity and consistency in intentionality on the basis of the phenomenological ego by which truth can lay claim to a status which is more than an ephemeral or haphazard congruence of knowing and being.

Husserl's acceptance of the phenomenological ego and idealism is an inescapable conclusion of the usage of the phenomenological epoche. Revealed in the thoroughgoing suspension of existence, which negates even the existence of the self, is a residue of the noesis-noema intentionality. It is an enduring consistency or unity which links intention with intention. Focusing on this residue reveals a transcendental unity behind intentionality—the phenomenological ego. Ever logical, Husserl's idealism follows from this. For, since being exists only within the constitutive relationship of noesis and noema, nothing can be said to exist except as is given in intentionality. As such the ontological status of all being is impressed with the character of noesis and the unseen unity of the transcendent ego. Simply put, the phenomena intended in consciousness no longer are to be merely "taken" as reality, these phenomena constituted under the auspices of the phenomenological ego *are* reality itself. The world, life, history and other persons have reality only as phenomenological objects constituted in consciousness under the phenomenological ego.

Scheler's Phenomenology

For all practical purposes Scheler's phenomenology begins with his 1901 introduction to Husserl, the impact of which led Scheler to withdraw an essay on logic from the presses. As he explains it, Husserl's elucidation of phenomenological intuition revealed the poverty of the Kantianism from which that essay had proceeded.[60] Yet, as both Edmund Husserl and he are quick to claim, Scheler cannot be said to be a student of Husserl.[61] Indeed, in accepting phenomenology, Scheler was already steeped in the life philosophies and was committed to an as yet undefined metaphysical position. From the very first, then, he includes in his phenomenology elements which are at some variance from Husserl's interpretation.[62] Nonetheless, although Scheler comes to understand phenomenology in a significantly different sense than Husserl, it becomes and remains the supporting methodological orientation of his philosophy, and his social and political theory. He finds in phenomenology a manner of approaching "reality" which neither stands transcendently beyond the object of inquiry nor stands reduced to the sphere of its object, as does psychologism. Concerned as he is with man, who functions as the linchpin between the transcendental and psychological for Eucken, little wonder that Scheler rejoices in phenomenology as the mode of inquiry most befitting the study of man, his world and his proper place. The greatest debt which contemporary phenomenologists owe to Max Scheler rests in this insight. It is Scheler who bears the primary responsibility and deserves the greatest credit for turning the concerns of the phenomenololgical movement beyond "things themselves" to the world of persons.

Something beyond a psychological difference in the attitudes and purposes of Husserl and Scheler is disclosed in this. Husserl epitomizes the professional scholar. Proceeding meticulously and methodically in the "doing" of his phenomenology, he laboriously clarifies his suppositions, gathers evidence and logical argument as support for his speculation and leads himself and his reader to a self-evident perception of each modest intuition, mortaring each as a brick into the imposing structure of his philosophy. Endeavoring to clear a hard foundation of certitude for the whole sweep of man's sciences, the appropriateness of his terming phenomenology "philosophy as rigorous science" cannot be questioned.[63] Matching his ends, Husserl's phenomenology approaches the precision of formulae, with strict and verifiable sequences of mental operations which complement his concern with logic. For Scheler, in contrast, a thinker more accustomed to smoke-filled cabarets or the conversation of a Latin quarter *Lokal* than book-lined studies, phenomenology is less formal and method-like and much more an attitude or stance—or a way of looking at the world. He writes.

> [P]henomenology is neither the name of a new science nor a substitute for the word "philosophy;" it is the name of an attitude of spiritual [*geistliche*] seeing in which one can see [*er-schauen*] or experience [*er-leben*] something which otherwise remains hidden, namely a realm of facts of a particular kind. I say "attitude," not "method." A method is a goal-directed procedure of *thinking about* facts, for example, induction or

deduction. In phenomenology, however, it is a matter, first, of new facts themselves, before they have been fixed by logic, and second, of a procedure of seeing.[64]

Phenomenology is subtly recast, then, in Scheler's thinking, not at first by any obvious, fundamental disagreement with Husserl's position,[65] but certainly by a significant difference of emphasis—as is demonstrated in the intensity which Scheler brings to his efforts to pierce through all "thinking" about experience in order to obtain the original "givenness" of things *in* experience. Highly distrustful of *any* pre-conditions to experiencing, especially any formal or ideal *a priori*, Scheler from the first appears more strident than Husserl in going back to the things themselves as they appear in experience. He writes that a "philosophy based on phenomenology must be characterized, first of all, by an intensely vital and most immediate contact with the world itself." In this sense, he continues, phenomenological philosophy is radically distinguished from any approach to philosophy "which takes concepts or formulas, or even science itself, as the basis of its procedure, and then seeks to reach the 'presuppositions' of science by reduction or to bring its results into a consistent system."[66] Theory, critique, idea and method must not precede the primal experience of "things." As with Husserl, Scheler is unrelenting in his criticism of empiricism for its failure to recognize the unseen metaphysics implicit in the rejection of universals out of hand, but Scheler is equally dubious of philosophies which proffer "critique" as a solution to the dilemma of metaphysics. For him, phenomenology must not in any fashion delimit the richness of experience. Utlilizing the terms in a very qualified manner, Scheler follows Eugen Fink in discussing this complete openness as "the most radical *empiricism* and positivism," and writes further that:

[A] wide gulf separates the radical empiricism of phenomenology from any and every kind of rationalism, insofar as phenomenology, by virtue of its principle of cognition, rejects the notion of giving priority to the problems of *criteria* when it deals with any question. A philosophy which does give criteria priority is rightly called "criticism." In contrast, the phenomenologist is convinced that a deep and living familiarity with the content and meaning of the facts in question must precede all questions of criteria concerning a particular domain, no matter whether these concern the distinction between genuine and false science, true and false religion, genuine and worthless art, or even questions like "what is the criterion for the reality of an intended object [*eines Gemeinten*] or for the truth of judgement?" He who is always inclined to ask for a criterion first of all—a criterion for whether this picture is an authentic work of art, say, or whether any extant religion is *true*, is . . . a man who stands outside, who has not *direct* contact with any work of art, any religion, any scientific domain. He who has not expended labor on some domain of facts is the one what starts off by asking for criteria (Stumpf).[67]

Contending that epistemological concerns, even a most basic epistemological distinction such as the truth-falsity antinomy, are not resolvable prior to experience, he argues for a phenomenology which seeks the originary experience of things prior to their manipulation in rational reflection, even prior to the epistemological categorization of truth and falsity. Nor, can any "criteria" for the appearance of "things" in the phenomenological attitude be asked for; doing so is not to understand phenomenology, because it begs the question of some measure of validity preceding the experience of these "things themselves."

Differences between Scheler and Husserl begin to stand out in some relief at this point, differences which hint that even in regard to their early thought (pre-*Ideas*) there might be unseen disjunctures at the roots of their phenomenologies. Husserl's concern with clearing an epistemological foundation for certitude seems to approach the error which Scheler finds in placing criteria before experience. More importantly, Scheler's claim that phenomenology must be intensely vital and in immediate engagement with the world would appear to accord little with Husserl's focus upon phenomena as they are presented within the intentionality of consciousness. Most crucial in addressing these differences is the question of the celebrated "thing themselves" in the context of Scheler's thought. Clearly not following him into the quasi-idealism of Husserl's later thought, what precisely is Scheler's stance relative to the status of particulars and universals, subject and object?

Initiating a consideration of these matters, Scheler remarks in 1922 that "phenomenology grounds a *new type of apriorism* which not only embraces [*umfasst*) the purely formal propositions of logic and axiology in their various sub-disciplines (ethics, aesthetics, etc.), but which also leads to *real* [*materiale*] ontologies".[68] Thus, he acknowledges the peculiar *a priori* "reality" of Husserlian concerns such as logical propositions, but extends phenomenological apriorism to a much wider field. The range of Scheler's phenomenology is uniquely revealed in this. Distinguished from mere empiricism, on one hand, by the acceptance of *a priori* essences; on the other hand, he claims by this acceptance that phenomenology is able to accommodate the validity of the idealist *a priori* of Plato and the formal *a priori* of Kant while surpassing both in the breadth of its encompassing reach. Yet, as Scheler asserts in 1913, a gulf remains between phenomenology and these theories, for in phenomenology "the *a priori* does not become a constituent part of experience through an 'activity of formation' or synthesis and the like, much less the acts of a 'self' or a 'transcendental' consciousness."[69] Perhaps covertly addressed to Husserl, these comments by Scheler are strong argument that phenomenology cannot distance itself from the world in the sense of Plato's *eidos* or Kant's noumena.

Scheler's conviction in this regard is illustrated in his extension of the apriorism of phenomenology to "real ontologies." With this the most basic and divisive difference between Scheler and Husserl is brought to light, for Scheler from the beginnings of his thought is, and remains a thoroughgoing *realist*. The path Husserl takes in phenomenology, from the realist corner toward the idealist, is directionally obverse Scheler's. Coming to phenomenology from idealism and neo-Kantian transcendantalism, Scheler turns increasingly toward realism. Specifically, it seems he is unsatisfied with the conception of the human subject and the existential world which the idealist position requires. Falling more than historically between Husserl's concern with epistemological certitude and Heidegger's concern with being itself, Scheler's pervasive concern is with the *ontological* status of man as both substantive (natural and historical) and metaphysical reality. For him, phenomenology has its major purpose in the uncovering of real ontology as it pertains to man in the world. Where for Husserl, phenomenology begins with an ambivalence toward the possibility of subsistent reality beyond the intentionality of consciousness and concludes with a transcendental idealism where "reality" is constituted in the relation of noesis and noema, for Scheler phenomenology ever affirms the ineluctable reality of the world and unique reality of persons acting within the world. The apriorism which Scheler perceives through phenomenology, is, therefore, one which is real and objective.

His purpose in phenomenology is disclosed in this. Edmund Husserl wishes to enable the acquisition of certitude while avoiding the Platonism of objective metaphysics and the reduction of psychologism, which leads him to overcome the subject-object dichotomy by appealing to an idealism expressed in intentionality. Scheler, rather differently, turns to phenomenology in order to clarify and uncover the objectively real ground of human being, and is led finally to posit an ontologically real junction where subject and object merge and where universals and particulars converge. Husserl's struggle with universals and particulars centers on establishing the possibility of drawing the universal from the particular. Fundamentally different, Scheler's problem is bringing the universal and the particular together and identifying the real ground of their linkage. To be more fully explored later, this ontologically real linkage or junction is the concept of the "person" upon which his "personalism as political theory" is based. He, for these reasons, refuses to circumscribe his phenomenology within a framework of method-like procedures precisely because such procedures would veil the givenness of his looked for deeper reality. Parodying Husserl's later phenomenology as illustration, it could be said that Scheler rejects Husserl's move to cut away from a grounding in the natural standpoint for fear of floating away from the ontological ground he so desperately seeks.[70]

Consequent from the inclusion of an ontology, Scheler's phenomenology, while on the surface remaining remarkably similar in appearance to Husserl's, varies significantly from the other thinker's at deeper levels. Although specific elements, such as Scheler's phenomenological reduction, his conception of intentionality and his personalism, are better considered in a more thorough treatment of Scheler's metaphysical position, four general remarks relevant to Scheler's phenomenology—which again illustrate the divergence from Husserl—might be usefully reviewed in concluding this section. *First*, Scheler's phenomenology demands an immersion in the world. His stress on phenomenology as an attitude of openness to the whole of experience very much requires that, whatever degree of subjectivity he allows, it be placed within the context of contingent reality. The focal point of this subjectivity, Scheler's notion of the "person," is much more intimately joined with the world than any purely transcendental ego would permit. Hence, Husserl's egology is criticized by Scheler for its isolation from the real factors of the world. *Second*, Scheler's phenomenology rejects the reductionism of psychologism and naturalism while at the same time foregoing the categorization and formalization inherent of rationalism and idealism. As the well-quoted Maurice Merleau-Ponty would later note, and as Scheler the realist admits, there *is* something to naturalism, something to psychologism, but neither naturalism nor psychologism are sufficient in themselves, phenomenology must be receptive, therefore, to the totality of experience. He acknowledges, for example, the *a priori* and universal "facts" of essences as well as the facts of the world of matter and history. What categories, hierarchies and universals are given, are discerned *directly* from the vantage of the phenomenological attitude as objective and subsistent realities in themselves. *Third*, the cognition which occurs in phenomenology is, at its core, an uncritical, passive reception of what appears in the phenomenological attitude. Absolutely nothing can be "known" which is not first naively and positively accepted in experience. Scheler contends that thinking "about something," can hardly precede a primal acceptance of the given "thing" in experience. *Fourth*, Scheler's phenomenology does not in any manner succumb to the phenomenalism toward which Husserl's thinking approaches in its later period. Given in the phenomenological attitude are not "pictures" of reality but reality itself, revealed in a clarity achieved via a reduction that has stripped away the symbols and theories with which the subject has previously veiled it. As will be seen, for Scheler the reality so experienced is affirmed in the resistance such givens raise vis-a-vis the actions of the mind.

REVIVAL OF METAPHYSICS, ANTI-EPISTEMOLOGY AND PHENOMENOLOGY

Turning to consider Scheler's metaphysical and epistemological thinking, it might be useful to briefly consider the third element in the background of his philosophy, the so-called "revival of metaphysics." Overlapping with the life philosophies on some points, such as in the philosophies of Eucken and Hans Driesche, and with phenomenology at other points, as in the works of Edith Stein and Peter Wust, the revival of metaphysics has its roots in a reaction to materialist and historicism relativism, on one hand, and in a reaction against the idealists and neo-Kantians, on the other. Comprised of a nebulous grouping of idiosyncratic scholars with little or no organization, the "movement" finds its unifying theme in the assertion of a positive, non-formal metaphysics which is disclosed in a process of induction, based on the direct and immediate experience of reality. Universals, essences and so forth are presented as objectively real and substantive facts which are gradually discerned, dialectically or teleologically, in the performance of acts and in the accumulation of experience. Pulling together a smattering of these writers in his own survey of the state of German philosophy during the Weimar years, Scheler writes of those associated with the movement that "all are epistemological realists," and that on the basis of this realism, the movement looks to construct "a metaphysics which rests upon the foundation of experiential science[71] [*Erfahrungswissenschaft*].''

The notion of "experiential science" is notable, for as Scheler describes it, the revival of metaphysics, while very much anti-empiricist, is not engaged in rejecting either the proper inquiry or the empirical validity of the natural sciences. Rather, the movement as a whole seeks to demonstrate that the confrontational "either-or" dilemma of choosing between the sensible world of the natural sciences or the invisible world of philosophy is an unfounded and inadmissable image of reality. Any difference between mind and matter is not to be identified with the idealist-realist dichotomy. Science and philosophy are not mutually contradictory in the pursuit of their common goal in truth. With some hesitation and qualification, Scheler includes portions of his own work under the aegis of the movement and he argues that the revival of metaphysics supports and welcomes the processes of the natural sciences which reveal and discover reality. In conjunction with the movement, however, Scheler also suggests that natural science errs in perceiving its special pursuit as the sole legitimate mode of inquiry or when it fails to recognize its dependence on a metaphysical position. The latter notion is crucial for Scheler, for to the extent that the sciences tacitly accede to the empiricist position that conceptions of being and knowledge are derived entirely from sense perceptions, the more the sciences undercut science's own metaphysical foundation. Similarly, in regard to the historical and social sciences, he cautions against the absolutizing of the objects of *their* study just as he rejects the natural sciences' absolutizing of the natural world. He is strident particularly in his criticism of those thinkers who are unable or disinclined to perceive that all such absolutizing only serves to raise empirical facts or history or economics to a metaphysical position. Metaphysics is inescapable in some fashion.

> Man does not have any choice as to whether or not he forms or does not form a metaphysical idea or a metaphysical *sense* [*Gefühl*], i.e., an idea upon which man himself and the world are grounded, upon which, as that reality [*Seiende*] that *is* only through itself (Ens per se), all other reality depends. Consciously or unconsciously, acquired or inherited, man *has* such

an idea and such a sense *necessarily*. . . .The sphere of absolute being [*Sein*], as present to thinking consciousness, belongs to the *essence* of man and establishes in conjunction with self consciousness, world consciousness, language and conscience, *one* indivisible structure.[72]

The revival of metaphysics, however, intends more than merely rephrasing the epistemological truism that some sort of metaphysical conception is fundamental to all cognition, for in another sense the movement, as Scheler notes, is diametrically opposed not only to the often unseen reductionist metaphysical realism of naturalism and historicism, but equally is opposed to the formal, transcendental "metaphysics" of the neo-Kantians. Arguing from Kant's thesis of the impossibility of knowledge of essences, the neo-Kantians claim that non-formal (i.e., objective) metaphysical knowledge is unattainable. Radically followed to its extreme conclusion this argument would permit no "positive," certain and universal knowledge of reality. Certainty and universality would be obtainable only in the critical processes of pure reason—reason divorced from the contents of experience. To what extent such sublime concepts are attainable, an unresolvable query for most neo-Kantian thinkers, they must therefore be formal and transcendental in character, entirely removed and "other" than the empirical world.

Agreeing with the revival movement, Scheler considers the neo-Kantian position as untenable. However, Scheler the phenomenological realist is also interjected into this conclusion. All knowledge, he claims, even knowledge of universals, must have its ultimate or radical source in the self-givenness of things in reality; it must begin in positive experience. As he puts it . . .

> There is no cognition without prior recognition; there is no recognition without the prior existence and self-givenness of the things recognized.

Unquestionably, the primary nexus between Scheler's metaphysics and his theory of cognition is given in this passage. Knowing is portrayed to be a genuinely positive reception of reality, and not merely treated as critical, analytic or synthetic. All knowing, however, follows some deeper primal awareness of the unique and inherent being of some "thing"—i.e., its *Selbstdasein*. In cordoning-off their "knowing" from this fundamental awareness of reality, Scheler holds that if the neo-Kantians actually were in fact capable of following their methodology this knowing would be extremely limited and suspect. He notes pointedly that "reality is 'transintelligible' for every possible knowing mind. Only the *what* of the being, not the *being* of the what is intelligible."[74]

Yet, in what sense is this reality of a thing "self-given"? On this question would seem to hinge the authenticity of the above nexus between metaphysics and the theory of cognition in Scheler's thought. The direction taken in this regard has already been tentatively outlined, for he asserts that the deepest awareness of reality is self-given in the primal experience of "resistance." Adapting the concept of resistance from life philosophers such as Dilthey,[75] it becomes the bedrock of the metaphysical realism which itself undergirds the general thesis of his philosophy. "Bedrock" is peculiarly appropriate, furthermore, because in turning toward this concept, he is making an anti-epistemological, ontological move. Running athwart many of the major philosophical trends of his day—critical realism, transcendental idealism and, perhaps most pointedly, Husserlian phenomenology—Scheler asserts that this primal "giveness" of reality is not present at the level of thought, or truth, or cognition in any strict sense. "It is important," Scheler asserts, "to express these problems, which are so crucial to metaphysics, in a purely ontological form and not confuse them with problems of cognition."[76] It is not an epistemological question. Rather, the primal givenness of reality is presented in resistance and, hence, is an *ontological* givenness. Reality, Scheler claims, is presented "in our instinctive [*triebhaft*] and conative conduct vis-a-vis the world, or, more broadly, in our dynamic-practical behavior."[77] More precisely, he adds elsewhere, reality is given in *"an experience [Erfahrung] of the non-spiritual, instinctive principle within us:* an experience of the unified, always specialized, *life-drive* inside us."[78] This most basic experience is the experience of resistance.

Resistance, thus, is the enduring obstruction which the reality of any being poses to life's most basic impulses. It is not a sensation, but an immediate and utterly undifferentiated experience where the substantial reality of objective reality "resists" one's intentional actions. Indeed, it is the central experience incurred in every action, and only in this resistance is "practical reality given" and any "practical object constituted."[79] Moreover, inasmuch as resistance occurs in the relationship between life and being, its roots reach beneath the box of consciousness within which Husserl and the neo-Kantians imprison "reality." By remaining at their "epistemological" level, Scheler believes that such thinkers are left ironically unable to resolve the very questions *of* epistemology—"What is it that is known? What is it which knows?

What is knowing?" Without real being existing beyond consciousness, one is lodged permanently in an endless circle of inquiry seeking after the conditions of knowledge; one remains unable to unravel the actual relationships between knowing and being. In oblique reference to Husserl, Scheler notes that "only a very definite historical stage of overreflective bourgeois civilization could make the fact of consciousness the starting point of all theoretical philosophy, without characterizing more exactly the mode of the being of consciousness."[80] Instead, the primal experience of reality "*is there—prior to all thinking and perceiving*," and it is on this very real basis that Scheler's own philosophy stands.[81]

From the perspective of his understanding of the concept of resistance, unique insight is gained into the special interpretation which Scheler affords ostensibly phenomenological notions such as intentionality and reduction. Unlike Edmund Husserl, for example, who comes to perceive intentionality as a cognitive and constitutive relationship involving consciousness *of* some thing—wherein both are inextricably bound together and essentially non-existent apart from the intentional relation—Scheler sees intentionality as less total, less all-encompassing. Like Husserl, he sees the relationship as involving acting—specifically *acting for* or *acting toward* some thing. Yet, Scheler's acts are not the narrowly cognitive acts of the phenomenological ego. Instead, in his phenomenology, acts are pre-cognitive and evaluative at root, and are fundamental preconditions for any subsequent cognition. This does not merely recreate Husserl's phenomenological ego and cognitive, constitutive intentionality in a new guise based upon a "willing" subject. Scheler's understanding is neither cognitive nor constitutive in the strict sense. Is is *not* cognitive—as amply noted previously—because knowing must follow the experience of the reality which is becoming known. Since the experience of resistance to acts is the primary medium through which this reality is conveyed, then the acts of intentionality are prior to cognition. It is *not* strictly constitutive because the experience of resistance implicitly reveals that the unique reality of the experienced thing is distinct in itself and precedes the acts of intentionality. Hence, not only, as in Husserl's version, is the transcendental unity of acts (Husserl's ego, Scheler's person) greater than what is encompassed in the bounds of intentionality, but the intended thing (the "object") is *also* greater than what is given in intentionality. Constituted in intentionality is strictly and only the givenness or awareness of the existential reality of the act and that which is acted upon. Even the givenness of this reality, moreover, never fully exhausts the full reality, existential and essential, of either the actor or the object. Their being, thus, is not essentially constituted in the intentional relationship.

It can be seen, once again, that the metaphysical realism in Scheler's thought is endemic to his philosophy. Intentionality is not concerned primarily with knowing and cognition, but with revealing the particular reality of what is given, laying only a groundwork atop of which cognition might later be established. Intentionality becomes for him the arena in which by revealing the particular model of being of a given thing as an object, the person obtains an awareness of his own mode of being as act.[82] Although being is conceivable only as objective being in Husserl's intentionality, in Scheler's, it occurs in two modes: as object and as act. It is this interpretation of reality, therefore, which lies at the heart of the differences between the two thinkers. Scheler's own interpretation, however, subtly is modified in the development of his thought, and can be perceived in two rather different phases. Through his middle period, roughly from the Munich years to the point of his final break with Catholicism, intentionality is portrayed with a strong emphasis on the deontological and volitional character of acts. His marvelous work on ethics of this period, *Formalism in Ethics and Non-Formal Ethics of Values*, presents intentionality as joined to a personal unity of evaluative acts. This understanding of intentionaliy, which will be treated in detail in a later section, sees all practical action as very much constrained and structured by the perception of values, values which are real and objective in their own right. Given before any other reality in the primal experience of resistance, Scheler argues, is a real value.[83] Conation of this real value must precede all other relationships with what is given in intentionality, including knowledge, instrumental utility and so forth. In his last period, this interpretation of intentionality is radically revised; he abandons much of the phenomenological "approach" in order to further construct his metaphysics and philosophical anthropology on the secure understructure of that which was previously clarified in phenomenology. Here, to the extent it may still be spoken of as "intentionality," the evaluative aspect of the concept is relegated to less prominent emphasis and, in its place, the arena of acts, resistance and the givenness of a powerful life drive [Gefühlsdrang] and a powerless intention of spirit comprise a more dialectical intentionality.[84]

The phenomenological reduction is also substantially tied to the concept of resistance in Scheler's thought. Recall that for Husserl and many phenomenologists the reduction involves the bracketing or suspension of the judgement that that which is given "exists." Scheler would wish to underscore the word "judgement" in this statement (about a quarter of any Scheler text is italicized). Crediting Husserl with posing this "basic problem of theoretical philosophy in a profound and original way," Scheler is still doubtful of the final validity of this understanding of the phenomenological reduction. He notes:

> The "elimination" or "suppression" of the positing of reality always implicit in the natural world-view is by no means satisfactory. It is a matter here not of suppressing existential *judgement*, but of stripping away the factor of reality itself which fulfills the meaning of the predicate in the existential judgement. Or, it is a question of eliminating the acts furnishing this factor. Merely to suppress existential judgement is child's play. It is quite another thing to set aside the factor of reality itself by putting out of operation those (involuntary) functions which furnish it.[85]

If Scheler's aim, however, is to go further than the bracketing of belief of judgement regarding existence, if his aim is indeed to "set aside the factor of reality itself," how is this to be achieved? Here, Scheler returns once more to the primal experience of resistance.

As noted above, the basic conation of reality is given in the experience of resistance. If, then, the factor of reality is to be set aside, the experience of resistance which furnishes it must be put out of operation. This is precisely the intent and process of Scheler's phenomenological reduction or "ideation." In the last of his works which Scheler saw published before his death, *Man's Place in Nature*, he explains the operation of this ideation process.[86] Missing in his portrayal is the method-like precision which is obvious in Husserl, for he sees the ideation process as a natural human function acquired in mankind's evolution and anthropological development. The spiritual aspect of man is able somehow to deny and reject the existential reality which is presented to him as a living creature. As Scheler elaborates, ideation is achieved by truly "deactualizing" reality—i.e., by withdrawing or restraining all intentional acts so that the primal experience of resistance, that experience which furnishes the givenness of existential reality, does not occur. In this manner, as in Husserl's early notion of ideation, essence is revealed behind the existential. "What remains after the deactualizing of the world," he remarks in another late essay, "is indeed the 'ideal' world of essence."[87]

Chapter Two
Person, Other, Community

S HORTLY BEFORE HIS DEATH, Scheler remarks that "the questions 'What is man?,' and 'What is his place in being?' have interested me, more than any other philosophical questions since the first awakening of my philosophical consciousness."[88] Here, disclosed, is the primary concern of Scheler's philosophical enterprise—understanding the human person, his place, his essence and his end. Unlike the broader ontological concern of Martin Heidegger, whose thought conveys much of the same resonance and shares a common philosophical heritage in the life philosophies and phenomenology, Scheler's concern with person betrays an interest not so much in being itself, but in the special being of being human.

Within the current renaissance of Scheler scholarship, this special dignity which Scheler grants the human person is increasingly and subtly muted in efforts to incorporate his thinking into the voguish antisubjectivism of present-day Continental thought. Such efforts, though not entirely bereft of merit inasmuch as he does much to bring the human subject down from the pedastal of the pure *cogito*, fail to appreciate the implicit intent of Scheler's endeavor. Indeed, it is but a few decades since Gabriel Marcel and other early French existentialists were sifting the works of Scheler in search of support for a thesis of subjective freedom. But, Scheler eludes easy accommodation within either the ontologist's or the existentialist's perceptions of the human person. The human person has his place within being and is, thus, locked in the embrace of nature and history. Yet, the peculiar being of being a human person is importantly different from the being of the world in which he is enmeshed.

This "specialness" associated with the human person is interpreted variously over the development of Scheler's thought. In his early years at Jena, he sees man as both a product and participant in a divine process in which by dint of his uniqueness man is engaged in the gradual revelation of being to itself. The first works of his early years in association with phenomenology see Scheler combining a Nietzschean portrayal of the failure of modern man with his own understanding of the human person as a unity of evaluative, spiritual acts. At the height of his Catholic period, Scheler endorses the Christian conception of man's end lying in salvation. This is bound, further, with his previous notion of person as a unity of acts. With this, since acts are intentional and inseparable from the world, an almost classical interpretation of person as link between the mundane and the divine is refashioned. Finally, this sense is given radically new meaning in his last period in the concept of the all-man [*Allmensch*]. Aptly named, Scheler's all-man attempts a total picture of man, and is posited as a model, or a leading figure [*Vorbild*], for a new age, the "era of adjustment," the seeds of which he sees about him in the revolutions of art, literature, and philosophy during the Weimar years. Reminiscent of Nietzsche's overman and perhaps certain themes of Aristotle, the model of the all-man is to serve as the guiding pattern not only for the spirit of the age, but for the transformation of man himself. A model for the completion of the special being of being human, as Scheler writes, the idea of the all-man "is the idea of a man who has realized all his essential capabilities."[89]

To be sure, the special dignity which he lends the concepts of man and person do not stretch to encompass a vision of man which sees him as wholly plastic and utterly devoid of essence. Nor, yet, does his understanding endow man with other-worldly faculties by which man entirely might escape living in the world. But, man's place in being is such that authentic, practical politics, is not only possible—but required. A consideration of this political element, however, must await a more fulsome review of the concept of man in Scheler's thought. Moreover, because it is Scheler's understanding of "person" which comprises the framework for such a theory of politics, i.e., personalism as political theory, it is the elusive dynamic of the human person toward which attention now shifts.

Act and Person

Scheler defines "person" as a "concrete [also 'ontic'] unity of acts."[90] At stake in this definition is a distinction between the way in which a person "is" and the way in which "things" are. As introduced above, such a distinction stems from Scheler's contention that being is of two modes: being-as-object and being-as-act. The person, a unity of acts, properly belongs to the latter mode. Things, in contrast, belong to the mode of being-as-object. Of the two, being-as-object, perhaps not too ironically, is more readily grasped and explained. Scheler identifies it as the predominant understanding of reality in the present day and he traces the origins of this predominance to the emergence of a type of man he terms "the bourgeois" and to the penchant of the bourgeois for appraising, ordering, classifying and counting.[91] At the same time, Scheler follows the deeper anthropological roots of the object to the species acquisition of the ability to distinguish and, thus, to manipulate objective elements in the environment. Unlike lower forms of life which survive solely by adapting to the surrounding world, man can also adapt and manipulate objective elements of the world environment to provide for his survival and livelihood.[92] Therefore, the origin of the object itself and the origin of the predominance of the object in modernity both arise in conjunction with a transformation of man, one being anthropological and the other historical.

It might be objected that there is little new ground trod in Scheler's argument, that, for example, Dilthey more thoroughly and originally treats the historical transformation, or that Bergson more sensitively discusses the anthropological. It might even further be argued that Scheler, in regard to both forms, is still locked, just as Dilthey and Bergson, in conceiving the object only as a "target" of some sort of thinking subject. This perception, while valid in a small sense, clearly misses the mark in a larger sense, for the uniqueness of Scheler's thesis arises from its non-dependence upon a thinking (or willing) ego. He asserts that the idea of object in the philosophies of most moderns follows from the positing of an *ego cogito* with every experience of the world.

> That is, this *ego* is not a correlate that is added to the unity
> and identity of the *object*. "Object" here *means* only a some-
> thing that is identified through the ego. *Identity* is not (as it is
> for us) an essential characteristic of the object. . . .[I]dentity is
> originally in the ego, and it is from the ego that the identity of
> an object is borrowed.[93]

Hence, Scheler contends that modern thought cannot escape the perception of object being a constitution of the thinking subject because it relies on the thinking ego as an individuated cognitive agency from which all action proceeds. To this Scheler responds, on one hand, that the being of an object is in no sense wholly a constitution of the subject. On the other hand, he contends that the thinking ego is itself only an object present before the subjectivity of the human person.

The first response, that being-as-object is not a predicate of the ego, is congruent with Scheler's renowned phenomenological realism and his even more non-Husserlian position that the reality of any thing is not exhausted in intentionality. Somewhat more radically, the response also envisions the being of an object as, inherently, objective. In other words, Scheler considers that objects are objects not because they are objectified by any subject, but because their very mode of being is being-as-object. An object is an object, ontologically. A cautious clarification might be interjected in this, however, for Scheler does not absolutely reject a constitutive relationship between person and world ("subject" and "object"). Such constitution *does* exist at a more superficial level. As noted above, the objects of the world, natural and historical, establish the framework of potentialities and possibilities for action. Actions, and by inference the human person, find expression only within the context of this situation in the world. Clearly, the specific potential activities of the person are, in fact, *constituted* by the objects of the world. Obversely, but in a similar manner, Scheler also grants that objects acquire meanings which are constituted for and through persons. The relationship between person and world at this level, therefore, is one in which the meaning of objects and potential for personal actions are constituted —indeed, are mutually constitutive. Yet, at the more primary, ontological stratum, Scheler adamantly insists that object and person are independent of each other and distinct in being. The meaning and function of objects in the world are constituted in relation with persons, but the objective essence of their being is not. The framework of existence in the world constitutes the medium and possibility of expression for personal actions, but the being of the person *per se* is autonomous.[97]

In consideration of the second response, Scheler argues that the ego is but another object amidst a world of objects. Anticipating similar pronouncements by later phenomenologists and existentialists and elaborated prior to any published accounts of Husserl's opposite turn, he speaks pointedly against the possibility of what he terms the "transcendental ego," whether as a "consciousness as such" or even a "species consciousness."

For the "ego," including the "egoness" in all individual
egos, is only an *"object"* (in every sense of the word) for acts,
especially for acts having the nature of "inner perception."
We meet the ego only in this perception. . . .[b]ut the ego is
neither the *point of departure* for this apprehension nor the pro-
ducer of essence. It is not an essence which unilaterally
"founds" all other essences or even all essences of acts.[95]

In support for this, Scheler in phenomenological fashion explores the
notion of "inner perception." He concludes that something is, in
fact, given in such perception, that among other things a self or ego is
perceived. Because it is thus "perceived," it *must* belong to the mode
of being-as-object. Rather insufficiently discussed by Scheler, the
thrust of this is directed toward making a sharp distinction between
the ego and the person—between the objectifiable aspect of man and
the non-objectifiable unity of acts which is the person. The unnamed
adversary in his efforts may possibly be Husserl's intentionality.
Scheler seems to foresee that Husserl's "consciousness-of-
something" necessitates a transcendental ego. Arguing elsewhere
that all cognition is a relationship between objects, an ontological
relationship, he apparently concludes that "consciousness-of-
something" is a perceiving relationship between a thing and an ego-
object.[96] This relationship, moreover, is not an object, but an activity.
Hence, the relationship between ego and other objects in the world,
or between any objects, rests upon a further ground.

This "further ground" is a unity in acts. Only as linked through
acts do objects exist in relation with one another. The separateness,
distinctness and individuation of objects is such that only that which
is non-objective can ground the relation between them. Illustrated in
this is an aspect of being-as-act which is of paramount importance for
Scheler's thought and, ultimately, for personalism as political theory.
As that mode of being by which objects are meaningfully related, act
is itself revealed to be non-objectifiable. Scheler notes, that "an act is
never an object; for according to the nature of the being of acts, they
are experienced only in their execution and given in reflection." Even
in reflection, he mentions further, an act is not an object. Reflection
accompanies an act, but does not objectify it, and no act can be perceived in the object sense by which ego is perceived in inner perception.[97] This latter is a keen insight, one deserving closer scrutiny,
especially from political theorists. *Reflection*, it would seem, does not

necessitate objectification. The acts of the subject are accessible only in their execution—or, as shall be seen, only in the co-experiencing of persons with persons.

The foregoing becomes crucial when it is remembered that the person shares act's mode of being and is discussed as a "concrete unity of acts." This is a key point, one which is too frequently misunderstood. Comprehendable solely as pure, unreified execution, act escapes any moment of hypostasis. It is beyond objectification and inconceivabale as a thing or substance. The person, a unity of acts, is likewise outside the realm of objects; it is not a thing or substance. And, imperatively, it cannot and must not be treated as such. Yet, to sketch the concept so negatively—e.g., *not* an object, thing or substance—affords only the barest glimpse of the person himself. What exactly is the unity of acts which defines the person? Scheler is perhaps over-much restrained in his answer. Every act, he explains, is intrinsically individual in itself and essentially different from all other acts. The root of this individuation lies in the fact that acts are ever acts *toward* some thing, things which themselves require acts to bridge their monad-like separateness. Just as Husserl, therefore, Scheler, would be faced at this point with the chaos of a cosmos of disparate phenomena devoid of meaning and unity. But, where Husserl turns to his transcendental, phenomenological ego to surmount this dilemma, Scheler is leery of the implicit idealism and the epistemological subject-object problem such an ego would bring in its train. Responding differently, he undercuts the subject-object dilemma be redefining the ego as an object among objects and by positing that any relation between ego and object would be constituted by a deeper mode of being.

To object, as many critics have done, that Scheler's move only postpones and does not overcome the subject-object dilemma—implying that he relies, and succumbs in the end to an obfuscated Cartesian subject—may be premature and not adequately sensitive to his argument. For, he does not stop with the redefinition of the ego as an object grounded on another substantial subject. Person is not a substance, and it is not separate from the world because it is a unity of essentially different acts which necessarily are joined to the world. Thus, he writes, "the person is the concrete [i.e., 'real'], essential unity of acts of different essences," "the 'foundation' of essentially different acts."[98]

The status of the subject, following from the above, becomes one which is quite different from the subject of Descartes, Kant and even

Husserl. It is not a cognitive process or agency, but an on-going constellation of acts which surrounds and gives unity to vastly differing specific acts. Nonetheless, it *remains* still a subject. Scheler contends that it is not exhausted in any particular action or in the sum of all actions. Serving as the "foundation" for all possible acts, it operates—using the term rather loosely—as *a priori* and transcendental for every specific act. While not entirely novel to philosophy, being reminiscent of Fichte's objections to Kant's noumenal subject, such assertions remain provocative, especially within the framework of what is ostensibly phenomenology. Yet, Scheler even more profoundly reaffirms the person's non-substantial and non-cognitive status, contending that his subject has being only in the performance of its acts. Thus, he comments in one place, that "it *belongs to the essence of the person* to exist and to live solely in the *execution of intentional acts*," and he recapitulates in another place, that "person 'is' only as the concrete unity of acts executed by the person and only *in* the execution of these acts."[99] Literally, it would appear, to be (in the sense of being a person) is to *do*.

Even though he succeeds in overcoming modernity's ego, the emphasis on acts, which are by definition intentional, coupled with a definition of the subject as a "transcendental" constellation of acts, lends a strong existentialist flavor to the place of subjectivity in Scheler's thought. Sharpening the focus on his subject, however, reveals limits toward understanding Scheler's project in this fashion. The person is "transcendental" only in his function vis-a-vis his specific acts. Furthermore, acts are themselves dependent on objects as the medium for their expression, and thereby occur only within the framework of a particular situation in the world. Along similar lines, Scheler elaborates three areas which reveal the need to comprehend subjectivity as embedded in, and existing through, objective being: in acts and values, in person and world, and in spirit [*Geist*] and drive.[100]

In the *first* area, the areas of acts and values, Scheler presents a theory of action which sees all acts as dependent upon the perception of and an inclination toward some value. Values are objectively real in his thinking and are perceived and evaluated prior to any and all other conation—including reasoning. Intentional acts are performed for the acquisition of these values. Consequently, in Scheler's theory, unlike the "act philosophies" of many other writers such as Schopenhauer's and Sorel's, acts are not seen to emerge from a blind willing, but from a "knowing" discernment of value. Accordingly, acts are demonstrated to be limited to the range of possibilities for execution which might be afforded by the complex of values which faces them.[101] This value-complex corresponds to what Scheler refers to as the "practical world," which in turn is the objective being with which the *second* area is concerned—the area of person and world. Just as act corresponds with an objective value, so too the person (a unity of acts) corresponds to a world (a complex of values). Like acts, the person is able to express his personhood only within the range of possibilities granted by his individual world. In other words, a person finds himself amidst a world which establishes the bounds of his personal existence. To this extent, the person is as his world is. Dependent upon the world for the possibility of his expression, moreover, person is inseparable from his situation in this objective reality.[102] Finally, in the *third* area, the area of spirit and drive, Scheler's later works depict a somewhat radicalized version of this same embeddedness of subjectivity in objective processes. The depiction centers on a discussion of the roles of spirit and drive, where man is seen as as the meeting ground of these two realities. Here, the claim is made that spirit—which is the realm of act and subjectivity—is powerless in and of itself. Spirit, by means of an almost Freudian sublimation, only acquires efficacy within the existential world by chaneling the potency of the objective life drive towards its ends. Like act and person, spirit as it exists in the world is very much a reflection of its situation and is able to impact upon its situation only to the extent that it can draw upon the forces of life which are ready at hand. Thus, in each of these three areas the subjective is constrained by the objective for both its medium of expression and its efficacy.

An intriguing picture of a *political* subject coalesces around the idea of Scheler's person. Not objectifiable, the person as citizen ought not be treated and manipulated as some thing or object. Existing only in the performance of acts in the world, yet retaining a reflective element as given in acts themselves, the person evokes images of the classical citizen of practical wisdom and of the more current understanding of political responsibility as praxis. Indeed, Scheler's understanding of the person lends support to those who would see a "transformed politics" lying beyond the so-called "end of politics"—one which perhaps would serve as complement to Scheler's looked-for "transformed man." Whether, however, Scheler is truly capable of establishing the person in the manner he attempts in his philosophy, remains an unresolved question. His presentation of the concept is far from being a tidy, systematic thesis. More than merely lacking the polish and attention to detail which one expects from academic philosophers, there exist a number of inconsistencies and inadequately developed arguments. These require careful consideration before any defense of personalism as political theory can be sustained. Further, any discussion of Scheler's conception of the person solely in regard to his objective and subjective status leaves the concept appearing altogether disembodied. Scheler, however, is sharply critical of any reduction of the richness of the concrete, real person to ghostly abstraction; and, thus, concerns himself not only with its ontological status, but with the person's place, history and destiny.

GENESIS OF PERSON—ONTOGENESIS AND MORPHOGENESIS

Drawing upon wide-ranging researches from as far afield as Gestalt theory and animal psychology, Scheler illustrates the place and genesis of the person in his own careful appraisal of many of the findings of psychology and biology. With regard to both of these, personhood emerges through an ascending hierarchy of pre-personal stages from the most contingent and determined to the least so. However, as will become clear, Scheler nowhere articulates an irrepressible historical or developmental process relative to the emergence of the person—despite the tacit teleology apparent in his hierarchical categories. Neither does he admit any sort of causal connection between these stages, for the lower orders are not the "cause" of the higher. This is not, however, to deny all dependency and order in his schemas. Despite what he sees as the difference of essence between each of the individual categories in his hierarchical typologies, Scheler contends that there is a chain of dependency which links them all, each higher category being possible only upon the fulfillment of the preceding, lower one.[103] The lower orders, thus, serve to make possible the conditions in which the higher might emerge, much as a plant requires soil in which to grow.

The ontogenetic or psychological grounds of Scheler's person are specifically explored in many of his works. Nowhere, however, does the rigor and care of his treatment of the topic approach that of his renowned work *The Nature of Sympathy*.[104] Here his investigation combines the then most current empirical studies of child development and linguistics with perhaps his most precise and thorough utilization of the phenomenological method. From his efforts it becomes clear that man's earliest experiences do not include an experience or awareness of the self.[105] Human consciousness begins without an ego, without reflection, completely at one with the stream of experiences acquired in its environment. An infant's first world, so to speak, is undifferentiated between ego and alter ego, or between the self and the surrounding social and natural milieu. Instead, Scheler contends, it is a completely unindividuated flux of experiences wherein the infant exists in seamless unity with its social and natural environment. It is only subsequently—curiously, by means of first isolating individual objects in the environment about him—that he is able to detach his individual personality from its previous immersion in its situation. Gradually, via this slow dissociational process, the human person is able to distinguish his personal subjectivity from the objective realities within which it is enmeshed. Inferring from this, a developmental sequence can be perceived where at its highest point even the isolation of the ego—an object among objects—is achieved. At this level the self, or *person*, emerges in full status as wholly "other" than the menagerie of objects, substances and things in which he finds himself.

Mirroring the ontogenesis of the person in psychology, Scheler turns to the biological underpinings of the person by partitioning the phenomenon of life into five categories as shown under the heading of morphogenesis in Table 1.[106] The lowest category, Scheler refers to as the "vegetative," and is seen as comprised of only the most primitive "vital impulse," a basic urge toward growth and the maintenance of life. Life which belongs purely to this category—plants and microbes—is wholly without consciousness, even without the true perception or sensation. The simple level of activity which occurs here is one which is little more than a blind response to the vagaries of the surrounding environment. Without any measure of reflective "feedback" in the performance of acts, life at this level exists as entirely submerged in its environment and as totally unable to differentiate its own being from the objective world in which it finds itself. This total submersion of the organism in its environment, which Scheler designates as "ec-static" existence, plays a crucial role in the development of the person. It is *the* origin from which all psychic life arises; all higher categories of life draw upon roots which burrow deeply into the primal life urge of the vegetative. Furthermore, it is at this lowest level that the most basic experience of the reality of existence is had; for the world is experienced—and for higher categories "known" to be real—by the resistance which the objective world poses to this vital impulse.[107]

More complex than the primitive "vegetative" category, the next level, "instinct," reveals two subtle distinctions from the lower level.

First, organisms are perceived as nascently able to dissociate or isolate certain elements in their environment from the flux of the environment as a whole. Second, following from the dissociation, organisms of the instinctive category possess the beginnings of purposive action. The capacity for this is not, however, an accomplishment of any individual organism *per se*, but reflects only a genetic "stimulus-response" pattern which is ingrained within the species. All flatworms, for example, would respond to a given stimulus in precisely the same manner, the actions of each organism precisely identical to the actions of others. Thus, for Scheler, instinct is integrated with the morphogenesis of the species and functions in close association with an organism's physiology and genetic evolution.[108] There is a unity of pre-knowledge and action at this level—i.e., there is no more

SCHELER TYPOLOGIES

Values	Ontogenisis	Morphogenesis	Sociality	Sympathy
Sacred	Person	Spirit (Geist)	Person Community	Personal Love
Noble	Adolescent Ego	Practical Intelligence	Society	True Sympathy
Vital		Habitual		Fellow Feeling
Useful	Emerging Ego	Instinctive	Life Community	Vicarious Feeling
Pleasant	Infantile Pre-ego	Vegetative	Herd	Emotional Identification

Table 1. Parallel Typologies Associated with Origin of the Person

"knowledge" at hand than that which is necessary for the performance of the next step of the action sequence given in instinct. Moreover, this knowledge is immediately given with experience, as if programmed into the genetics of the species. Life at this level, nonetheless, is able to direct its actions toward specific objects or aims which
are distinguished from the background of its situation in the world.

The third category of life is a continuation of the development of
the capacity for dissociation. This level, which Scheler designates as
the level of associative memory or "habit," is the level of conditioned reflec.[109] Actions by organisms corresponding to this level
demonstrate the first evidence of individuation. Each organism is able
to establish a specific individual pattern of behavior or habit based
upon feedback sensations associated wtih acts of "trial and error"
directed toward something perceived in experience. In performing
some tasks, thus, a pigeon is able to modify its behavior and establish
a habit of certain actions when repetitive positive or negative rein-
forcement is experienced. Habitual actions represent a furthering of
the dissociation of the organism from the environment, requiring the
organism to interject a degree of preference in at least some of its actions.

The fourth category of life involves what Scheler terms "practical
intelligence."[110] Scheler argues that an organism behaves intelli-
gently if it acts spontaneously and with a purpose when faced with a
previously unexperienced situation. So doing is a qualitative leap
from the "trial and error" behavior which would characterize
organisms of the previous level. Practical intelligence is seen as a
problem solving enterprise which results in actions which are utterly
new and unlearned. As Scheler describes the activity of organisms of
this category, there is presupposed an ability in the organism to
analytically draw out useful interrelationships between various objects in the environment, and on this basis to synthetically
manipulate the environment to the organism's particular purposes.
Additively accumulating a store of learning from this process, the
organism would further be able to usefully build upon previous experiences for the acquisition of even greater utility. Hence, there is
again at this level an increase of the ability of the organism to
dissociate itself from its situation in the world. Animals behaving in-
telligently are able to utilize such elements outside of reference to the
here-and-now.

The fifth and final category in Scheler's schema of life is the level
of spirit, or *Geist*. Here, as is seen with the highest level of the onto-

genetic schema, a fundamental transformation occurs. In some manner, Scheler even finds it inappropriate to include this category with the others of the biological schema, for it represents much more than merely another incremental advance in an organism's capacity for dissociation. It radicalizes dissociation, as the organism—the person—is able to dissociate even his own ego and psychological functions. Perhaps the level of *Geist*, therefore, might be perceived as inherently and essentially *opposed* to the objective realm to which life generally belongs. Indeed, in his last period, Scheler makes such an argument, claiming this new level

> ...transcends what we call "life" in the most general sense. It is not a stage of life, especially not a stage of the particular mode of life we call psyche, but a principle opposed to life as such, even to life in man. Thus, it is a genuinely new phenomenon which cannot be derived from the natural evolution of life, but which, if reducible to anything, leads back to the ultimate Ground of Being of which "life" is a particular manifestation.[111]

Clearly, Scheler invokes his duality of being in this passage. Spirit is of the mode of being-as-act, and cannot be understood as derived from the almost evolutionary sequence of stages which mark the lower categories. Spirit—the level of person—becomes the basis by which man is possessed of a special place in reality. Although absolutely powerless in and of itself, requiring a sublimation of the potencies of the lower levels of life for its efficacy, spirit yet represents the origin of personal freedom in acts. The peculiarity of this freedom is its utter dependence upon the objective being of the world for its operation. Spirit is utterly inseparable from life and life's place in the world, while it is never wholly immersed within it.

Returning to the ontogenesis or psychological roots of the person, it can be concluded that the person similarly draws upon the more primitive psychological stages of the personality for his efficacy as does spirit on life. Responsible and free personhood requires deep reservoirs in the rawer lower levels, just as the mature individuality of the person stands atop an initial milieu where the self is undifferentiated from the social and natural background.[112] Personhood is not, then, a severing of the roots to these more primal psychologies. It draws on the undefined experiences of the pre-self and pre-person as taproots for its more rare and subtle existence.

PERSON AND OTHER, SOCIALITY AND INTERSUBJECTIVITY

Scheler's work on the nature of sympathy also outlines a phenomenology of the relationship between the person and the other in the guise of an extended critique of ethical theories which rest on the feeling of sympathy.[113] In addition, the work initiates a discussion of an approach to the problem of intersubjectivity which has its basis in what Scheler finds as the genuine person-other relationship. In subsequent works, the insights gleaned in these areas are elaborated to form integral elements of his ethics, his epistemology and his sociology, and establish the substance of the community which is the necessary ground for turning personalism to the problem of the *political* community.

Briefly discussed in the previous section, the starting point for Scheler's understanding of the person-other relationship, and all sociality, lies in his investigation into the ontogenetic stages of the person. As was noted, he perceives the initial stage of the process to be one which is wholly devoid of individuation, where the human is without self-consciousness or other self-awareness and is unable to differentiate its own experiences from the web of experiences of its social milieu. Scheler at one point writes of this stage, that it is ''an immediate flow of experiences, *undifferentiated as between mine and thine*, which actually contains both our own and others' experiences intermingled and without distinction.''[114] Man's *a priori* world, so to speak, is a totally social one—one which Scheler terms the *Mitwelt*. In his genesis, at least, man's image in Scheler's thought somewhat resembles the ancient picture of the *zoon politikon*. Yet, as was also noted, the human being on the basis of this primal social world is gradually able to dissociate his individual ego and ultimately his person from the enveloping social milieu, much as a child first discovers and greedily rejoices in the self only ideally to mature into personhood that is able to appreciate and care for the concerns of others. He does not see, of course, any guarantees in this process. Humans cannot be programmed like automatons to climb step-by-step toward personhood. It requires neigher a psychologist nor a sociologist to recognize that civilization is not possessed of an abundance of ''ideally mature'' persons. Scheler suggests only that this is the pattern of the emergence of the person. The genesis can unfold from an unconscious and unitentional milieu without distinction between self and other, through aggressive and adolescent egoism, toward genuine individual freedom and the concomitant acceptance of other-directed concern and social responsibility.

Complementing the ontogenesis of sociality in the person, Scheler proposes a similar typology of stages as evidenced in the phylogenesis of human sociality. Going beyond Ferdinand Toennies' dochotomous division of sociality into *Gemeinschaft* and *Gesellschaft* and even beyond the tripartite analysis of Hegel to which it is obviously indebted, Scheler's is a four-tiered typology. As presented in his *Formalism in Ethics and Non-Formal Ethics of Values*, the bottommost level of sociality is the *herd*, at which level the individual is totally submerged in a beast-like social organism.[115] Above this, at the next level, is the *life community*, where the barest shadow of the individual can be discerned. What small measure of individuality is afforded in the life community, however, would be an individuality determined and created by the community for the larger purposes of this social whole. Scheler describes such individuality as an appendage of corporate community, much as one's hand has an individual character but is meaningless without the whole body.[116] At the next level of the typology, the *society*, which Scheler likens to the modern individualist society, more completely differentiated individuals appear. Individuals at this level succeed in transcending the understanding of themselves as only objects or means for the various ends of the community. However, in so doing, the community ceases to exist in its own right and becomes merely a means to the many disparate ends of the numerous individuals. Men, similarly, by asserting the primacy of the self, isolate themselves from their fellows who at best become objectified means for the ego's ends. In denying the community to assert the self, Scheler contends that the individuals of the society fail to achieve a fundamental aspect of the true individualism of the person—i.e., the personal dignity and respect for the self which is only freely given in the eyes of one's fellows. By viewing others as objects the individual here is himself objectified in the perspective of each of his fellows.[117]

Person community, the highest level of sociality, envisions a transcendence not only of the self as an object of the community, but of the community and others as objects of the self. In this instance, the community which disappears as a separate existence at the level of the society, is reformed and transformed. In one sense, accepting the personhood and inherent dignity of others eliminates the subject-object relationship between the self and others. In *another* sense, however, personal individuality is most deeply affirmed in the acceptance of one's own personhood in the eyes of others and in the embrace of the community. [118] This conception of the person community is somewhat reinterpreted by Scheler in the subsequently published

Formalism under the term *Gesamtperson* [collective person], which he defines as "*the unity of independent, spiritual, and individual single person 'in' an independent, spiritual, and individual collective person.*"[119] It is a collectivity in the sense of the life community, but it is actually and historically incorporated by the free intentions of individuals as is reminiscent of the society. The *Gesamtperson* or person community, however, is not so much a creation of individuals (as would in fact be the case in the society) but is rather concomitant with the existence of the person himself, owing to the character of personhood. Thus, he claims, that "an individual person *and* a collective person 'belong' to every finite person," for "both factors are essentially necessary sides of a concrete whole of person and world."[120]

In more familiar terminology, it is clear that the parallel characters of Scheler's ontogenetic and phylogenetic stages of person and sociality offer an intriguing complement to a theory of intersubjectivity involving person, other persons and the communal person. In circular fashion, he illustrates that the individual is possible only on the foundation of the engulfing natural sociality and, yet, that the highest sociality represents the choice of individual persons who forego their narrow selfhood by joining in the person community.

Scheler the phenomenologist, however, is not content with uncovering merely the social and individual background of intersubjectivity. His main concern, indeed, is the illustration of its actual operation and functioning. More importantly, he seeks to clarify the status of the relationship between the person and the other by which the person is able ultimately to join in the person community. Toward this, Scheler's thesis, again, begins with the concept of the person. As noted previously, the person cannot be reified or objectified. It is "essentially" different from all objects—including the psychophysical object which is the ego—because person's mode of being is being-as-act. As a constellation of acts and existing only in the performance—the "doing"—of acts, the person himself is beyond objectification. *In the same way, other persons are also beyond objectification.* As pure execution, the being of others escapes the objectification to which even one's own ego succumbs. "if act can therefore never be an object," Scheler writes, "then the *person* who lives in the execution of acts can *a fortiori* never be an object." Equally, " if we are concerned with *other* persons," he continues, "there is no objectification."[121] Agreeing, thus, with Immanual Kant that the other "must *never* be considered a *thing*," Scheler belongs in the rich tradition of those who find a moral imperative in that the other ought never be treated as a means but always as a unique locus of subjectivity equal in dignity with one's own person.[122] There are, however, immediately encountered limits in representing Scheler in the Kantian analogy, for in the end Kant's person is found by Scheler to be no more than a cognitive ego, an ego in light of which others, too, are able to be perceived as merely thinking objects. Here Scheler argues that Kant's failure lies in the formalizing of the subject. In dutifully considering all "persons" as formally identical in regard to their essential nature, the other is understood as less than the full person he is. Kant's formalism, like all formalisms, ineluctably can conceive of men only as "the X of certain powers" or the "X of some kind of rational activity"—i.e., as an object.[123]

Scheler's revelation of the essential non-objectifiability of the other opens wide vistas of possibility for ethics, morality, social philosophy and poltical theory. Little imagination is required to foresee the character of a political community and its politics wherein each person is afforded treatment appropriate to the incomparably unique dignity of her personhood. On this basis, is suggested a transformation of the practice of politics. Scheler's personalism would see citizens recognizing their follows *not as equal* to themselves, but as entirely transcendental to the objectification by which any measure of equality might be achieved—an idea which in some sense may be more revolutionary than mere equality. At this juncture, the radical nature of Scheler's personalism—his "radical humanism" as one author terms it—becomes startlingly evident. [124] Where the liberal movements were founded on the radicalization of the medieval understanding of man, i.e., endowing man with formal or sovereign equality, and where the socialist movements similarly radicalized the liberal conception by endowing man with material equality, Scheler would transcend the notion of equality itself. Beyond equality lies the inestimable dignity and absolute uniqueness of the other as a person.

Yet, the very radicalness of Scheler's notion of the status of the other, despite the utopian social and political landscape which it reveals, poses a number of troubling questions. Foremost among these is the dilemma which appears relative to the understanding or "conation" of others. How is "knowledge" of other persons to be arrived at when all knowledge of others as objects is precluded? Or, better put, what is the means or process through which the person is able to recognize his own primitive social character, see the other person as a sharing partner in the social milieu, and resonsibly join with the other in a fully personal community? If others cannot be rendered as objects for knowing, then on what basis can a coming-together [*Miteinandersein*] of any sort become possible?[125] In answer, a most provocative aspect of Scheler's personalism is introduced—an aspect which remains central to his thought from his student years at Jena until his death. Speaking to the apparent dilemma, he writes in a late essay...

> Other people, too, as *persons* cannot become objects. (In this sense Goethe said of Lili Schoenemann that he "loved her too much" to be able to "observe" her.) We can only come to know them by entering into their free acts, through the kind of "understanding" possible in an attitude of empathetic love, the very opposit of objectification—in short, by "identifying," as we say, with the will and love of another person and, thereby, with himself.[126]

Through co-acting or co-experiencing, therefore, a "knowledge" is gained of the other by which the person perceives his own social character and origin. Through this "knowledge," in perceiving the immeasurable dignity of the other as person, the person is able to join responsibly and intentionally and to accept the highest sociality of the person community.

In the *Nature of Sympathy*, Scheler discusses this same "co-experiencing" in its highest form as a "non-cosmic personal love," a concept which he locates atop a hierarchy of types of sympathy—which he sees as the grounds of intersubjectivity.[127] Again, he parallels the stages of this hierarchy with the stages of the ontogenesis of the person and the genesis of sociality itself. At the lowest stage, corresponding with the sociality stage of the "herd," Scheler contends that the nature of this "intersubjectivity" rests upon a totally unconscious, unintentional and undifferentiated emotional *identification* [*Einsgefühl*] between peole, so much that the individual subject and the other are emotionally indistinguishable.[128] Familiar with the mass movements of the Weimar years, Scheler casts this stage in a rather perjorative light, taking the torchlit, leaderless, nighttime mob as a contemporary example of this unconscious emotional identification of one human with another. Above such radical identification of one with another, the next stage of sympathy, corresponding with the sociality of the life community, is one which is established on what Scheler calls *vicarious feelings* [*Nachgefühl*]. As with the lower identification stage, this level sees an unintentional sharing of experiences between all subjects, but the completeness and directness of this co-experiencing is vitiated by a relatively greater emotional distance between subjects. By way of illustration, Scheler depicts the passing from the lower identification level to the higher vicarious feeling level by referring to the chthonian mysteries of Greek antiquity. In the earliest period of these revels a genuine "identification" was experienced among participants as each individual surrendered to the emotional rhythms of the amorphous whole. With time, however, history sees a gradual formalization of these rites, congealing into the ritual art of tragic theater, where direct indentification passes over into the vicarious participation of the audience in the drama.[129]

With the attainment of the next two stages of Scheler's hierarchy of sympathy-grounded intersubjectivity, the term "intersubjectivity" itself becomes appropriate. In identification and vicarious feeling, the individual subject cannot be said to be viable in itself, and it lacks the self-consciousness necessary for intentional (i.e., responsible) action. The emergence of the self-conscious subject, however, would seem to underlie the *fellow-feeling* [*Mitgefühl*] which is the sympathetic bond at the next level of intersubjectivity. Scheler remarks that "it is through fellow-feeling, in both its mutual and reciprocated forms, that 'other minds in general' [already previously given as a field] are brought home to us in individual cases as having a *reality equal to our own.*" Vicarious feeling is not sufficient to confer this sense of the other's equality. The basis for possible intersubjectivity, which corresponds with the individualism of the "society" stage of sociality, fellow-feeling is an intentional reaching out from one subject toward the other. Through it "self-love, self-centered choice, solipsism and egoism are first overcome."[130] Above fellow-feeling, yet still beneath the highest possible ground of for intersubjectivity, is *humanitarianism* [*Menschenliebe*]. Humanitarianism is higher and more all-encompassing than fellow-feeling precisely because humanitarianism recognizes the intrinsic, special dignity of the other as a fellow and equal human. Is is the peculiar sympathy one experiences when the equality of the other is recognized in his humanity—despite the existential differences in which this equality may be cloaked. Thus, for example, Scheler cites the watchphrase by which Goethe would allow entrance into heaven: "For I was a man and that is to be a fighter."[131]

Humanitarianism, however, is not the highest of sympathies. Scheler's early works, in fact, are unrelentingly harsh in their appraisal of humanitarianism, identifying the concept with the bourgeois and romantic notion of universal brotherhood—an ethereal fraternity which inevitably never quite reaches to the flesh-and-blood humanity of the everyday world of practice. One could imagine the humanitarian professing love for mankind while incapable of recognizing the personal humanity of those encountered in daily life. In his most Nietzschean work, *Ressentiment*, Scheler argues that humanitarianism is but a disguised outgrowth of the resentment which darkly issues from the bourgeois recognition of the uniqueness—and thereby possible superiority—of the other. "Modern humanitarianism," he explains, "does not command and value the *personal* act of love from man to man, but primarily the impersonal 'institution' of welfare."[132] And, although Scheler later retracts the extreme vitriol which he directs here toward humanitarianism, he maintains that humanitarianism is locked into the perversion of formalism—treating the other as *merely equal* in his humanity with oneself. As noted, the radicalness of Scheler's thesis lies in its transcendence of mere equality by its recognition of the essential and absolutely unique dignity of each person. Hence, the sympathy which forms the basis for the highest intersubjectivity is one which accepts and rejoices in the other's infinite dignity, one which allows for more direct and personal co-experiencing with the other, and one which retains the preservation of individual personal responsibility. This highest stage of sympathy, the concept of *personal love* with which this inquiry into sympathy was initiated, Scheler equates with Christian love: for him a synthesis of the Greek senses of *agape* and *eros*. Against humanitarianism, he states, this sympathy "is sharply distinguished from the generalized love of humanity which merely regards individuals as lovable *qua* "'specimens' of the human race."[133]

The foregoing portrayal of Scheler's understanding of intersubjectivity is incomplete without the perception of its close linkage of his theory of values. By way of this linkage, further, he endows his thesis with ethical imperatives through which it becomes at least equally a normative as an explanatory theory. Scheler's ethics is a "material" ethics. Unlike Kant's non-substantial and formal "goods," values are seen as real and objective, and as intrinsically lexical according to an *a priori* rank order. Scheler's typology of values, however, (utility-vital-spiritual-salvational) does not afford a category for assessing the value of the other. This is consistent with Scheler's notion of the non-objectification of others, for values have objective status in his conception of reality. Other persons *are not* objective even as values, and the other ought never be treated as a value for oneself. Instead, Scheler speaks of "personal values" as those values which belong or are carried by a person, both one's own the person of the other.[134] Hence, in the personal love which marks the highest intersubjectivity, one co-experiences the values of the other, thereby mutually sharing in the pursuit of the highest values appropriate for each unique person.

In the community of persons, or *Gesamtperson*, in which each individual person partakes, the implications of Scheler's value theory paint a somewhat fabulous, albeit attractive, vision. For, in the corporate person, as an intentional and responsible communion of free individual persons, a moral solidarity is achieved. Here the whole assumes the moral responsibility for the actions of each part and each part accepts the responsibility for the whole. The *Gesamtperson* and the individual person are freely entered into what can only be described as a "loving" relationship, where each pursues (in coacting through the other) the fulfillment of the highest value of each. Not a dreamy utopia, Scheler contends that

> If one takes a look at the *relation* of this highest form of social unity—as the idea of a solidary realm of love of individual, independent spiritual persons in a pluality of collective persons of the same character—compared to the ideas of life-community and society, one can see that life-community and society as essential forms of social unity are *subordinated* to this highest essential social form, and that they are determined to make it appear, but, to be sure, in different manners. Although the idea of the highest form of social unity is not a "synthesis" of life-community and society, essential characteristics of both are nevertheless cogiven in it: the independent, individual person, as in society; and solidarity and real collective unity, as in community.[135]

Further insights into Scheler sociological and political thought follow from his theory of intersubjectivity. Since others are non-objectifiable and opaque to cognitive knowing, understanding of the other stems from a primary sociality (as ontological ground) and from an intentional participation in the acts and experiences of the other. Abandoning self-centered inwardness and accepting the unique personhood of the other, it is through co-experiencing and co-acting with him, sharing in his practices, that all "knowing" of the other is possible. Moreover, it is in this manner that the community, politics and (presumably) social and human sciences can occur. For politics, Scheler's phenomenologically unearthed intersubjectivity tenders an opportune alternative for those theorists dubious of the legitimacy of political theories which celebrate the formal reason of post-Enlightenment bourgeois liberalism, or which depand upon the so-called "rational man." For social scientists, Scheler's intersubjectivity proffers convincing evidence of the inadequacy of objectivist and positivist methodology and strong support for the absolute primacy of a type of *Verstehen* as the basis for all inquiry into man and the human condition.[136]

WORLD: NATURE AND HISTORY

For every person, as a constellation of acts, there exists as a correlate a "world," as a constellation of objects.[137] The world in Scheler's thought, roughly speaking, is the existential framework inside which the person is presented with the medium and "limits" whereby acts are able to be performed. It establishes the boundaries and opportunities for being-as-act (or spirit) to be *realized*. The world is that constellation of objective reality which is *present* to the person, to which the person is always a correlate, but also with which no person can utterly be "identified." In his penchant for finely defined distinctions, Scheler assigns the many objects of a given person's world with numerous labels—objects of the inner world, outer world, bodiliness, ideal objects and value objects. However, in light of immediate concerns, the details of his analysis may be put aside and Scheler's thesis of the "enframedness" of the person in the world might be valuably discussed in the terminology of the twofold distinction between nature and history.

Scheler's concept of nature has already attracted passing consideration in this study, especially in regard to the morphogenesis of the person and the relationship of spirit and drive. In the first instance, it was seen that the person holds a privileged position in life by virtue of the ability to dissociate his subjectivity from the objects of the natural world, including his own ego and psychology. In the second, it was seen that person, as a locus of spirit, must draw upon the potency of drive and the natural world for the expression of personal existence and the accomplishment of personal ends. The spiritual core of the person, his being-as-act, is *realized* in the body and through the natural world. Curious and compelling as this perception of man's place in the natural world is, the passing consideration given it fails to convey the full intent behind Scheler's thinking.

Quite open in his rejection of the modern concept of nature, one which he states "first bludgeons nature into a corpse and then claims to have discovered the innermost secret of its life," Scheler with the romantics bewails the tragic alienation of modernity where man appears disjointed from his proper place in the natural world.[138] Like many of the romantics, moreover, he traces the origin of the perversion of the modern concept of nature to the roots of modernity itself—seeing the brightest flowering of the concept in the "pure spirit" of the Enlightenment and in the philosophies of Berkeley, Kant, Hegel and Fichte, while finding the most disquieting results of the concept in the mechanistic scientism of Newton and Edison and in the positivism of Comte. Yet, Scheler is no romantic. His own conception of nature is *not* a pining for a unity of man with the unspoiled natural world; nor even is it an escapist retreat from the here-and-now to a presumed halcyon antiquity. In the *Nature of Sympathy*, the clearest glimpse of his own understanding is lent in an analysis of past and present theories of man's unity with the cosmos.[139] From a primeval understanding of man as ecstatically submerged in nature, through the Greek awe-inspired wonder at the myriad of natural forms and their order, through the Judeo-Christian perception of nature's subordination to man, to the modern conception of nature as something to be mastered, dominated and utilized—Scheler follows a thread that culminates in something rather different. Where others, from Max Weber to Jacques Ellul, perceive an inevitable development of the concept of nature from an organic model toward an increasingly mechanistic, Scheler wishes to include a further stage.

Paralleling, once more, the stages of his several typologies, it can be supposed correctly that Scheler's preferred understanding of nature complements his notions of the person and the person community. Man's most primitive attitude toward nature is one which sees him immersed in the natural world and indistinguishable from it. This is supplanted by a subsequent stage wherein man still belongs to the natural world but is distinct within it owing to his peculiar place in the vertical hierarchy which is seen in the cosmos. In the modern conception, this too is supplanted; the vertical sense is initially retained, but an essential difference of kind is introduced by which man no longer belongs in nature but is an alien in its landscape. At first elevating humanity above the being of the natural world, nature is reduced to objective "thingness," to the status of a mechanical process which must be learned and mastered. Like many others, Scheler sees inner contradictions and depersonalizing tendencies in this understanding. Coupled with the later collapse of the vertical schema of man over nature in scientific materialism and positivism, modernity's attempt to dominate the natural world proves ultimately to be a double-edged endeavor. For, as Scheler writes:

> With the devleopment of modern civilization, *nature* (which man had tried to reduce to a mechanism for the purpose of ruling it) and *objects* have become man's *lord and master*, and *the machine* has come to dominate *life*. The "objects" have progressively grown in vigor and intelligence, in size and beauty—while man, who created them, has more and more become a cog in his own machine.[140]

What, then, is the non-romantic and non-mechanistic understanding of nature that Scheler would propose to supplant modernity's *Wille zur Herrschaft über die Natur*,[14] and to complement his understanding of the relationship between the person and other persons? Curiously, it is in the oddly fraternal outlook of Francis of Assisi where Scheler finds the attitude toward nature which informs his own analysis.[142] In his evaluation, Christianity as a whole is recognized as drawing the Jewish conception of man's dominion over nature, the Greek worship and indentification with the order of nature, and the Roman sense of legal mastery, into a convergence which in Thomistic scholasticism would claim that *omne ens est bonum*, but which placed man authoritatively atop, and not completely inside, the pyramidic hierarchy of the cosmos. In this, as Nietzsche noted before him, Scheler contends that the stage is set for the scientism and human alienation of the modern conception. The Franciscan understanding, however, moves in a remarkably different direction. Contrary to the vertical hierarchy which pervades the earlier attitudes, where nature manifests a divine "chain of authority," the Franciscan would see a horizontal fraternity. Not as the embodiment of divinities as the ancients perceived, nor as mere objects to dissect and utilize as is the predominant contemporary perspective, the Franciscan hymn speaks of the sun as "brother" and moon as "sister." "What is really new and unusual in St. Francis' emotional relationship to Nature," Scheler comments, "is that natural objects and processes take on an expressive significance of *their own*, without any parabolic reference to man or human relationships generally."[143]

To what extent Scheler accepts the conception of nature which he finds in Franciscan thought is uncertain. The notion of fraternity with the natural world is appealing, but there would seem to be difficulties in accommodating such a position with his ontological dualism. The distinction between being-as-act and being-as-object appears contrary and prohibitive for the equality of status which a horizontal fraternity presumes. Granted, Scheler does speak occasionally (in later years) of a "Ground of Being" which would apparently undergird both modes of being, hence, suggesting support for the possibility of fraternity between person and nature. But, would not this notion erode the special dignity of personal subjectivity which Scheler seeks so desperately to preserve? Indeed, would not true fraternity, in this light, suggest more than a semblance of subjectivity in the objective world of nature? Correspondingly, does not this leave the person much closer to the mode of being-as-object than even most phenomenologists would admit? Perhaps, this is precisely the direction which Scheler's thought would travel given the bearings of his last years—despite his own early efforts to link human dignity to a "special" perception of values and their hierarchy. At best, weighting the emphasis he places on the Franciscan inspiration, the often misunderstood Heideggerian analogy of "the shepherd of Being" might be more valuably utilized to describe the relationship between the person and the natural world in Scheler's understanding.[144]

Unfortunately, Scheler himself never fully explores the many implications of his conceptions of nature. To be sure, in the philosophical anthropology of his last years, he develops in great detail a sketch of man's place in nature—but he indicates only circumspectly what mankind's attitude toward the natural world ought to be. Furthermore, his sociology of knowledge goes far toward demonstrating that a radical reconciliation with nature, an achievement of true fraternity, is utopian. From the vantage of both his anthropology and sociology, Scheler argues quite convinceingly that one aspect of man's biological, anthropological and historical makeup is a directedness or interest in dominating and controlling objective being—especially objects of the natural world. Interesting passages hint at other directions, but overall Scheler laments man's alienation from nature while offering scant concrete grounds for viable alternative attitudes. Similarly, he is quick in his criticism of the methodological approach and theoretical vanity of modern science, but one searches in vain through Scheler's works for more than passing, oblique reference to the possibility of some "new science."[145]

In regard to the *historical* context of the person's world, Scheler is far less circumspect. Oddly, however, history is not seen as an entirely independent element in the composition of the world, but is itself enframed—as human spirit generally—within the confines of nature. Writing in 1917, he notes that "all human history races within the bounds of the *essential structure* of human natures."[146] A key insight into Scheler's own theory of history is unearthed in this remark, for history is revealed to be something that is in no sense an independent, "apersonal" absolute. It is something which *is itself* very much mundane and contingent, tied-up closely with persons themselves. In Scheler's understanding, history, *on one hand* is very much haphazard and very much a product of the chaotic interplay of objective factors. Owing to the duality of being, there is an ontological "otherness" to history by which it far less knowable than the orthodox Hegelian or Marxist would admit. *On the other hand*, while Scheler allows only limited influence for spirit (superstructure) in the process of the world (substructure), the impact of spirit and person cannot be disregarded. Persons perform actions which change history and alter development. Persons, further, are not "things" amenable to explanation and prediction by any objective "human" or historical science. There is, then, a twofold opaqueness to history intself for human knowledge, because objective aspects of history possess a mode of being which is distinct from the person, and the subjects of history cannot be counted on to march lockstep with *"dem Gang Gottes in der Welt."* History, as it were, exists rather intimately with both persons and nature and cannot be conceived as a truly transcendental process; Scheler is loathe to extend subjectivity beyond the borders of the person. History, thus, must be understood as a complex dialectic involving real, material necessities and conditions conjoined in tension with personal insight and responsibility. Borrowing Comtean terminology with approval, he finds in the realm of the person, the *cultural and spiritual* sphere, "'freedom' and autonomy of events with respect to quality, meaning and value." "Yet," he continues, "in their practical expression these can always *be suspended* through the causality of the 'substructure' proper to it; *'liberte modifiable'* (suspendable) one might call it." Conversely, Scheler perceives "in the sphere of real factors only that *'fatalite modifiable,"* which Comte aptly and correctly discussed."[147]

Scheler substantiates the personal aspect of history, the field of *liberte modifiable*, by illustrating that that which is called "history" is in large part "made" by the present. History is not an inert reflection of the past because the very gaze of contemporary man alters it. An event in history does not present itself as a constant unchanging reality; it depends on the present for its continued existence and its coming-to-be. Plautus slept, Scheler notes, until he was reborn in Moliere.[148] More significant and subtle than the commonplace notion that all interpretations of history have existential roots, his point here is a counterthrust against the implicit metaphysical argument of historicism. Not only does *knowledge* of history ebb, flow and change with existential values and interests, but history itself—as contingent upon such values and interest—is, thus, relative. In other words, "not only our cognition of 'historical fact' but *'historical fact' itself* is *relative to the being and essence*—not just the mere 'consciousness'—*of the observer*. Or, as Scheler comments further,

> [H]*istoricism*, as a world-view and as a bad cryptic meta-physics, pervading all true metaphysical problems, has been uprooted with this view. . . . The historicism that relativized all cognition, first in metaphysics (Dilthey), then also in natural science and mathematics, and finally even in its own cognition (Spengler), is *itself* relativized by the above insight. Historicism has made history into a "thing in itself." And what else does this mean but that it attributes to historical reality and to its cognition a *metaphysical* meaning and sense? If, as we stated earlier, all positive historical *goods* become relative, viz. relative to the absolute system of non-formal [*materialen*] *values*, historical whatness and value-being is *itself relative*.[149]

In, therefore, undercutting all claims that history is an absolute, Scheler is effectively presenting the subjective aspect of history as a result of personal actions—past actions and present actions interm-ingled, mutually constitutive, *and conjoined with an absolute order of values*. As he claims elsewhere, "without man, there is no history."[150] Does this then grant them person a transcendence relative to the con-stitutive web of history?

Scheler is clear in his response. Although person and the historical world are bound in a mutually constitutive relationship, there ever remains an aspect of personal acts which reflects the sub-jectivity and responsibility of the person, an aspect which, while en-framed by history (and nature), in some fashion is more than any possible combination of the real elements of the world. In an early passage, Scheler states that "there remains an exteriority to our true, deep 'self;' and the holiness and unholiness of this lies sublime and still beyond the weather-storm of world history." "The wonder and the question," he continued, that "'I am' and that there is a 'world'—what we open up [*anfangen*] with both together is an *eternal constant* within history and weltanschauung."[151] Enmeshed in the historical world lies a spark of personal subjectivity by which aspects of human action can be said to be responsible and not merely historical. Man is not simply a product of history. History like man is comprised of subjective and objective aspects. Sharing a similarity in essence, man and history are together enraveled in a mutual "making" process. Hence, although personal action has historical actuality and efficacy only by accommodating and drawing on the real factors of the world, Scheler nowhere abrogates personal subjectivity or its concomitant responsibility.[152]

A late essay, "Man and History," lends detail to the background of his understanding of this "sublime and still" special responsibility of persons in history. He differentiates five conceptions of history based upon five philosophical anthropologies: the Judeo-Christian conception of free will and fallen nature, the Platonic and Enlightenment conception of *home sapiens* and transcendental reason, the positivist and naturalistic conception of *homo faber*, the romantic-pessimistic conception of human decline, and the Nietzschean conception of the overman. It is the Nietzschean overman with which Scheler, in this late period, identifies his own understanding. The freedom of the person in history here is not the Western religious conception of "free" will which Scheler sees as tied to a fundamental fear of the world and of man's own fallen nature, nor is the freedom of the person to be equated with the negative freedom of the transcendental *logos* in either its Platonic or Enlightenment forms. At the same time, Scheler also declines the "freedom" of the naturalists, one which is perceived as only a tool for the adaptation of the organism, and the "freedom" of the Marxist, where it is perceived as an *ad hoc* product or tool to be used in conjunction with the class and economic dialectics of history. Nor, finally, does Scheler accept the romantic decadence model where this spark of subjectivity is seen as the origin of man's alienation from the vital currents of his nature and where, as a result, personal actions are seen as the motive force in the regression and decline of human nobility. Instead, this late work postulates a subjectivity in history of "the greatest imaginable increase of *responsibility and sovereignty.*" Where the Christian and Jew see such responsibility as stemming from man's divine nexus, where the Platonist and Kantian see it stemming from man's transcendental reason, Scheler with Nietzsche finds man radically responsible for his acts precisely because he is *only and solely* a being in the world. As if in emphasis, he chooses to express this thesis in the then still shocking Nietzschean motif of man and the "death of God." To posit the death of God, Scheler remarks, does not release man from his subjectivity and responsibility; it radically makes such responsibility *personal and his alone*. As Nietzsche, Scheler too proclaims, *"Ecce Homo"*—the overman, the all-man.

> The full reverence, love, and adoration, which men once expended on God and their gods, are due, then, to this kind of person. In icy solitude and absolute self-reliance, not a derivative being, the person stands between the two orders, the realm of mechanistic reality, and the realm of an objective order of values and ideas, freely suspended in itself, and not posited by any living, spiritual Logos. In order to set the direction, meaning and value of history, man must not, in thought and will, rely on outside forces.[153]

In this, the historical and categorical personalism of being and values is considerably deepened. Collective, real forces in history are not denied—as in Carlyle's assumption that "men make history;" they are fully recognized. It remains only that history is no escape from personal responsibility.

Scheler also distances his thinking from the second horn of the historicist dilemma—i.e., the relativity of norms issuing from an infinity of historical interpretations. It is precisely this face of the dilemma which has drawn the closest scrutiny of many *political* philosophers. Struggling for a terminology in which to describe his theoretical enterprise, Scheler at various period adopts certain lables and terms as catch-phrases for central themes of his broad undertaking. His conception of history is no exception to this, and in his late period the conception is subsumed under what he calls "philosophical anthropology"—or, more enigmatically, "meta-anthropology." Inasmuch as the present study concerns itself with the political theory of his personalism, such phrasing is especially worthy of attention.

From the earliest beginnings of political theory, its endeavor can be seen as an effort to clarify for politics an aspect of human being which is "special" by virtue of it being more real, complete or absolute than the dross, changeable, mortal background in which it is seen imprisoned. Taking this aspect of human being as an absolute standard, the theorist then attempts either to engender a transformation of the political realm so as to reflect this standard in the political order, or to structure the political order in some manner which maximizes the potential in the community for members themselves to pursue such a standard.[154] Seemingly, this equally applies to the ancient and medieval theorists as to the moderns inclusive of Kant.[155] In other words, the theorist acts on the presumption that there is a permanent and unchanging aspect of human being upon which a permanent and enduring political order can be structured. Following many others—from "Hegel to Nietzsche" as Karl Löwith has remarked—Scheler rejects this notion outright, fully admitting the historical character of human being.[156] Taking history seriously in this fashion is claimed by many to leave mankind bereft of internal criterion (or apparatus) by which truth, goodness and so forth—political and otherwise—are to be ascertained. It removes all certainty of direction according to which human actions—political actions—might be best guided. Hence, persons are denied access to any unchanging absolute owing to their own participation in the flux of history, and all "orders," political and otherwise, are seen as reflecting only an infinitude of individual, situational interpretations.

On the basis of his meta-anthropology and his material value theory, however, Scheler skirts this "infinitude of interpretations." He points to what he perceives as a "foundational order" in man's anthropology.[157] In accordance with this, being human remains fully historical in character, but the "order" latent in the anthropological background of the person, which is reflective of the absolute order of values, serves to deny any purely relativist position. It is in this that the importance of Scheler's term "meta-anthropology" begins to be understood. Since Kant, if not since Descartes, the predominant thrust of all inquiry has been toward analysis and clarification. From Dilthey's hermeneutics to Husserl's early phenomenology, the immediate background of Scheler's own thinking fits with this push. Man and man's experience set the limits of what is acceptable for analysis. Obviously, the turn toward anthropology as the foundation for knowledge and norms has clear rationale. Scheler, in large part, moreover, follows this thrust as is evidenced by his sociology of knowledge. Yet, insofar as man is a historical being, the foundation sought in anthropology is suspect. Where some thinkers turn to history itself as an order lending structure to anthropology, Scheler denies the existence of any absolute in history. He turns, instead, to a foundational order which is inseparable from anthropology itself and linked with the responsibility and creativity of the person—an order which parallels the order he finds in values.

History is intimate with persons, relative to personal subjectivity. What order is found is given it by the present. And, while Scheler concedes the possible narrowing of personal responsibility in the development of history—man, is, after all, enmeshed within it—such responsibility, Scheler insists, "will never become a nothing."[158] Personal responsibility will never utterly disappear.

Chapter Three
Personalism as Political Theory

BEYOND A SCHELERIAN POLITICAL THEORY

CONTAINED IN MAX SCHELER'S understanding of the person is a theory of politics. Unfortunately, it remains rather implicit. For, although Scheler indicates an awareness of the radical implications which his personalism poses for the theory and philosophy of politics, and although as a philosopher of *engagement* he is embroiled in the tumultous political affairs of his day, at no time is a fully systematic political theory outlined in his works. There is no Schelerian "Politics" wherein "personalism as political theory" is found sandwiched between a preface and postscript. This state of affairs is not, however, without its own merits. In a day fraught with bitter conflict between political "systems," perhaps the lack of systematic political theorizing on Scheler's part can be construed to underscore the reflective and philosophical character of the political theory derived from his thinking. Moreover, Scheler is by no means entirely aloof from political theorizing. As is well-known, Scheler offhandedly *does* discuss political imperatives drawn from particular aspects of his personalism. In similar fashion, his writings *are* salted and punctuated with reflective and polemic tracts addressed to themes of the political world: socialism, liberalism, Marxism, democracy, war, pacifism, freedom and power. Furthermore, (despite the heterogeneous nature of his political writings) vis-a-vis his personalism, a coherency of directon and intent gradually becomes evident. Nonetheless, great care must be exercised in appraising the theoretical underpinnings of Scheler's political pronouncements. It remains unresolved to what extent many of Scheler's political writings find their roots in his philosophy of personalism. Thus, although the present study attempts to bring to light the significance and degree of this connection and will carefully weigh many specifically political passages in his works, it is the political theory of Scheler's personalism itself which comprises its predominant inquiry.[159] The present chapter of this study, in this light, tries to draw together various strands of Scheler's personalism which reflect its significance for political theory. In so doing, it is hoped that personalism as political theory can be brought to clarity.

As political theory, personalism can be seen in part as a continuation of the ostensibly modern notion that all inquiry must begin in anthropology. The particular inquiry of political theory would appear especially to accentuate this notion of the fundamentality of anthropology. Indeed, it is claimed widely in the discipline that (at least since Kant's rejection of noumenal knowledge) political theory is an anthropological debate, or a series of interpretations of human and social anthropology. Within this vein, the far-reaching and insightful philosophical anthropology of Scheler's personalism serves well as an antrhopological foundation for political theory. It opens new avenues for the comprehension of political practices and counsels new meaning for the "doing" of political acts. Less clearly, Scheler's personalism—as political theory—outlines certain possibilities which would belie the so-called "end of political theory" or "end of politics," reaching (perhaps toward what might be designated as a *transformed politics* or a *transformed political vision*. This latter remark is *transformed politics* or a *transformed political vision*. This latter remark is intended frankly; the image of politics glimpsed in the interstices of Scheler's inquiries into the person and the person's place is an image at some distance from and at odds with what is now widely taken as politics. Curiously, however, the possibility of such transformation is joined closely with those premises of Scheler's thought which reach beneath anthropology toward ontology and realist metaphysics. As will be seen, the transformations drawn from the political theory of personalism pursue an accord not only with the reality of man's character and development (man's anthropology), but also with the reality of the cosmos, to which the person entirely belongs. Nonetheless, the transformational aspects inhering in personalism as political theory require the closest scrutiny. The specific character of such transformation cannot be glibly (or even neutrally) treated. Pursuing this thread, in elaborating the political theory of personalism, the following pages consider the transformation of political order, authority, fraternity, equality and power. Yet, rigorous care must be exercised; undeniable political dangers stalk the borders of such transformations—a fact which political theory cannot responsibly dismiss.

MODELS AND LEADERS: EXTENDING THE PURVIEW OF POLITICS

Some sense of the nature of the transformation latent in Scheler's personalism is grasped easily. Following the illustration of the origin of the modern subject as discussed in the previous chapter, a pattern or "order of foundaiton" can be observed which suggests an outline of the so-called "transformed politics."[160] Ontogenetically, the person emerges only after a succession of stages where personal responsibility swells as the person is dissociated from naive identity with the experiential world, from the corporate unity with mother and family, and finally from the individuality of the ego. Equally, if sociality (or intersubjectivity) is discerned to have a foundational order which proceeds from organic homogeneity, through hierarchical corporatism and possessive individualism, to the free solidarity of the person community, then a similar sequence in the ontology of the political order hardly could be unforeseen. The transformations associated with "personalism as political theory" must clearly reflect that leap in mutual autonomy, freedom and responsibility which Scheler sees accompanying the emergence of the person and the person community. On the basis of this argument, an order of foundation relative to the political aspect of human being likewise might be postulated. Thus, politics can be pictured in a sequence of transformations which follow a foundational order from amorphous and aresponsible herd activity to hierarchically structured and corporately responsible feudal virtue, from feudal virtue to economically structured, material self-interest,[161] from self-interest to a freely and personally structured political order which celebrates the uniqueness and radically different contributions and needs of each special citizen.[162] It goes without saying, of course, that it is the latter transformation which the current study offers as a likely outline for the transformation of politics inherent in Scheler's personalism.

Several of Scheler's works discuss politics in a fashion which supports this supposition. From his unpublished *Nachlass*, he writes in an essay entitled "Models and Leaders" [*Vorbilder undd Führer*] of a parallel schematic pertaining to the obviously political concept of "leadership." The work, as the title indicates, is uncomfortably poignant. Concerned as it is with a theoretical appraisal of social and political guidance and leadership, Scheler's inquiry obliquely invokes the clamor of the Weimar political community in its frenzied search for the which might bring order and direction. In the work he distinguishes leaders from models precisely as he distinguishes real factors from ideal factors in his appraisal of the sociology of knowledge. Leaders are actual living men who authoritatively inspire and draw their followers to action. Leaders are actual, temporal and historical. Citing Robert Michels, Scheler sees leadership, then, as a sociological fact, "a law, that in the last line of analysis is grounded in the nature of organic life."[163] Designated as "the law of the small number," Scheler finds it a plainly factual principle that "in any given [bewusst] human sociality, in any group conscious of its unity, there is a small number which rules."[164] Hence, biologically and anthropologically, leaders and leadership find their origin in the biological-anthropological character of the human animal.

Models are quite different in Scheler's estimation. A model is an exemplar for a certain way of being human. As such, it is a framework which orders values and structures noetic experiences. Accordingly, every model tacitly raises certain criteria for what might count as "valuable" or "meaningful " for the way reality and human being are and the way they could and should be. A model may be false, incorrect or even evil, but its reality is such that it can never be understood so by those who truly subscribe to it.[165] At the highest level, further, models are not even so much determined or abstracted from historical experiences as they are reflective of the special being of the person—who is, however, enmeshed in history and nature. As Scheler remarks, "the model is ever a *personally formed value gestalt,*" by and through which one's being, living and doing are consciously or unconsciously organized. Thus, "leaders do not determine models, but rather the reigning models (in conjunction with outside powers [i.e., real factors]) determine who and what becomes a leader."[166] Or, as Scheler states in contrasting fashion, "leaders ultimately direct practices [Handeln], performance and behavior," while "the model directs *being,* a gestalt of the soul."[167]

To some extent, Scheler's distinction between leaders and models supports the traditional distinction which political theory discerns between politics as the art of ruling and politics as education. *Seemingly,* Scheler opts here, at first blush, for education—models being conceived as structuring human being itself and as *a priori* frameworks for leadership. Such an interpretation, nonetheless, is insensitive to the fine line which Scheler sketches. His philosophy, as should be clear at this point, is not an unrepentant idealism. Just as his sociology of knowledge denies the efficacy of *ideal factors* except insofar as they find expression in and through the *real factors* of nature and history, so too models require "realization" in order to affect mundane human actions. Rather melodramatically, Scheler illustrates, contending of models that these

> delicate, ghostly [*schattenhaften*] images must indeed drink blood at the primal spring of history and experience. For, if models drink of this blood, they become *concrete models*.[168]

More prosaically phrased, models which are somehow *abstracted from* or essentially *transcendent to* experience and history are powerless and merely utopic.[169] In order to affect the world, models must draw on the power and assume the particular reality of the world. It is, then, inappropriate in this context to think in terms of either leaders or models as naively primary or secondary vis-a-vis each other, as if in some capacity one causes or even temporally precedes the other. As has been made clear in regard to many aspects of Scheler's thinking, the relationships between any sort of noetic reality and historical, physical reality admit no manner of either aspect of reality dominating or fully determining other other. Furthermore, these "superstructure-substructure" relationships are also neither dialectics of mutal opposition nor sophomoric Platonisms of form and matter. As has been seen, Scheler understands the relationships as *mutually* constitutive. The superstructure constitutes the parameters of values by which the substructure is given deontological order and meaning. The substructure constitutes the parameters of efficacy by which the superstructure can find material and historical expression. Hence, returning to the concern with models and leaders, the noetic reality of models must "fit" the historical, material reality of available leadership, and the leader must "fit" his or her leadership within the framework of values established within the reigning model. Any primacy which models have relative to leaders is non-temporal, non-causal and reflective of an order in being itself.

The crux of this understanding for personalism as political theory is the centrality of the image of man, as a foundational concept and as an actual living individual, both for models and for leaders. Central for every model is a particular understanding of man relative to which actual leaders must be congruent. Characteristically, Scheler illustrates the range of these understandings or images by elaborating a typology of such images, "a great, general schema of possible model-types," which include the "guilding-models [*Vorbildmodelle*] of: the saint, the genius, the hero, the leading spirit of civilization and the artist of enjoyment [*Lebenskunstler*]." Such guiding-models, further, are perceived by Scheler as belonging *essentially* to the being of the human person. These guiding models, in Scheler's comprehension

> are not the resultants of abstracting from the experience of particular historical men. Even less are they the "innate ideas" perceived by Plato. Rather, they are to be viewed as they are perceived by any actual men, as eternal value-ideas of persons [*Wertpersonideen*], by which we can recognize the degree of distance of historical men from them.[170]

Clearly, Scheler pictures this schematic as an objective and eternal foundational order which is perceived in the essence of the person himself. As with the previously considered "orders of foundation," each higher type is possible only upon the shoulders of the lower types, which enables understanding the order as a non-causal sequence of transformations. At the base in this typology stands the guiding model of the person as an artist of "enjoyment." Politically, it would seem that such a model envisions a polity comprised of individuals directed toward the immediate satisfaction of their assorted physical needs and desires. Generally structured by the values associated with the necessities and enjoyments of life, this model regardless forms the primal soil from which succeeding types might emerge. Recognition of the value of life and being (*omne ens est bonum*) at this level, makes possible an appreciation of the more subtle, invariably less tangible and less immediate values associated with the higher types. In other words, the next higher guiding model—the leading spirit of civilization—does not negate or overcome the artist of enjoyment as much as it swells up from the lower type.[171] Arising from the lower's appreciation of the immediate values of life, the leading spirit of civilization sublimates the immediacy of satisfaction in the values of the present for perceived greater future satisfaction. At this junction a transformation occurs. The artist of enjoyment *remains*, in a substantive sense, but is equally transformed into that which is "higher." Where the lower model settles for the pleasures of immediate gratification, the leading spirit of civilization defers satisfaction and looks ahead to the possibility of more gratification to be acquired through planning and temporary sacrifice. Hence, the model is intricately tied to notions of progress, accumulation of wealth, technical achievement and mastery over the physical world. A polity organized according to such an image of the person is likewise one which is utilized by its citizens as a tool for their individual accumulation of wealth, domination of nature and acquisition of surplusses of security and utility.

At the next level, "the hero" can be recognized as a transformation of the "leading spirit." The lower type's concern with progress is an interest in *more*, in greater "quantities" of those things which offer values of a relatively less lofty variety—more wealth, more utility or convenience, more "goods and services" in the time-honored usage of the terms. Seen in the best light, the progress toward more-and-more at the level of the leading spirit is valued for what such progress lends to the interests and desires of individuals generally. In contrast, the hero finds greatest value not in the number or accumulation of the "good things" of living, but with the quality of life itself; not with the lives of individuals generally, but with the life of the whole of a particular community above and beyond any aggregate of the interests of individuals. Only atop, however, the foregoing appreciation of quantity is an appreciation of quality possible. In the same way, the hero's concern with and perception of the value of the whole is a transformation of the leading spirit's perception of the values of individuals generally. Referring to the hero as a personification of the values of "nobility," Scheler discusses the model in the terminology elsewhere associated with his sphere of "vital values," and illustrates an appropriate historical setting for the hero in situations reminiscent of the traditional, ritualistic pre-modern communities which figure prominently in the sociologies of Weber, Sombart, Mannheim and others. In addition, such settings also find Scheler invoking a certain understanding of *political* order and activity. The level of the hero, he contends, is the level of politics as understood in a strictly etymological sense—revolving around the life of the *polis*, as contrasted with the less (and possibly non-) political politics of the lower models. Further, there exists an unmistakeable Nietzschean ambiance to Scheler's portrayal; the heroic model of the person is impelled and drawn by an abundance of "spiritual will" as opposed to more physical forces. Like homeric mythic heroes or platonic guardians:

> The hero is a man of *will* [*Willensmensch*], meaning equally: a *man of power* [*Machtmensch*]. A hero-structured soul can reside in any body, but it can never be conjoined with a weak vitality. Potency, strength, power, fulsomeness and an inner, almost automatic ordering of the vital life drives, all belong to the essence of the hero.[172]

Hence, Scheler closely joins the model of the hero with the renowned premodern virtues of nobility, honor, patriotism, courage, and with the Stoic and Renaissance notion of *virtu*.

By "genius," the next ascending type in the schematic, is meant a guiding-model of the person which reflects the values of purely spiritual *ideas*—the noetic values of the beautiful, pure knowledge, the "right" [*Recht*] and so forth.[173] Once again, moreover, a transformation is seen between this model and the preceding. Indeed, just as Aristotle uncovers the soil for the philosopher in the *zoon politikon*, Scheler discerns the concern for the values of purely spiritual character to succeed, in the sequence of transformations, a concern for the values of the community as a whole. As seen, then, the model of the artist of enjoyment pursues the immediate values of the self's desires and needs, the leading spirit of civilization pursues the prospect of satisfaction for individuals generally, the hero pursues the values of the life of the whole and, the model of the genius, in like manner, pursues the values of pure spirit. Central to the model of the genius are objects of value which are perceived to be somewhat less historical and less circumstantially relative than the value-objects of the lower types. While Scheler demonstrates in many places that knowledge, beauty and similar notions are very much rooted in the dynamic realities of sociology and anthropology, he affirms the obviously more enduring and more "universal" nature of those things which carry noetic value. An appreciation of those things which bear values appropriate to the model of the hero—a given historical community or nation, for example—is to a great extent more relative to a particular time and place than an appreciation of the beauty conveyed in a work of art or the knowledge conveyed in measurements of the heavens. Likewise, the politics of the hero, relative as it is to the life of the community within the walls and boundaries of the polis, is transformed in conjunction with the character of the genius and the political becomes what Scheler terms "the cosmo-political."[174] Where the politics of the hero is associated with a chauvinistic and likely aggressive patriotism, the genius is directed toward others not with an eye which adjudges them brother or foe, "Greek or barbarian" *in patria*, but with an eye toward their supra-"political" common ground as perceivers of the values of pure spirit. The politics of this type, thus, would seem to be one which reaches beyond the historical and geographic specificity of any given political community to encompass the macro- or cosmo-political community of other persons as persons like one's own person. In other words, the "politics" of the model of the genius, itself a transformation of the politics of the hero, is a politics which might in a limited sense be called a politics of personalism. As *cosmo-political* its sphere and its footing is in some sense more "foundational," than the brute-like sphere of individual needs and desires, than the sphere of utility calculation and exchange values, and even than the otherwise very basic human sphere of traditional polity and politics.

Curiously, Scheler does not conclude his typology of guiding-models with the figure of the genius. In contrast to his previously reviewed typologies, his schematic of personal models here lists five rather than four types. Above the model of the genius, in order of foundation, Scheler locates the guiding-model of "the saint." At the root of the essential difference between the saint and the preceding model of the genius lies a distinction regarding the nature of the *subjectivity* of both and a parallel distinction regarding the character of the *intersubjectivity* appropriate to each. Contending that the genius only "lives actively in its works," and that it is then "truly not its spiritual personhood, but utterly its *individuality* given perceptively therein," Scheler finds the distinction to be of fundamental importance. The genius, despite its recognition of others to be persons in the narrow sense of being fellow perceivers of the values of pure spirit, still approaches its world, its values and its others only from the perspective of its own personhood. In Scheler's estimation, the genius ever begins with its own subjectivity-personhood as *a priori*. "The saint," he presents in contrast, "in a most god-imaging [*gottebenbildlichsten*] sense, in a model sense, has no individuality."[175] Here, therefore, a further transformation in Scheler's foundational sequence becomes apparent. The genius, constrained by its active, individual subjectivity, can understand the personhood of others only from a comparison with its *own* personhood. Its activity begins as "its" activity, starting *a priori* at its individuality. Essentially different from this, *the saint begins with the person of the other.*[176] What transformation occurs is a transformation, again, of the nature of the person itself. No longer only a perceiver of the values of pure spirit, the person as revealed in the guiding model of the saint participates directly in the personal being of the other.[177] Too, the nature of intersubjectivity becomes other than the recognition of the other as a fellow perceiver of such values; instead, it finds its origin in the direct, mutual participation of persons in the personhood of others. Aptly, Scheler refers to this new intersubjective relationship as a *Liebesgemeinschaft*—a "loving community."[178]

Surely, the transformation of the polity from the cosmo-political to the "loving community" would be reflected in a similar transformation of the practice of politics itself. Scheler, however, is rather silent in this regard. It can be postulated that the saint's pervasive concern with—love for—the person of the other would require the development of new or transformed conceptions of such obviously political notions as community, authority, justice and so on, which would manifest this peculiar new intersubjectivity. Along these lines, this study would like to refer to the new character of such notions with the modifier of "personalist," and see the general aegis under which such concepts might be grouped as itself a model for personalism as political theory. There is, however, an inescapable quixotic quality to such thinking; it strikes the modern ear odd, or fabulous, to designates as "political" that which does not involve domination, competition or the calculation of costs and benefits.[179] Scheler, moreover, as will be made painfully clear in his inquiry into the matter of "political power," certainly recognizes that a political theory derived from the personal model of the saint would not accurately depict the empirical reality of twentieth century politics, or the empirical political realities of any given historical time or place. Perhaps, however, the present's expectation that political theory must of its essence be limited to issues of conflict, domination and so forth, is in part a reflection of the embeddedness of the current understanding of the political within the anthropological limits of the personal model of our times. Might not political theory concern itself not only with the way politics is, and has been, but with the way politics can be? Few theorists, surely, would limit political inquiry to the encyclopedaeist's task of analysis of the empirical political activities of current events. Most, certainly, would at least accede to the possibility of including human actions other than those intended with domination or competition with the proper purview of political theory. From its most obvious profile, Scheler's personalism is a philosophical anthropology which provides profound and intriguing insights into certain ways in which humanity is, has been, and can be humanity. As political theory has grown accustomed to appraising the politics of human anthropologies, this side of personalism as political theory ought to be familiar. To the extent that Scheler's personalism as political theory is more than anthropology, personalism as political theory must be considered from a somewhat different perspective.

POWER, MORALITY AND POLITICS

In the last years of his life, Max Scheler reconsidered many of the vaguely political themes which has been his concern during and immediately after the period of the war. Unfortunately, no published materials ensued from this reconsideration during his lifetime. It is evident, however, from the loosely organized collection of materials which he gathered, that a substantial study of politics was envisioned. Fortunately, various lectures arising form this reconsideration were delivered at the university in Cologne, and ironically at the Weimar government's Ministry of Defense and at the German Institute for Political Studies. More fortunately, many of the materials from this collection survive in Scheler's archive and two excerpts have appeared in print, one a brief assortment of lecture sketches and notes, *Gedanken zu Politik und Moral* (Thoughts on Politics and Morality), and one a more polished essay, "The Idea of Peace and Pacificism."[180] Together with available information from presented lectures, these materials lend a more distinct outline to the notion of personalism as political theory.

The argument made in the sketches and notes of the *Gedanken* excerpt concerns the important distinctiveness of politics relative to morality. This distinction has its origin in the further origins of both morality and politics. "Morality," Scheler claims here, "is a technique," a technique for "realizing in an ethos the given order of values." But, politics is not a technique—not something *contrived* or *adapted* by man to achieve some end. Rather, politics is a fundamental aspect of human being with its own anthropologically rooted end. It is a "striving for power, a wanting grounded in power-seeking, with a goal in sovereignly actualizing positive values in the commonweal within the boundaries of the order of values."[181] Owing to its different character, politics is not responsible to the moral order. To argue otherwise, from the standpoint of personalism, would be reductionist, for the highest purpose of personal existence is not a moral one. The highest purpose "*is* the realization of values," Scheler argues, "but not exclusively of the moral." There are other intrinsic values for the person. Indeed, "the 'good of the person' is not highest, but rather the good, whole man."[182] Yet, inasmuch as Scheler finds politics to be an aspect of the very being of the person, it would seem that politics would be essential to the existence and emergence of the person in a manner more fundamental than morality.

Subordinate to the highest value of the "good, whole man" (or person), politics and morality share a common end. Each, however, concerns itself with a different facet of the totality of values intrinsic to the full reality of the person. Obviously, then, Scheler finds politics to require that sort of direction which he finds the perception of values to provide for persons generally. As an aspect of being human, politics, as it were, has its own proper perspective on the order of values. But, what are the values rightly to be perceived from the stance of politics? Moreover, what is the role which politics plays for the larger whole of the reality of the person? Here there is suggested an important difference of understanding between Scheler's argument (in the *Gedanken* excerpt and elsewhere) and the interpretation of personalism as political theory developed in this study.

Scheler contends that the values which are proper for politics are those vital values which are concerned with the welfare and preservation of the commonweal.

> Within the rank-order of values there are common *vital* values (i.e. the values of development and of the objective welfare of the nation), which are primary for all politics in question, and for which the common lower and higher values [beneath and above vital values] are secondary. The higher levels of value are not realizable through political action—which can only cultivate or create their preconditions. The lower, especially the utility values, are secondary since they *are* important for the values of life.[183]

In other words, the perspective appropriate for politics on the order of values is partial, and limited to the sphere of the values of life (also called "vital" values); it is limited still further to those vital values pertinent to the life of the polity as a whole. Congruent with his other typologies, Scheler intends to locate politics in a particular niche—one parallel with the niche he finds for vital values, the life community and so forth. Were this approach to be elaborated to resolve the question of the role for politics in the larger reality of the person, politics would be seen as but one type or manifestation of mankind's anthropological concern with power. Likely, it would be found to be a manifestation of human power-seeking which aims at the actualizing of the values of the polity.

While this actualizing is vital for the existence of the polity itself— and *a fortiori* for the existence of the person—it overlooks other elements of Scheler's own reflections on person and *polis*. To consider politics only in terms of its narrow niche within the larger human concern with power-seeking, fails to recognize that the "type" of power-seeking which is politics is part of an order of foundation in the sense that these types have been interpreted in his other typologies. That is,

Scheler appears to concern himself with politics as if it were a phenomenon independent and delimited to narrow range of functions. But, as was noted in the last chapter, Scheler's "types" are better understood not as separate and isolated categories. Instead, they ought to be interpreted as intrinsic, foundational elements of a larger whole. Hence, a better understanding of politics from this interpretation would begin with a picture of politics not merely as an isolated stage or type of power-seeking, but as an interdependent, inherent aspect of all human concerns with values inasmuch as the relations of power are a fundamental aspect of human being.

The groundworks for such an interpretation of politics and power are well-laid in Scheler's investigation of the function of power relative to the existence of noetic realities, which is a central issue of his later works. This investigation leads Scheler in two intriguing directions, both of which have been alluded to earlier in this study. The first direction is toward a recognition of power's role in the deepest experience of subjectivity. The second is toward Scheler's determination that the most sublime realities of human experience— the loftiest values and noetic reality in general—are impotent in themselves and come to *effective* existence only by way of the power sublimated at lower levels of reality. Together, these two directions outline a provocative interpretation of power—and analogously of politics. Inside the *first* direction is the Scheler thesis that the primal experience of subjectivity is one of "resistance" to acts. As noted in previous pages, the resistance that reality poses to one's acts, the awareness of which is pre-cognitive, is the deepest core of the awareness of our subjectivity.[184] Moreover, because the person is essentially a constellation of acts, this experience of subjectivity is the experiential root of personal consciousness. As Scheler describes it, this experience of resistance is not a defined sensation, but an immediate and undifferentiated demonstration of the exteriority and substantiality of the world which is revealed as a resistance to the very being of the person. Befitting the present topic, in other words, the foundational experience of both subjectivity and world is an experience of power. The world reveals its presence as a power to resist one's acts. The person's awareness of his own subjectivity rests finally upon an experience of difference conveyed by the power of the world to resist the person's acts. On this basis it is easy, then, to understand Scheler's identification of an inherent human concern with power-seeking, of which politics is but a particular manifestation. If the primary experience of both subjectivity and world is one of power, then our relations with world, self and others, too, must be in some manner relations of power.

To accept this thesis, in keeping with personalism's concern to overcome approaches of domination and repression relative to the world and others, power in itself must not be negative or repressive. Here Scheler's *second* direction is revealing. This direction is the thesis of the essential powerlessness of spirit, high values and noetic reality in general. As discussed in previous passages, these noetic realities are discerned to be impotent in themselves and come to efficacy only by deriving potency through the sublimation of the power of more substantial realities. Even in the *Gedanken* notes, for example, despite hesitations concerning the consideration of politics, the argument is put that "power has—in contradistinction to powerlessness—the means value for spiritual values."[185] Power is not to be comprehended as a negative or repressive force. Instead, power is shown to be a necessary and postive value by which the pursuit of all other values is possible; power is productive and creative, even to the extent that the experience of power is at the root of subjective self-awareness. That is, power does not bring these more sublime realities into being, but power is the means by which they become actualized in the world. As Scheler notes, "only to the extent that 'ideas' of anykind are *united* with interests, drives and collective drives or 'tendencies,' as we call the latter, do ideas *indirectly* acquire the power of being realized." Hence, it is the power of the basic, mundane levels of reality which provides the impetus by which noetic realities can be realized.

> Raphael needs a brush—his ideas and his artistic visions do not create it; he needs politically and socially powerful patrons to employ him to exalt *their* ideals: otherwise he cannot act out his own genius. Luther needed the interests of dukes, cities, territorial lords leaning toward particularlism, and the rising bourgeoisie; without these factors nothing would have come out of the doctrine of *'spiritus sanctus internus'* reading of the Bible and of *'sola fides.'*[186]

These two directions which Scheler takes in his investigation of power and noetic realities do much to demonstrate the central function which power plays at all levels of the person's relationship with reality. Power is both the character of the primal experience of reality and the means by which higher reality acquires efficacy. Yet, the revelation of the ubiquity of power within the personal experience of reality does not itself complete the broadening reinterpretation of politics as an inherent aspect of all human acts. To say that power is inherent in this fashion, does not confer similar status on politics. Indeed, though Scheler defines politics as a variety of power-seeking, politics is determined to be only that power-seeking concerned with the values of the life of the community. Needed still, in the effort to broaden the politics of personalism beyond this narrow delimitation, is a linkage by which power relations themselves can be presented as essentially political. Scheler, unfortunately, does not directly propose such a linkage. Nonetheless, this understanding is clearly in keeping with the elements of personalism outlined in this study. In the ontogenesis of the person, for example, it was found that the person exists from the first only in relation with others, that individuality is but an outgrowth of sociality and is completed only by a return to sociality with the person community. Similarly, Scheler notes that each individual person is equally a *Gesamtperson*—an aspect of the common person which is the polity. On these grounds, it fairly can be inferred that the relations of power between person, world and others (relations which inhere in every personal act) are also ''political'' in a unique sense of the word. Hence, personalism as political theory would find man's fundamental relationship with reality to be characterized by an experience of power, and that this relationship and experience would be, in a peculiar way, political.

The understanding of the political character of the experience of reality, inferred from Scheler's personalism here, has in recent years garnered support from diverse quarters of contemporary philosophy. From Hans-Georg Gadamer's philosophical hermeneutics, Michel Foucault's linkage of reality to the relationship between power and discourse, Peter Berger's social construction of reality and so forth, there has arisen a substantial literature which stands in general accord with this thesis. The literature offers various insights relevant to the question of the political character of the relationship with reality which may valuably deepen personalism's own hesitant steps in these directions.

The ambiance of the thesis of the political character of man's relationship with reality is also evident in the only published political essay of Scheler's last years, ''The Idea of Peace and Pacifism.''[186] Intermixed with ideological yearnings for a unified Europe, the essay's theme is an exhortation for world peace based upon a balance of pluralistic differences and powers among individuals, groups and states. Such peace is possible only by way of recognizing the unique and rich distinctiveness of every person, group and state. In common Scheler fashion, the essay takes an oblique approach in its rhetoric, coming to its position by way of outlining the inner contradictions of all other forms of pacifism. That is, Scheler demands a pacifism which grows from a ground in the full reality, or totality, of the person. He rejects, then, the viability of what he terms "instrumental" pacifisms: the self-centered pacifism of individual conscience, religious pacifism, liberal pacifism, juridical pacifism, Marxist pacifism, imperialist (*Pax Romana*) pacifism, capitalist pacifism and cultural-intellectual pacifism. Each of these instrumental pacifisms rests upon a reductionism; each rests upon a utilization of one, narrow aspect of the human being as its mechanism by which conflicts would be resolved and wars avoided. Failing to build peace upon the totality of the person, Scheler judges that each is unable to achieve these desirable ends. As with the *Gedanken* materials and the discussion of the models and leaders essay, Scheler in this context closely joins that the sphere of the political to the notion of person itself—and inferentially to the meta-anthropology of the Allman. Politics, therefore, would derive its legitimacy through its foundation in and reflection of the full reality of the person. Even in this essay on international affairs, seemingly far removed from headier philosophical works, Scheler opts for a personalist foundation and criterion for responsible politics.

With the "Models and Leaders" essay, these later materials lend a rough outline to the picture of politics from Scheler's personalism. Still, there remains much ambiguity. With care, then, a turn to the more directly political works of Scheler's corpus, from the period immediately following the war, is revealing for present concerns.

PERSONALIST SOCIALISM, PERSONALIST DEMOCRACY

This study has amply noted the difficulty with any consideration of Scheler's overtly political tracts, which were largely composed during and immediately after the First World War. Many of the earliest of these works, as discussed previously, are little more than chauvinistic or propagandistic apologies for the German war efforts, occasionally with allusions to themes in Scheler's earlier philosophical writings. Yet, in the post-war period, Scheler abruptly shifts from the ideological themes of his early political pieces toward a more theoretical appraisal of the place of politics in the future of Western civilization and the future of Germany. Within this appraisal, various political topics are touched upon which bear directly on the possibility of personalism as political theory, including such notions as personalist socialism and personalist democracy. Two interrelated essays are especially worthy of attention: *"Chancen und Mächte des Aufstiegs und Niedergangs"* (Prospects and Potencies for Ascent and Decline) and *"Christlicher Sozialismus als Antikapitalismus"* (Christian Socialism as Anti-Capitalism).[188]

The catalyst for the *Chancen* essay was the then wide popularity of Oswald Spengler's thesis of the decline of western civilization. Objecting to the despair of Spengler's work, Scheler nonetheless takes a curious stand on the notion of decline itself. The essay reviews the many expressions of the thesis of the decline. Surveying evidence in support of each, Scheler begins with that of the *biological* decline of the European population as revealed by Europe's declining birthrate. This decline is attributed to capitalism and capitalism's need for the establishment of a mass society as its base. A similar argument is made for the potential of *cultural* decline, the immediate cause of which is perceived to be mass society's reduction of qualitative difference to numerical differences of quantity. In this vein, the rising Weimar German trends toward romantic nationalism and toward German bolshevism are only complementary poles of mass society's cultural reductionism. But, cultural decline has impact beyond the mass level. These harbingers of decline point toward a possible narrowing of western man's opportunity for responsibility and creativity. The reduction of qualitative diffrences within the sphere of human life, a possibility apparent in both poles of mass society, would preclude avenues for personal expression, which comprises the character of those acts constitutive of the person himself. Finally, Scheler also turns to consider the likelihood of a *political* decline which would be joined with these trends in the coming of mass society. He remarks with fear that of the major, contemporary currents in politics, "bolshevism, fascism, the movement which the new military dictator of Spain leads, the South-German people's movement, all are anti-democratic and anti-parliamentarian."[189]

The failing light of democracy and the decline of politics itself are presented as inseparable, suffering a common base in the emerging mass society. Foremost evidence of the possible decline of politics, in this analysis, is the growing predominance of economic over truly political concerns. This predominance robs politics of its proper focus; politics is reinterpreted only as a mechanism for economic distribution. In the wake of such reinterpretation, Scheler foresees citizens fleeing from the responsibilities of genuine political participation toward a politics of mysticism, amusement and private material interests. In the retreat from genuine politics, however, a bitter irony becomes apparent. Fragmented by private interests and by the irreconcilable ideologies derived from mysticism, democracy becomes deadlocked and non-functional. Faced with such deadlock, Scheler's great fear is that he people would turn to ''a charismatic dictator—not arisen from a conscripted army, but from an elite powerful youth who would place themselves at his disposal, in military formation, as his bodyguard and as his highest executive organ.''[190]

Notwithstanding his obvious sensitivity to the signs of impending horrors in the contemporary age, Scheler rejects any argument of the inevitablility of decline. Spengler's vision, with its despairing philosophy of history, is judged not to be an accurate perception of the future of the West-only of Schwabing in 1921. Indeed, with the potentials for decline, potentials for ascent are to be seen as well. The same world war experience which Spengler used as a buttress for the thesis of decline, for example, Scheler perceives as a catharsis out of which a rebirth for the West is possible. A profound experience common to the mind of all citizens of the world, the war offers the people of the West a fertile soil for a new consciousness of unity and solidarity from which a ''genuine democracy'' could grow. Hence, the essay cites the contemporary, widespread concern among peoples for ''solidarity''—among religious groups, political groups, the literati and many other circles. This solidarity, it is contended, stands as counterindication to the reductionism of mass society and to the tendency for decline which it signifies. Particularly, solidarity undercuts the primary dynamic of decline in the West, which is identified to be the spirit of capitalism. Out of its reification of persons and personal labor, in its materialism, in its furtive psychology of an anarchic human drive for private accumulation of wealth, Scheler finds the spirit of capitalism behind the outward symptoms of a pathology in the age. The decline of politics, the increasing failure of democracy, the decay of high culture and so on, are derivative ills of the problem of mass society. But, mass society and its problems may be avoided, Scheler claims. These developments are not inexorable; Marx, Spengler and deterministic philosophies of history in general are judged incorrect. Capitalism need not have come into existence, nor bolshevism, nor need come the decline of the West. Scheler asserts that the spirit of solidarity suggests the possibility of another future. Further, such solidarity suggests also the possibility of a new politics and a ''genuine democracy.''

The focus of the essay on capitalism is not new ground, of course. In the period from 1912 to 1915 several studies critical of capitalism appeared, *Der Bourgeois, Die Zukunft des Kapitalismus,* and others. These earlier studies, like the *Chancen* essay, revolve around the argument that the contemporary social order reflects a peculiar inversion in the order of values, which in turn accompanies the appearance of capitalism. For Scheler, plainly, capitalism represents not merely an economic system of private ownership and enterprise, but a manner of living which actualizes a spirit that, like a virus, imbues the entire socio-cultural order with its character. The new ground of the essay is the notion of solidarity and personalist democracy as an antidote to capitalism and its mass society. Overlooking the rhetorical excess of the foregoing, the gist of Scheler's political thinking here is an idea of a democracy which functions within an intersubjectivity based upon something other than the epistemologically difficult notion of overlapping self-interest (the theory of capitalism and modern liberalism). Genuine or "personalist" democracy, in other words, operates within the context of a *polis* which is not a happenstance aggregation of individuals pursuing parallel private interests. In conjunction with other aspects of the present study—the understanding of the person, person community, the order of values and so forth—personalist democracy has an unmistakeable outline. This thread of analysis is continued in "*Christlicher Sozialismus als Antikapitalismus,*" in which Scheler's thought moves from analysis of capitalism to reject Marxism as but capitalism for the proletariat. The study concludes, however, by affirming a Christian (or "personalist") socialism, in contrast to both capitalism and Marxism. Personalist socialism is proffered as that social order for our age which avoids the twin paths to mass society. In such a personalist socialism, personalist democracy and solidarity meet to suggest some prosaic substance, at last, for personalism as political theory.

The *Sozialismus* manuscript is incomplete and hastily composed. Care must be taken in regarding it as more than an indication of Scheler's mature and considered thought on this subject. But, its argument fits easily within the broad interpretation of personalism as political theory taken in the present study. Written in whole to contrast the repressive socialism of Marx and others [*Zwangssozialismus*] with Christian, personalist "expressive" socialism, the essay's central argument is found in the last few pages. Appropriately, the greatest contrast between personalist socialism and repressive socialism lies in the nature of the intersubjectivity upon which their respective political communities stand. Personalist socialism would understand individual persons to be concerned with others not out of shared material needs, primarily, nor out of overlapping self-interests. Instead, persons are concerned one with another out of a disposition to love each other [*die soziale Liebesgesinnung*].[191] Explored in the second chapter of this study, the roots of this disposition are found in the notion of person as a constellation of acts and in the idea of acts being directed toward values. The highest values are not values of things, but the unlimited value of persons—a value which transcends even objectification and is perceived only in coexperiencing the personal subjectivity of the other. Moreover, this disposition reflects the social character of persons generally, whose own individuality is possible only in a community with others and whose own individual person is equally a *Gesamtperson*. The contrast between repressive and expressive socialism follows from this idea of the person. For Scheler, other socialisms are achieved by external constraints to mold man to fit their perception of what his anthropology ought to be. Personalist socialism, in contrast, is the social order reflecting the order in the anthropology of the person; it comes to be not by external repression, but issues from the being of the person. Where the external socialisms would contend regarding the distribution of goods that "What is yours should—indeed, must—also be mine." Scheler claims of personalist socialism that "What is mine would also be yours (*Sozialismus*, p. 673). That is, personalist socialism is an outward giving of oneself to others as a free expression of personal being.

Interesting as the thesis of the *Sozialismus* essay is, there is ample room for further clarification. Perhaps, approaching personalism as political theory more obliquely by way of comparison with dominant contemporary theories of politics would prove useful.

Chapter Four
Scheler's Person and
The Modern Political Paradigm

THE UNDERSTANDING OF THE person presented in Scheler's thinking obviously corresponds with an interpretation of the political subject, the political community and politics itself which is fundamentally unlike the dominant interpretation of these in our times. A political theory is implicit in this personalist interpretation. To sketch in the outline of the political theory which Scheler's understanding of the person suggests, however, might be most easily approached obliquely—by way of contrast and comparison with modern political thought.

Owing to the dominance of a particular type man in the current age, Scheler perceives the character of modern politics *not* as fragmented into several essentially distinct theories (such as liberal, Marxist and so on), but as generally coherent in character and rooted in a singluar paradigm.[192] Modern politics, regardless of the particular form or political movement in which it finds its expression, is concomitant with the value-complex and peculiar weltanschauung of what Scheler terms "the bourgeois man."[193] Bourgeois liberalism, bourgeois Marxism and the mass-based extremist politics of the left and right, in Scheler's estimation, are at root only differing manifestations of a common underlying understanding of the politics of this modern man.

The essential core of modern politics is laid bare in Scheler's somethines virulent and sometimes coolly dispassionate inquiry into the character of modern man. In his considered appraisal, modern politics appears epiphenomenally with the emergence of the bourgeois. This "new" man, he argues, is the product of an anthropological transformation which, at least in part, issues from personal creativity and responsibility.[194] According to Scheler's thesis, the fused Greco-Christian understanding of man of the Middle Ages is stripped of both its sense of communal solidarity and its teleological

95

linkage and hierarchical structure of world-man-God. Bourgeois man is thus left with irresolvable breaches between himself and others, and between himself and the world. Recognizing this alienation and fueled by the passion of *ressentiment* which is entailed by such alienation, the bourgeois man's attitude becomes one of domination toward both the world and others. He seeks frantically by way of force and cunning, in this regard, to re-establish a semblance, however artificial, of the earlier world-man-God linkage.[195] The frantic scurrying leads to a boundless acquisitiveness and, with the loss of hierarchy, to a blind and indiscriminate greed for quantities of objects.

Likewise, with this responsible and creative evolution of the new man comes the emergence of a conceptual and normative framework, a paradigm, by which the world view of the bourgeois is rationalized and according to which all questions of self, world and others are resolvable. This paradigm establishes the broad context in which politics takes place, and involves a number of different dimensions. Following the primacy of value perception with which Scheler underpins his personalism, the primary dimension of the paradigm is portrayed as an array of values and as the particular "appearances" of these values in the objects of the everyday world. As has been considered in previous passages, from the perspective of personalism, he concludes that the absolute order of values has been turned on its head in the world of bourgeois man. Utility values, which represent the lowest values in Scheler's schema, becomes the sole criteria by which every action, every virtue and every good must be measured. Even "life itself," Scheler claims in an early work, "the sheer *existence* of an individual, a race, a nation—must be justified by its *usefulness* for a *wider* community." Where "according to the earlier notion," he continues, "life in its aimless *activity*, its mere 'respiration' and its characteristic inner processes, represents an instrinsic fullness of value," with the appearance and dominance of bourgeois man and his yardstick of utility, "the pure expression of life is only ballast and evil luxury—a kind of 'atavistic survival' of forms of behavior and action that were useful long ago."[196] Modern politics, whether as bourgeois liberalism, bourgeois Marxism or the mass politics of the extreme right and left, reflects this same fundamental error. Revealing their origin in the anthropology of bourgeois man, each succumbs to the "perverse" value order of the bourgeois. Modern politics, thus, despite its surface differences, is ineluctably imprisoned in the single dimension of utility values.

In looking solely upon the *value* dimension of the paradigm of modern politics, however, important *conceptual* aspects of both comparison and contrast between personalism as political theory and modern politics are lost. Even in relation to Scheler's own political inclinations, there stands much more room for reviewing affinities and disaffinities than his uncompromising rejection of modern politics on value grounds permits. Indeed, though widely touted as a conservative, Scheler ardently argues for a religious socialism and adopts an increasingly liberal political stance as the Weimar republic devolved into a babble of extremist voices. Close consideration, therefore, may prove valuable regarding the conceptual dimension of personalism as political theory vis-a-vis modern political thought. Since, furthermore, it is largely liberalism and Marxism which have come to be viewed as the major political movements and theories of the modern era, these serve here as the principal foci for comparison.

BOURGEOIS LIBERALISM

By and large, Scheler determines bourgeois liberalism to be the purest exemplar of modern politics, a variety more attuned to the reality of bourgeois man than other strains of modern politics.[197] His early antagonism and later ambiguity toward liberalism illustrate a continual, if peripheral, concern with the phenomenon associated with his general concern with the status of man in the modern world. Drawing on his research, four conceptual aspects of bourgeois liberalism seem to stand at great variance for the picture of personalism as political theory sketched earlier. These four (formalism, individualism, needs-utility motivation and modern rationalism) offer interesting contrasts with personalist politics.

Formalism

Although there would appear to be a little need to restate what even its proponents are willing to admit to be the "formal" character of liberalism, no need certainly to duplicate the exhaustive scholarship on the topic by other researchers, it is worthwhile for present purpose to take a perspective of some distance from the many debates regarding liberalism and to paint quickly with a broad brush the major features of its formalism.[198] Especially from the angle of personalism as political theory, liberalism is "formal" in two important ways, both of which draw close scrutiny from Scheler in many of his inquires into the phenomena of politics and community. Liberalism is theoretically formal *in process* and *in its basis in formalized elements*. Accordingly, the *process* of liberalism is an operation which follows a strict formula of established rules and procedures. This is epitomized in the works of early liberal writers where the actions of politics are conceived as the results of the processes of individual interactions coordinated through contracts. In the theories of the later liberal writers, where the operation of the polity is in some sense more concrete owing to the consideration of actual utility or pleasure, the process remains in large part formal when the motor of political action is reduced to a formal, mathematical aggregate of individual human desires. Even more clearly, later liberal thinkers arguing for a categorical imperative, to the extent that it can be construed as a maxim for the political order, can also be perceived as adhering to the formal character of liberalism. Despite the various and sometimes important differences among the several versions of liberalism, therefore, there exists a commonality in their process; each counsels the determination of proper political actions via a methodological following of certain principles. Political actions are legitimate, regardless of the particulars of outcome, if the proper methods have been followed. Political practice is considered ''good'' if it issues from the appropriate, established processes—a point applicable for both society as a whole and for individual political actions within the liberal schema. There is no acknowledgement of the legitimacy of social goods and values apart from this adherence to formal procedure. Hence, political practice can never attain more than the status of an *ad hoc*, formal tool devised by its citizens as a means toward their separate ends.

Max Scheler's most thorough investigation of ''formalism'' appears in his master work on ethics, *Formalism in Ethics and Non-Formal Ethics of Values*.[199] Taking Kant's formalism, ''a colossus of steel and bronze,'' as his starting point, Scheler demonstrates the possibility and necessity of a flesh-and-blood, substantively human approach to questions of deontological significance. Despite the impressiveness of Kant's colossus, and while acknowledging the validity of much of his conclusion, Scheler finds the colossus to be inadequate precisely because formalism offers no ''down to earth'' value for real men faced with actual normative choices.[200] Formalism, in this concpetion, is a denial of knowledge or any conation of the ''right'' or ''good'' action itself, and an assertion that only the rightness or wrongness of the method or process of choosing any given action can be known. This inadequacy of Kant's and all other formal approaches to normative issues lies in the chasm which is drawn between formal procedures and material facts. Scheler remarks that the character of such procedures (general, abstract, inflexible) is itself illustrative of its in-applicability to the uniqueness of each person and each particular human situation. Personalism, in contrast, is chary of the lodging of human responsibility solely in such methods and processes and would seem to require a greater emphasis on the responsibility of persons for the actual results of their actions—above and beyond any responsibility associated with the means by which such results are attained. More particularly, by way of convincing phenomenological presentation, as discussed earlier in this study, Scheler reveals that special material "facts" are directly perceived in every normative experience. These facts are "values," values which are immediately given and which offer concrete guidance for action. The proper course of action is that on which the "higher" value lies. When in conflict, for example, and all else being considered equal, one ought to pursue the relatively higher value of social welfare over the lower value of individual utility.[201] Hence, Scheler contrasts the formalism of liberalism with his own non-formal, direct perception of values. In the place of liberalism's process of politics in terms of artificial constructions, it would seem that Scheler is holding out the possibility of a politics based on actual, though deontological, "facts."

As noted, however, liberalism is formal in more than its *process*. It is formal as well in what might be termed its basic structural elements. Common to much of liberal theory is the conception of the civil society as only a network of contracts or covenants, rules or procedures. As classically phrased, its government is one of laws, rather than of men and women. Beyond, then, the concerns which Scheler voices over the formal methods and procedures of liberal political theories lies a more disquieting implication. In Scheler's estimation, liberalism inevitably reduces actual, human persons to less-than-human abstractions of themselves. The formal character of liberalism requires that unique personal needs and talents be ignored in order that individual men might be more effeciently handled by the political process. In democratic liberalisms, men would be treated as radically equal units of political demands and inputs—as identical, faceless, voting digits in the counting of numbers which constitutes liberal democratic policy-making. Even a formalism which claims that persons must ever be treated as ends—and never as means—may be in the final regard a depersonalizing contruction. Scheler agrees with Immanual Kant that the person "must *never* be considered a *thing* or a *substance*," and asserts along similar lines that the person must be the "immediately co-experienced unity of experiencing." Nonetheless, he contends that efforts by Kant to overcome the objectification of the other by dutifully considering all men as identical to oneself (in regard to possessing the same structures of reason) ironically leads to a conception of the other as less than the full person he or she is. Kant's formalism, like all formalisms, ineluctably can only conceive of men as "the X of certain powers" or "the X of some kind of rational activity." The depersonalization occurs, therefore, because the X, "that 'something' which is the subject of rational activity, must be attributed to concrete persons—indeed, to all men—in the same way and as something *identical* in all men."[202] Regardless of its intentions, it seems that the formalism of bourgeois liberalism unavoidably reduces the person to a ghostly caricature of his or her full personhood and distorts and narrows the practice of politics by relegating choice to blind procedures removed the reality of human experiences and the reality of values.

Individualism

As with formalism, individualism is not so much a causal factor in the devlopment of liberalism as it is an aspect of the conceptual and normative framework of bourgeois man. As was discussed above, Scheler percieves bourgeois man to approach the world and others always from the perspective of the self. The bourgeois self ever begins with its own subjectivity, emphasizing its "ownness" in regard to the otherness in which it finds itself. In liberalism, to differentiate it from the subjectivity which Scheler sees in Marxism, it is the individual human, understood as a reasoning and desiring locus of subjectivity, in which this subjectivity finds its expression. Liberal political theories divide the political community into standardized and formally equal chunks of rights, liberties, duties and so forth—chunks that are individual men. Because liberalism looks at the polity in this fashion, because it seeks to explain politics and direct political action in accordance with this model, the subjectivity of bourgeois liberalism aptly is termed "individualism."

Scheler illustrates the modern notion of individualism and its relationship with liberalism by contrasting the ideal of the liberal society with the dominant ideal of society existing prior to the emergence of the bourgeois type of man.[203] The previous conception was one of a natural community wherein members partake of social rights and responsibilities proper for each member's determined place in the social order. Much different from this, Scheler's portrayal of the liberal society finds rights and responsibilities relative not to one's proper place in the political order, but to a procedural or formal understanding of one's rights and responsibilities *without* the political order—indeed, outside all association with others. In this picture, responsibility for other can only be a secondary consideration which follows and is built on a primary concern for unilateral self-responsibility. In the same way, rights are no longer to be understood as "social rights" (the only manner of understanding them prior to bourgeois man). Rather, rights in the liberal paradigm are understood as wholly lodged in the individual. As a result, the polity is "not a special reality outside or above the individual." It is, in fact," only the similarity or dissimilarity of *individuals'* interests... [a] fabric of *relations* that represent 'conventions,' 'usage,' or 'contracts,' depending on whether they are more explicit or more tacit."[204] Scheler's response to the concept of individualism is not to romantically hearken back to the so-called natural polity or to an organic community. Individualism in many ways must be seen as an improvement to the stultifying, static hierarchies of the previous medieval conception. Neither, however, does Scheler champion the notion of individualism as it is presented within the framework of bourgeois man. While he acknowledges that both the earlier conception of the polity *and* bourgeois individualism offer valuable insights into the context of man's social life, it is believed that both conceptions ultimately fail to encompass the full range of human sociality and individuality. Both too narrowly delimit the possible relationships between person, other and the community. In addition, Scheler contends that neither the individual nor the community can be entirely understood by isolating one from the other. For Scheler, both are merely separate and incomplete manifestations of man's anthropologically based sociality.[205] Both, moreover, are subject to the destiny of man.[206]

From the perspective of personalism as political theory, as has been clarified with some detail in earlier discussion, the primacy of the individual, which is a central premise of bourgeois individualism, is untenable. Despite the emphasis on the special dignity of the individual person, Scheler's personalism sees the genesis of the individual person in a gradual emergence from community—through a series of transformations whereby the person acquires the ability to "dissociate" or objectify the world, then others and, finally, the self.[207] Likewise, viewing the acquisition of individualism in the development of the species, human sociality is perceived most

primitively as an amorphous herd, then as a specialized life community, and only subsequently in the form of the familiar individualism of society.[208] Both in the origin of the individual character
of the person and in the origin of individuality which is obvious in the
human species, the social or communal is discerned, at least foundationally, to precede the individual. Hence, bourgeois liberalism errs
in a very basic sense, when it endeavors to found the civil society on *a
priori* individualism.

This is *not*, however, a full elaboration of the distinction between
personalism as political theory and bourgeois individualism on the
subject of individualism. Not only does bourgeois individualism fail
to comprehend the contingent and developmental nature of individualism itself, it equally does not recognize that individualism is
but a moment or aspect of the larger reality of human sociality. In this
error, no quarter is granted for considering the possibility of the
transformation of the sociality of individualism to the persons community. Just as the individual personality may overcome its self-
centered adolescent individualism maturely to recognize the subjectivity of others and its own roots in the enveloping community, so too
the individuality of bourgeois liberalism may be overcome in a person
community where persons recognize the origin of their individuality
in the community and, with the responsibility such recognition en-
tails, would creatively constitute the person community itself.
Human individualism finds its genesis only in community, in other
words, but the highest community—the person community—has its
origin in the creative overcoming of mere individualism by individual
persons. The person's individuality is an achievement of his or her
sociality; the person's highest sociality is an achievement of his or her
individuality. Hence, the person community must be seen as inherently "political" in the best sense of the world. Each person
creatively partakes in constituting the person community (itself a corporate personality), acknowledging and accepting the constitution of
his or her own individual personality *by the community*.[209]

Returning to the question at hand, three counterpoints to the individualism of liberalism can be derived from the foregoing. *First*,
because the background of the individual is the community, liberal
individualism is incorrect in viewing the individual as prior to the
community. Although only by order of foundation, personalism
demonstrates that the social experience is primary and the individual,
secondary. Liberalism is mistaken in regarding the individual as the
theoretical ground and most basic building block of society and

politics. *Second*, individualism fails to do full justice to the individual. True individuality requires the mutual acceptance of the unique personhoods of one's own person, other persons and the person of the community as a whole. Because the liberal scheme sees the community as dependent upon the parallel but separate actions of distinct individuals, the dignity of the unique personhood of the others and the community is precluded. Denying the subjectivity of the community and others undermines the possibility of the individual's own subjectivity. *Third*, individualism in the liberal scheme is substantively unachievable.[210] Because each individual discovers himself only aginst the backdrop of the community, then any conception of the individual as isolated from the community would be but an illusory abstraction. Although Scheler's personalism does not claim that there is a causal dependency between the individual and the community, or even a circular interdependency, he does assert that both the community and the individual are necessary for a full understanding of the person. As illustrated by these counterpoints, personalism as political theory rejects the simple individualism of bourgeois liberalism.

Motivation

Within bourgeois liberalism, two differing explanations for the motivation behind the polity and behind all political action have figured prominently among theorists. Typically, however, the difference between these two explanations of motivation is often blurred by such thinkers. Even at best, distinctions between these motivations are only vaguely noted. Yet, from the perspective of Scheler's phenomenological studies on values and, more importantly for present concerns from the perspective of personalism as political theory, a sharp line must be drawn between liberalism which is motivated by the *negative* value of "need" and liberalism which is motivated by the relatively low, but *positive* value of enhanced utility or pleasure.)[211]

Need-motivated liberalism would conceive of men and women as motivated in their political actions by an effort merely to escape from a present great evil toward future conditions with potentially less evil. In this pessimestic protrait of human existence, the status quo is perceived to be forever a scene of woeful circumstances that is tolerated only out of fear of degeneraton into worse situations. There is no tranquil, resigned acceptance reflected in whatever toleration might be granted to the present. Indeed, the circumstances of the present are an eternal goading for humankind to seek progress toward predicaments of lesser evil.[212] All political actions must therefore be understood as directed at minimizing or blindly avoiding the discomforts of existence. Hobbes, in this vein, sees humankind acting politically due to fear of violent death, Spinoza out of fear of aimless anarchy. It might be objected that any identification of a pure need-motivated liberalism is itself an abstration, that no liberal thinker completely ignores motivation from positive values. Hobbes, for example, might also be cited for his stress on the desire for a commodious life. But, while it will be acknowledged by Scheler that a number of need-motivated political theories also consider some minor positive values in motivation, such positive values are very much secondary motivations for these theories. Moreover, when present in these schemes, such positive values—pleasure, physical satisfaction, etcetera—remain values of the lower levels in the foundational order of values which is conjoined so closely with Scheler's personalism. Thus, a need-motivated liberalism might discuss a motivation such as fear or anxiety. Indeed, more typically, such of lesser importance in the explanation of motivation than a negative motivations such as fear or anxiety. Indeed, more typically, such thinkers despair of truly positive values and come to name that which fulfills a need as a "positive" value. Whatever the particulars, all need-motivated liberalisms operate according to the principle of ameliorating the deficiencies of existence which can never be wholly overcome.

Again following Scheler's inquiry and surveying all other theories of liberalism it might be said that what is not definable in terms of needs motivation can be roughly catergorized under the general heading of utility motivation.[213] Under this heading, political practice is motivated by a recognition of only a narrow range of what for Scheler are the lower, materialistic utility values. Due to the nature of such values and the failure to consider values beyond this level, motivation in such liberalisms aims toward the amassing of greater and greater *quantities* of those things which carry these values—i.e., property.[214] Unlike need-motivated liberalism, which pictures men engaged continually in seeking (though never completely finding) easement of the evils of life, utility liberalism finds the basic motivating factor in human action to be an atraction to perceived values such as "pleasure." They operate not on negative values, therefore, but on positive ones. As with the needs version, however, there are seldom pure examples of this utility-based explanation of human motivation. Most liberal thinkers in this category also admit the negative value of "pain" and assign it a secondary role in the motivation process. Some more complex examples of utility liberalism contend that negative values predominate in the operation of civil society until a certain level of civilization is attained at which point utility values come to dominate.[215] However, regardless of its various guises, utility liberalisms remain based upon the notion of "utility seeking" as the primary motivation of individuals and the purpose of politics.

Scheler's evaluation of these two different explanations for motivation in liberalism varies with each. In regard to need-motivated liberalism, Scheler begins by investigating the feeling of need itself. He contrasts the feeling of need with instinctual impulses such as hunger, terming it an experience of displeasure which accompanies the perception of a lacking.[216] Although such an experience occurs as well in hunger and thirst, Scheler notes a profound difference in that "needs" are not a physical, natural experience of lacking, but rather are in some sense an artificial product of minds and cultures. He supports this point by way of very convincing examples, noting that a starving tribe of primitives does not "need" the fish in nearby lakes if their culture has not come to consider fish as food. Similarly, pre-Columbian, American aborigines did not "need" the horse, despite the reality that their children's children of the American plains truly did have this need. Needs, thus, are *not* innate, but are developed in psychology and history by men's actions.

Such revelation in these regards cuts to the heart of the need-motivated concept of liberalism. If needs are a product of psychology and history—if there are no common "innate" needs—then needs can hardly be taken as the foundation of culture or the motor of historical processes. Needs cannot be the basis for explanation of civilization or political practice when they themselves arise in history and reference to human acts.[217] Furthermore, needs are certainly incapable of explaining *true* growth, whether historical, cultural or individual. Such growth is measured in the attainment of new height, in the coming to know of that which was previously unknown. Yet, as Scheler makes evident, one can only need what one has known or experienced before. As negative, reaction-like feelings focused on what are perceived as the lackings of the present, needs are unable truly to look forward; they are unable to guide action in anticipation of the new "heights" of growth. While the need-motivated model of liberalism is characterized by a state of constant agitation due to men's continual reaction to the inadequacies of the status quo, such a scenario would result not in genuine forward-looking growth but rather only in aimless, incremental flux. To suppose that the polity arises haphazardly from such a process is to deny it positive purpose and to reduce its existence to the status of happy accident.[218]

In opposition to this understanding, personalism as political theory would contend that all actions by men have their basis in the perception and subsequent pursuit of *positive* values. More than this, the subsequent pursuit of positive values itself has its "source in a *surplus* of positive feelings at the deepest stratum."[219] Human action springs, accordingly *not* from *need*, but from *surplus*. True development or growth (physical or spiritual) occurs when the present situation is not only "tolerable," but when there exists in the present a great enough overabundance of positive value so as to begin reaching for that which is greater than the present. Civilizations do not arise where humanity is in greatest need, but instead where there exists a great surplus of resources. Polities do not arise of out of needs, but out of vision—vision freed from the ball and chain of necessity. Politics is properly a pattern of human actions, *not* reactions.

At first glance, utility liberalism would appear to be in concurrence with Scheler's response to the needs variety. The needs model, after all, fails in Scheler's estimation precisely because of its blindness to positive values. In contrast, utility liberalism finds the pursuance of positive values, in this case *utility* values, to be both the mainspring and the proper end of human action and (so-called) development. Oddly, however, it is exactly because utility liberalism finds *utility* to be both the motive behind individual action and the ultimate end of human sociality, that Scheler utterly rejects such liberalism as an explanation and normative guide for social life and politics. Utility liberalism, he claims, rests upon an "inversion" of man's hierarchy of values. Thereby, Scheler sees it as only a "perversion" of the proper means and end of the social order. Scheler traces the historical grounds of this inversion in a number of early works to the feeling of *ressentiment* which comes to predominate the constitution of man as he emerges as the *typus* of the bourgeois. Like Nietzsche, Scheler finds *ressentiment* to be a self-poisoning of the psyche issuing from the suppression of the smoldering hatred of a lesser man for one greater.[220] *Ressentiment* in time undermines the normative framework of the greater man/lesser man (master/slave) relationship. If only by the weight of their numbers, the masses, filled with *ressentiment*, come to subvert the order of value which marks the greater, exceptional man as superior to themselves. The common virtues of the multitude are extolled while the secretly-envied virtues of the superior man are held up for ridicule. The proper order of values is overthrown through appeals to the most base values (i.e., "utility") and lower values are placed in ascendancy over the higher. Usefulness is celebrated over nobility, quantity over quality, homogeneity over creative diversity. Moreover, Scheler argues that the art of ruling is thus rendered as "economics;" science becomes "technology;" development becomes not growth but "gluttony" and truth itself becomes merely "pragmatic truth."[222]

The significance of this becomes clear in considering the pattern of values itself, which Scheler divides into five modal levels: the agreeable, the useful, the vital, the spiritual (geistliche), and the holy.[223] From the agreeable as lowest to the holy as highest, each level corresponds to its own distinct sphere of acts and values. At the same time, the array of values itself must be seen as an order of sorts, a foundational sequence of stages where the values of the lower levels are to be considered as directional signs pointing toward the highest levels. Utility liberalism, therefore, greatly errs in its consideration of the value of utility (pleasure, agreeableness) as the proper *end* of the polity or as the ultimate goal of political action. The implicit imperative of Scheler's order of values requires that every positive action be done in consideration of the highest values, or, as he states elsewhere, in consideration of the "destiny of man."[224] Although Scheler certainly does not object to the intrinsic importance and independence of each modal level, in a situation of conflicting values, the lower must give way to the higher; the utility values must be subordinated to the vital, the vital to the spiritual and the spiritual to the holy.

Crucial here is the recognition that personalism as political theory, to the extent that it shares Scheler's value theory, does not deny the importance of the value of utility per se. The distinction to be made is that personalism as political theory does not narrowly delimit itself to an understanding of politics motiviated only by utility or any other single category of values. Rather, it perceives a variety of motivating values in the practice of politics—indeed, the entire range of values. Scheler himself struggles with this extension of the political. In his early writings he conceives of politics, in the narrowest usage of the term, to operate wholly within the sphere of what he calls "vital values." In large part, following from this, his dismissal of utility based liberalism stems from a perceived perversion where bourgeois man raises the utility values of economics above the vital values of politics. From the implications of Scheler's personalism, however, it would seem that the concept of the political cannot even be constrained to the single category of the vital values, but must be seen to encompass the entire array of values—and always in light of the higher values. The motivation of political action, thus, has many sources. For personalism as political theory, whatever the immediate motivation for political action, political practice occurs in an arena which recognizes the highest values.[225]

Rationalism

According to Scheler, the interpretation and understanding of reason also undergo profound change with the emergence of the bourgeois man. Where previously reason was somehow understood as very much intertwined with faith, love, man's ultimate values, goods, ends and so forth, with this new type of man reason is stripped and isolated from such heady concepts. Reason being conceived in a much more narrow and restricted sense, Scheler contends that with the bourgeois man, it "*emancipates* itself from both emotional and organic-schematic guidances."[226] Reason, thus, becomes estranged from the world and others. Theory is distanced from nature and practice. Facts are thoroughly severed from values.

Two somewhat different *but essentially interrelated* versions of this new interpretation of reason are evident within the paradigm of modern political thought, both of which directly evidence themselves in bourgeois liberalism. According to the first, reason is rendered a mundane, instrumental and calculative tool serving the interests of individuals' needs and utility. This "reasoning" is, therefore, only conceived as an instrument of the underlying needs and utility motivations which were earlier considered and rejected by Scheler. Indeed, Scheler only sketchily treats this particular version of modernity's transformation of reason.[227] The second version, however, attracts his closest attention. Perhaps in awareness of the inadequacies and dangers of establishing ethics and politics upon a foundation of utility or need, this second version of the new reason takes the "purified" reason of the bourgeois man *itself* as a guide and starting point for practical action. Liberal thinkers in this "rationalist" vein would stand approvingly with Scheler in opposition to the claims of other liberals regarding a universal need or utility motivation. Such rationalists contend that needs or utility motivations belong in general to the world of sensory experience and, thus, are dangerous grounds for political principles and untrustworthy bases for the legitimate polity. The rationalist skirts the problems of such empirically-based social and political theories by claiming that "the ground of obligation must not be sought in the nature of man or in the circumstances in which he is placed, but sought—*a priori*—solely in the concepts of pure reason."[228] In other words, Scheler's rejection of those liberalisms which operate on the assumptions of need or utility motivation is inapplicable to liberalisms based on the *a priori* imperatives of universally shared reason. Rationalism here, a derivation of rules for action from reason itself, becomes the explanation of and justification for society and politics.

Operationally, this understanding conceives of humankind as molding the sensible world, through the innate processes of reason, into general categories which reason itself can subsequently work with and manipulate. Rationalism contends that the raw world is unsuitable as a location from which to make social and normative judgements because it is particularized and individuated. Indeed, so much is each bit of experience in the everyday world understood as an individual and unique occurrence, that the world of these experiences is taken to be only a meaningless chaos of disparate phenomena. To make normative decisions in the midst of such an unsettled state of affairs and on the basis of such incoherent data, the rationalists reason, would be folly. To establish a political community on a foundation of this sort—the chaotic, raw facts of the sensible world before reason has digested them—would be absurd.[229] Similarly, the rationalist liberal thinker looks to reason for a common frame of reference by which humankind can acknowledge and act in accordance with others. Without such a frame of reference, the rationalists argue, that each individual man, being isolated from his fellows by space and time, would perceive an utterly different world than that of his fellows. It is in this sense that humans are individuated. Without reason, they content, this individuation would be such that every man would be radically alienated from every other man. Politics and ethics are only possible, therefore, where this radical individuation is circumvented by the possession of the faculty of reason among all persons. Because both the empirical perception of values and the derivation of the "good" from nature are dependent upon the relativity of human experience in a suspect world, normative choice is seen to require some firmer footing. The rationalists find such "footing" in reason itself. The ultimate ground (or, better, "criterion") for norms and action *must* be found in reason. By reason, therefore, the world can then be dealt with, society with others can be possible, and human actions can attain normative significance.

Political institutions and structures for political practice follow upon these rational suppositions. Since politics involves the exercise and conditioning of choice, its domain (in classical parlance) is that of the will. The rationalist position conceives of the will, however, only in terms of it being merely a creature of reason. Reason determines the ground of will, constituting the objects to which choice applies. For politics, reason thus posits practical principles which generally determine the conditions of political practice. Inasmuch as such principles are established on and through reason, the rationalists contend they are valid and binding for every rational being—they are, in other words, "universal." The ultimate criterion of the validity of political practice, the ultimate test of the legitimacy of any political institution is therefore the measure of its universality, its generality in regard to all rational beings. In this context, it follows that there are no political goods in themselves, "good" being only those principles which stand the test of being rendered universal. General rules and procedures would follow from such principles. Yet, the farther such rules and procedures stretch from the universalized principles toward the particular situation in the world, the less valid they become. Hence, an apparently liberal political landscape emerges.

Scheler raises serious objections to this whole process—objections which go beyond his previously considered rejection of the formalism implicit within it. He questions the very applicability of such reason to practical affairs. He claims, *first*, that the rationalist conception rests upon an antiquated, static understanding of man which wrongly assumes all men in all times possess equal access to reason. *Second*, he questions whether reason is the secure haven from the world of experience which the rationalists seek. *Third*, he denies the assertion of the *a priori* place of reason in normative concerns.

Beginning with the *first* of Scheler's points, he notes that the rationalist pictures mankind to to be something firm and stable in its possession of certain faculties. Though most rationalist writers contend that they are concerned not with human reasoning, but with reason itself, their works offer little evidence to support the possibility of reason existing outside of actual men.[230] With scant few exceptions, to be a man is seen to be a rational man regardless of personal development, culture and so forth. As Scheler writes, in the rationalist view "the concept of man was, in a way, involuntarily idealized, and a real species was subsumed under this ideal concept as a correlate, which today seems possible only on the basis of insufficient knowledge of the fact. This results in the 'universally human,' 'humanity,' and the 'all too human.'"[231] Scheler cites a growing body of empirical evidence which undercuts this rationalist position. Men differ from one another across time and space. Mankind evolves genetically and anthropologically. Just as the child grows and changes in reason, so too do men in culture and mankind as a species. "Mankind is, like any race, people, or individual, changeable in principle, and its constitution is a product of the universal development of life."[232]

Suspicion is therefore warranted for the rationalists' effort to utilize men's faculty of reason as a secure and universal base. Since mankind itself is no unchanging thing in the world, but is instead a dynamic, developing entity, any assumption that men's access to reason is identical for all humankind is hard to swallow. Fire might burn equally in Persia as in Athens, but the rationality of the Persians was suspect even in ancient times, and little imagination is required to speculate on the Persian conclusions regarding Athenian rationality. Scheler rejects, on these and other grounds, any notion of an unchanging, *factual* unity of human nature and rejects, therefore, any "notion that there is a certain *fixed*, 'inborn' functional apparatus of reason given to all humans from the beginning—the idol of the Enlightenment as well as Kant."[233] There is no fixed and frozen human nature, and rationalism cannot disregard this fact by pontificating on the universality of reason. Reason may or may not itself be always and everywhere the same, but man's faculty of reason is locked within his dynamic and developing essence. The mere possession of the faculty of reason by man does not avail the hopes of the rationalists for finding in reason a ground for norms and actions.[234]

The *second* objection which Scheler raises against the use of such reason as the primary guide to practical affairs radicalizes the first. For not only, he argues, does does the faculty of reason change, but *reason* itself changes. The key to Scheler's claim is what he terms the "functionalization of essential insight." [*Funktionalisierung der Wesenseinsicht*).[235] As Scheler explains the concept, reason exists much more intimately with man than the rationalists would admit. Reasoning affects reason, on one hand, and the objects of reason, on the other. Reason itself is pulled and stretched to accommodate both forces. Subjectivity/experience constitutes the conditions of reason; reason becomes what it is required to be by both man and world. It develops and grows. "The *functionalization* of essential insight enables us to understand that there can be an *evolution* and growth of reason itself —growth, that is to say, of its property in *a priori* rules of selection and function."²³⁶ Contrary to the hopes of the rationalist, reason is not immune from the flux of experience. Nor is it immune from the actions of men. As Scheler puts it, reason "grows and diminishes, 'evolves,' and 'regresses,' because certain of the essential insights by whose functionalization its progress is controlled are attached to this or that particular locus in the concrete world-process and are possible only at those points."²³⁷ Ironically, adding insult to injury, Scheler concludes that the particular reason upon which the rationalist liberal seizes, is but the peculiar reason of the European Enlightenment and only a cul-de-sac in the development of reason in Western civilization.²³⁸

The *third* point, which Scheler raises against the utilization of reason for practical matters, concerns the rationalists' assertion of the primacy of reason. As noted, rationalism utilizes reason as both the guide *to* action and the justification *for* action. The will follows reason and depends upon reason for its legitimacy. Reason, for the rationalist conception, is thus the *a priori* source of acts. Scheler, of course, denies this. Scheler's rejection of the priorness of reason in regard to action and norms does not succumb to the voluntarist charge that a blind, unknowing will is primary. Both will and reason for Scheler are inherently in the domain of the individual ego and, as discussed previously, the individual is itself not primary. He admits freely, concurring with the rationalists, that all willing is a "striving for that which is known." Yet, is the "knowing" which precedes willing a rational knowing? Scheler thinks not. Examples can be imagined which illustrate a "knowing" unknown to reason. Such "knowing" can lend itself to willing and action beyond articulation in terms of rational purpose. Scheler, however, does not establish his rejection of reason's primacy on a single category of examples. As remarked early in this study, at its deepest root knowledge is a relationship of being, specifically, the relationship of one being partaking in the essential character [*Sosein*] of another being without incurring any change in the character of either the knower or the known. What is thus presupposed in knowing is a primal act of abandoning the self in order to come into experiential contact with the world. As a relationship of being, knowledge *follows* the peculiar act of *overcoming the self* in order to reach out for something perceived in the world. And, at this deepest stratum, the perception which precedes rational knowing, is a perception of value. Rather than reason constituting the conditions of will, as the rationalists claim, Scheler convincingly argues that the conditions of reason are constituted by the perception of values.[239] Even the perception of value, however, cannot be seen as sufficient grounds for reason, for there must be a tendency in the knower to rise beyond itself to participate in the known. There must be an ''evaluating'' or ''taking interest in'' that which is becoming known. In the most mundane sense, Scheler refers to this tendency as ''interest;'' in the highest sense, he calls it ''love.'' It is only by way of this fundamental tendency that man is able to overcome the self, in order to reason. He claims that man ''before he is an *ens cogitans* or an *ens volens*, is an *ens amans*.''[240] Reason is, therefore, not as the rationalists see it. The bedrock of our relation with an other is always the perception of the inestimable value of the other and the tendency to deny the self to partake in the other's essential character. The root of our relation to the world is always interest. Reason cannot be the primary ground of normative choice and action. Reason follows the ''knowing'' of the heart, and the rationalist liberal errs, therefore, by establishing the legitimacy of politics on the priority of purified reason.

Personalism, Liberalism and Polital Legitimacy

On the basis of the foregoing inquiry into the conditions of ''bourgeois'' liberalism, it may appear puzzling that there might be found any affinity between liberal political thought and personalism as political theory. Yet, it is the peculiar image of bourgeois man and the value-complex of the bourgeois which has been revealed to lie at the root of the untenability of these conceptions of liberalism—and not explicitly liberalism itself. It is then curious to reappraise Max Scheler's own growing liberal inclinations as the German political environment of the 1920s grew increasingly dominated by extremist voices. The period is one of growing reflection in Scheler's own writings, and while in no sense is it marked by any retrenchment, he is seen to be increasingly careful to distance his own thinking from certain misinterpretations of his earlier works. Notably, he takes pains to clarify that he is far from being the irrationalist that some reviewers of early works, such as *Ressentiment*, had designated him.[241] Similiarly, this period marks the final break between Scheler and Catholicism, one which he very clearly explains to be congruent and even founded on his continuing philosophy of personalism and realist phenomenology.[242] This same thread is also apparent in his chastisement of the German youth movements, whose spirit he had previously applauded, (groups such as the *Wandervögel*, and various religious and political groups), for their growing mysticism, irrationalism and blind obedience to their leadership—all while still lauding their rejection of the bourgeois values of their parents.[243] Likewise, the times find Scheler engaging in bitter renunciation of the mass-based and mob-like political parties of the right and left—fascist, racist and communist.[244] In these examples and many others, there is evidenced a growing emphasis on the importance of considered reflections, individual liberty, and what might be called personalist "pluralism" in Scheler's thinking, especially as these qualities relate to political practice. As such, a vaguely "liberal" quality to his position is discernable.

Unresolved, however, is whether by any sense of the word, personalism as political theory might be described as "liberal." The question is troublesome and in no way is its resolution fundamental to this study. Obviously, a personalist liberalism would be one shaken loose from the moorings liberalism now retains in the paradigm of the bourgeois, for the crux of personalist thought is the possible transformation of man. More particularly, personalist liberalism would be one which recognizes utility values as but a narrow slice of an array of values which stretches to the values of the sublime and holy. What such a liberalism would resemble is best left to speculation, but attention might be paid to the foreground sequence of transformations which precede bourgeois liberalism itself. The high virtue world of liberalism, "legitimacy" is illustrative here. Where the bourgeois liberal can conceive of legitimacy only as based on convention due to a happenstance convergence of various individual interests, the word has intriguing roots: *legitimatus, legitimus, lex, legere, legein, logos*.[245] The legitimacy of the politics of personalism may in some manner include and transform each of these notions. Hence, a personalist liberalism, seemingly, may differ from bourgeois liberalism more plainly in its essence than its appearance.

BOURGEOIS MARXISM

A political theory which has as its basis Max Scheler's personalism, stands in an ambiguous relationship with Marxist political theories.[246] In large part, the relationship would be one of much affinity and many parallels. Like Marxism, for example, personalism is very much an argument for the situatedness of subjectivity and its many attributes within the contours and circumstances of world and history. In this vein, Scheler posits a sociology of knowledge, a functionalization of essential inquiry, and anthropological philosophy of man, and a rejection of both pure idealism and ethical-political formalism. Additionally, he finds, as does Marxist theory, that the material conditions of class, economics and labor are of central importance for understanding the actions and practices of persons in the world. With the so-called *Kathedersozialisten* of Weimar academia, Scheler is also closely engaged in the application of elements of Marxist cultural theory in a broad and critical analysis of bourgeois man and the often unperceived ideals of bourgeois society. Moreover, and finally, there are readily obvious parallels between the Marxist notion of the emergence of true communist society and Scheler's own thesis of the transformation of the person and the constitution of the person community.

Yet, in no sense can Scheler be termed "Marxist." Although he freely utilizes Marxist theory for his own purposes and adopts certain elements of Marxist thought which are congruent with his own philosophy and his social and political theory, he rejects Marxism in a general sense because he finds it mired in the curious value-complex of bourgeois man.[247] Marxism, in other words, may be a useful and powerful instrument which is valuable for its insightful dissection of certain pathologies in the social, economic and political structure of modern society, but from the perspective of personalism and realist phenomenology, Marxism—as it is widely interpreted—is also found to be enmeshed within the shortsighted value systelm, if not the worldview, of the bourgeois. More specifically, Marxism (which is associated with terms such as "scientific," "mammonistic" and "economic" in Scheler's usage) unwittingly and without reflection accepts bourgeois man's myopic focus on the values of utility as the "measure" of all things. Contrary to the understanding of many Marxist thinkers, in fact, it may be claimed on the basis of this insight that the political theory of bourgeois Marxism is only a diguised and new triumph of the bourgeois psychology of *ressentiment*, where the moral and political and (patently) the economic agenda of bourgeois man is sinisterly extended beyond the actual, historical class of the bourgeoisie themselves. In Scheler's reading of Marx, it is economic values and the patterns of their historic maldistribution, the experience of alienation grounded in the unequal exchange between labor and the ecnomic value of such labor, and a very bourgeois calculating rancor over these admittedly real and inexcusable inequities, which are understood to combine and drive the Marxist engine of history. Obviously, if the validity of Scheler's reading is affirmed, Marxism operates primarily at the lower levels of possible values. Whatever inconsequential frictions might exist between "bourgeois Marxism" and bourgeois liberalism, therefore, do not reflect an underlying essential difference, but stem instead from only what is clearly a bourgeois competiton for the inevitably scarce objects of utility values.

This study, although cognizant of the many faces of Marxism in recent decades, follows Max Scheler's own understanding of what is here referred to as "bourgeois Marxism." Just as with the inquiry of bourgeois liberalism, bourgeois Marxism must be recognized as a facet of an essentially unitary modern politics, a unity which is itself founded on the conceptual and deontological paradigm of bourgeois man. Like the previous consideration given liberalism, then, bourgeois Marxism also stands to be valuably compared and contrasted at certain points with personalism as political theory. The following pages consider dialectical materialism, class subjectivity and the critique of ideology from this standpoint. As with liberalism, and as ought to be expected, the results of the comparison reveal a general disaffinity, but equally indicate possibilities for curious and thought-provoking affinity.

Dialectical Materialism

The heart of bourgeois Marxism is disclosed in its emphasis on the primacy of material reality and in the constitutive (even determinant) role which the processes and conditions of material reality play in the formation of noetic reality. Ideas, consciousness, metaphysics and morality are understood as entirely dependent categories—without intrinsic histories—existing only as products of what is termed the "material dialectic."[248] Occurring in this, relative especially to the general direction of the Western understanding of man's place in the cosmos, is a thoroughgoing delimitation (although not *quite* elimination) of the range of human creativity, responsibility and subjectivity, coupled with an obverse broadening of the scope of that which is necessary, scientifically explainable and objective. Particularly, the process of historical change is greatly distanced from *subjective* human activity and is instead associated with the dynamics of the material dialectic.

In the acquisition of the necessities of human living through labor, it is argued, men and women are found involved in definite relations with each other which are ineluctable and independent of their will. These relations, which are Marx's celebrated "relations of production," correspond to the material realities of the given historical stage of production. Together such relations comprise the economic structure of society, which is the basis for the specific non-material realities of society's social structure, politics and, indeed, human consciousness itself. The rest is well-known. The nature of such relations engenders certain objective antagonisms or tensions. Following Marx's purported "righting" of Hegel's upside-down dialectic, bourgeois Marxism conceives of material reality as developing through a "dialectical" process where any given structure of relations internally foments a negative counterstructure. Because human consciousness is but a reflection of the material conditions of reality as manifested in a given economic structure, the particulars of men's and women's consciousness of themselves, their world and their history—their ideologies, as it were—are determined by the specific character of economics in a causal manner. Hence, inasmuch as non-material realities such as ethics, politics and so forth are objective in character and are unvarying resultants of the dynamic processes in material reality, they can be known and explained in the same scientific manner that a physicist might explain the necessary transformation of hydrogen into helium under certain empirical conditions.[249]

Despite certain affinities which will become apparent, for the personalist theory of politics as discussed above, the theory of dialectical materialism as rendered in bourgeois Marxism is untenable. From this perspective, both bourgeois Marxism's materialism itself *and* the operation of the material dialectic are suspect. Of the two, it is materialism itself which draws Scheler's most rigorous scrutiny.[250] He reveals that materialism's origin lies in the emergence of the bourgeois type of man; indeed, it is fundamentally linked to the formalism which has earlier been shown to have its source in the bourgeois. It is linked, in his estimation, with that subject-object or self-non-self alienation where bourgeois man divorces his subjectivity from the world and from solidarity with others. Issuing from "the unrestricted tendency of the city-bourgeoisies toward a *systematic,* and not only occasional, *control over nature,* and an endless accumulation and capitalization of knowledge for controlling nature and soul," the physical world is perceived as an encirclement of alien things—as *objective* things—to be used, dominated and gathered up for future use.[251] For bourgeois man, nature is transformed into a collection of objects which are entirely separate from himself and which are devoid of intrinsic value. The objects of the material world, moreover, acquire value only when they in some way are put to the use of, or are seen to serve the interests of bourgeois man himself—only when "owned," at which time they can be granted an exchange rate relative to other owned objects or unresolved interests. "That is to say," Scheler adds, "everything appears first as *merchandise.*"[252] Likewise, the divorce of the subjective from nature is equally at the origin of modern formalism. As Scheler remarks, "the 'forms'— which during the Middle Ages were ontic and God-given and had fixed meanings—become, throughout bourgeois thinking, consequences of acts of human *subjects*, viz. they become regarded primarily as forms of human thinking only." In other words "objectively one regards them as containing 'laws' that can be mathematically formulated, or at least of a *formal-mechanical* type."[253] Thus, modern materialism and modern formalism are but different faces of the same coin. More importantly, both are to be recognized as pursuing the same interests, in light of a sharing of the bourgeois complex of values.

The particular values or interests which arise with the coming of the bourgeois man—interest in control, acquisition and utility—give rise to a parallel type of knowing, which Scheler designates as *Herrschaftswissen* (a knowing with regard to how things might be controlled, dominated or put to use.)[254] From this standpoint, formalism (as discussed above in the discussion of bourgeois liberalism) and materialism are both apparently extensions of *Herrschaftswissen*. For formalism, which is closely allied with idealism, the direction of *Herrschaftswissen* is one which turns away from the difficult project of knowing and controlling the material things in the world and the particularity of others in favor of the categorization and *objectification* of varying phenomena within unchanging, knowable and controllable "forms." In this way, the supposed flux of material, phenomenal reality is able to be ordered and put to use.[255] In bourgeois liberalism, as was noted before, this is the path by which *Herrschaftswissen* is applied to the ordering, controlling and dominating of political practice. For materialism the direction of *Herrschaftwissen* is somewhat different it means, *but identical in end*, because the end stems from a shared common ground in the value-complex of bourgeois man. Materialism in its essence is, therefore, an endeavor seeking the objectification of the world and others which blossoms from the bourgeois interest in utility, acquisition and domination.

As Blaise Pascal remarks in a perceptive epithet from the *Pensees*, reflecting on the character of modern man: "There is nothing which we cannot make natural, and nothing natural which we do not destroy.''[256] Nature, in the understanding which Scheler assigns to the type of man he terms the bourgeois, is the realm of things, of objects. To be natural, from the locus of this understanding, means to exist solely at a level which responds to unvarying causal laws—to be absolutely, in a word, ''necessary.'' This state of affairs is eminently ''useful.'' To know the causal laws and necessities which operate among the objects of material reality enables such objects to be put to use. Recognizing this, materialism is an extreme effort, in Scheler's evaluation, to reduce all reality to the level of the causal laws and necessities of physical objects—to the level of that which is knowable within the strictures of *Herrschaftswissen*. Bourgeois Marxism, therefore, to the degree it pursues the reduction of human consciousness, creativity and responsibility to the causal forces of the physical world, to the degree it presents the development of history and the political practices of persons at the level of necessary and scientifically ''knowable'' laws, and to the degree that the material dialectic is conceived as only an objective material process, succumbs to the self-same reification of persons and world which it finds to be a perversion in modern capitalist society.

Scheler, of course, is aware that such possible results run counter to the ostensible intent of bourgeois Marxism. In some sense, it is the dichotomy which bourgeois man raises between self and non-self, between subject and object, which bourgeois Marxism maintains to be the underlying problematic of capitalist society, and to be the origin of the alienation which is seen behind the sundering of the worker from the products of his labor. Consistent with these points, he admits that the dialectical materialism of bourgeois Marxism is somewhat different from any pure materialism. He remarks, for example, that the Marxist material conception of history [*materialistische Geschichtsauffassung*] is seldom understood correctly. The general objection to the materialism of Marxism, he notes, is its finding ''the prima causa and the independent variable in historical evolution in the so-called 'economic relations' which are equally seen as the highest *value* and highest *end* of human existence. This conception, however, (regardless of whether it is true or false in itself) is a basically erroneous interpretation,'' because, ''only previous history, according to the Communist Manifesto, is a history of economic class struggles and is unfree, such struggles having been merely illusory 'ideologies.''' This is a crucial point, he continues, because Marxism secretly shares the same dream as German idealism. Hence, for bourgeois Marxism the belief is retained that ''the new socialist society ought to bring about an immediate 'leap' into freedom."[257] It is exactly the uncritical reliance on the value-complex of the bourgeois which accounts for the failure of bourgeois Marxism to achieve its intent. Bourgeois Marxism is keenly insightful in its bringing to light the hidden bourgeois dichotomy of self and non-self latent in modern idealism. But, just as idealism's effort to overcome this dichotomy through reduction to pure spirit is only a radicalization of the bourgeois interests and values from which the dichotomy springs, so too is a reduction to materialism. Both a radicalization of the self (in spirit) and a radicalization of the non-self (in matter) are furtive manifestations of *Herrschaftswissen* and the narrowing of value perception to the values of utility. Both approaches, therefore, raise internal contradictions for their goal in maximizing personal creativity and responsibility.

Some image of Scheler's own thinking in these regards is offered in his all-too-hasty treatment of the notion of the dialectic itself.[258] Beginning with his sociological analysis of knowledge, his preliminary approach to dialectics is to conceive of the process as a reasoning which proceeds from the material and historical conditions of the lower class. Finding it plausible "that the lower class tends to reflect upon *becoming* while the upper class tends to reflect upon *being*," he contrasts the *historical* understanding of the lower class with the upper class which looks at the process of history as a "static 'realm of the past,' which resembles a 'hall of fame' for great men and works." For the lower class, however, the process of history is seen as "what is *becoming*, i.e., from the 'dialectical' clash of dynamic possibilities."[259] In this he finds that the error of bourgeois Marxism's absolutizing of the dialectic resides in its uncritical exchanging of merely one class-based understanding of history (the vision of the upper class) for another. Marxism, thus, does not extend its class analysis of knowledge to its own clay feet.

Nor is his recognition of the sociological relativity of dialectical thinking the sole factor in his hesitation. Behind this hesitation, more deeply, lies the pluralist character of personalism. Unlike many other objections to the dialectic, Scheler affirms the validity of its understanding of history as a successive engendering and overcoming of antagonism. As in Marxism, historical change in his theory of personalism follows a certain order or pattern of maturation where tensions can burgeon in an arena of striving personal drives and the exercise of power.[260] All of this Scheler finds incontrovertible—although he very much finds its impetus to be much more than a matter of economics and its loci to include much more than class antagonisms. The rub, for Scheler, is that history and human affairs generally cannot *only* be understood in this fashion. Change occurs which does not result from pitted struggle and the dialectical resolution of antinomies, and human practices are motivated by other values than utility for self. Scheler's "change," it is made clear, is also not simply explained by absolute laws of development. Revolutions in this are transformations of man himself, and wittingly or not must partake of personal creativity and shoulder personal responsibility. Bourgeois Marxism, then, is seen to be oblivious to the historical-anthropological ground from which its absolutizing of the dialectic stems, viz. the bourgeois notion of competition, and the struggle by which the self endeavors to dominate the non-self. Scheler is especially fearful of those interpretations of the dialectic where it is viewed as a process of frictious grinding away in a linear march toward a chiliastic progress. Rather than a dialectic which posits the eventual overcoming of differences (between persons, ideas and so-forth) in conflict, personalism would subscribe to a celebration of differences among utterly unique and special persons. This would likely entail a politics which seeks the radical unraveling of the conflictual knots and relationships of domination which spring from the peculiar character of bourgeois man. The gravel-grinding machine of bourgeois competition, in Scheler's portrayal, has already succeeded in grinding the creative differences among persons into the common sand of mass-society. In absolutizing the dialectic, and in conceiving it solely as an objective process, Scheler's obvious fear is that bourgeois Marxism may be only unwittingly extending this process.[261]

Class and Species Subjectivity

By "class and species subjectivity" this study refers to the bourgeois Marxist rejection of the individual subject of liberalism in favor of the human species as a subjective whole and the peculiar subjective role of certain classes within this whole. Some symmetry is, therefore, intended between the expression of subjectivity in liberalism through the individual and Marxism's locating of subjectivity in the species, and in particular groups within the species. It may be remarked, of course, that Scheler's personalism does not only assign subjectivity to the social being of the person, but to the totality of the person—both social *and* individual. From this, since Scheler in his early works sees the Marxist species-subject as swallowing the individual in the maw of organic community, it might be supposed that the clearest contrast between personalism and Marxism resides in this distinction. Yet, as Scheler comes to realize in his later works, the species-subject of Marxism does not deny a subjective role for individuals, and in this regard the distinction between the relationship of individual to species in Marx and the relationship of individual to *Gesamtperson* in Scheler becomes somewhat foggy. As before, the matter at issue is one which has received attention for its centrality to Marxism, and one which has attraced all manner of interpretation.[252] Concerned as this study is with *bourgeois* Marxism, the general body of these interpretations may be usefully divided into two approaches: an approach which sees the corporate subject as the individual subject writ large, and an approach which sees the corporate whole as but an objective agency, not as a true subject in the usual sense. Briefly, from the vantage point of personalism, Scheler's evaluation of the Marxist position reflects the ambiguity among Marxists themselves in the interpretation of this concept. He dismisses the individual subject writ large notion on roughly the same grounds by which he elsewhere dismisses liberal individualism. The approach which denies true subjectivity and locates the vehicle for change in an objective corporate agency, however, proves rather more treacherous. Hence, this second notion might receive first attention.

The explanation for the difficult which Scheler's personalism experiences in wrestling with the corporate "subject" as an objective corporate agency has its source in the proximity of this interpretation to his own theory of the sociality of the person. To be sure, the concept is untenable for personalism from the first due to its implicit reliance on a materialistic reduction—as was addressed in the previous section. But, at the same time, the conception conforms in an important way with aspects of Scheler's own social theory. He confirms, just as does Marxism, that anthropologically a human being is, *a priori*, a social being.[253]. Moreover, at the level of the species' anthropological origins, the behavior of this social being is objective in character and determined by the conditions and realities of being. He rejects, plainly, "any theory (reminiscent, for example, of Hegel) that holds that the course of cultural history is a *purely* spiritual process." The behavior of the human social being at its deepest level is determined by real factors, "realities which follow their strictly *necessary* course with respect to existence," the latter being "a course that is 'blind' from the viewpoint of the notions of value and meaning belonging to the subjective *human* spirit."[264] Personalism, however, finds this conception of human social being—albeit true and valid as far as it goes—to be only one perspective or aspect of the full, total reality of the sociality of the person, a sociality which is equally social and individual, and which is a subjectivity atop an objectivity. In other words, for personalism the objective agency of the primeval human social being is only the root of the total person. From this root, personal subjectivity grows by way of a series of transformations that issue out of a process of *dis-sociation* from the objective realities of existence. Likewise, from this root, the sociality of the person passes from the organic sociality of the herd to the specialized corporate sociality of the life community, from the life community it passes to the individualist sociality of the society, and from the society, ultimately, to the creative and responsible establishment of the person community.

The most troubling error from the personalist perspective, in this understanding of Marxism, is the abnegation of personal subjectivity. Personalism recognizes the essential sociality of personal being, and it acknowledges the objectivity of man's social being within its primeval origin. Yet, the "highest" social being, the personal community, is precisely the most sublime because, regardless of its original necessity, it is *not* necessary in itself and *not* simply an objective reality. Moreover, unlike those interpretations of bourgeois Marxism which scientifically predict the emergence of personal subjectivity in the coming of true communism, Scheler's personalism is premised on a growth of subjectivity through a series of transformations. The result is that even bourgeois man's society is not necessary —although it fails to achieve the full creativity and responsibility of persons in a person community. The real potency of personalism's analysis of bourgeois man, modern culture, society and politics rests on this insight. Despite the myriad of *real factors* involved in the constitution of human social existence, for personalism there remains an undeviating perception that the pathology of man's social being is not necessary at its core—that man as a species is, at heart, *responsible* for his own making. In Scheler's understanding, finally, the burden of this responsibility does not fall only on the ambiguous shoulders of humanity in general, or only on more tangible shoulders of the social being of the person, but falls with equal weight upon the individual being of the person. The social being of the person in personal community can then be spoken of as a "moral solidarity." The intimate person bears the responsibility for the *Gesamtperson*, and the *Gesamtperson* for the intimate person—because the *Gesamtperson* is creatively constituted (at this juncture) in the solidarity of intimate persons and each intimate person is open to being constituted in his or her individuality by the *Gesamtperson*.[265] Scheler's personalism is differentiated from *this* Marxist conception of social agency, therefore, not for an outright rejection of the Marxist thesis but due to a recognition that fundamental aspects of personal social being lie beyond the amorphous and necessary sociality of the objective human species in the world.

On the heels of this differentiation, it might be imagined that personalism as political theory would admit a greater affinity with those bourgeois Marxist theories which portray the human species in history, and particularly certain economic classes, as subjective in essence. Yet, the matter is very much more uncertain. In part the uncertainty reflects the varying differences among these theories relative to the character and degree of subjectivity discerned, but equally it reflects the ambiguity of Max Scheler's own conception of personal subjectivity. To the extent that class and species only replace the individual subject of bourgeois liberalism, however, there is a certain reciprocity between the theories of species as subject and the theories of species as objective agency. Just as Scheler rejects the theory of social being as purely objective in nature because it fails to recognize the subjective aspects of man's social reality, so too he rejects the simply subjective theory because it fails to recognize the inescapable objective features of that same social reality. In Scheler's eyes, foremost among approaches which subscribe to the latter theory are those interpretations of Marx which elevate the proletariat (often with the maieutic assistance of [save us!] intellectuals) from a position of object in the world to the role of genuine subject in capitalist society.

In his response, anticipating many of the later criticisms of Karl Mannheim, Scheler contends that there is no privileged or central economic position for subjectivity in the world and history.[255] He argues first, from the basis of his sociology of knowledge, that the particular circumstances of the proletariat do structure the agenda of *interests* relative to that class—interests in accord with those of the bourgeoisie: material welfare, greater quantities of goods, domination of the natural world and other men. Sharing the same interests as the bourgeois man and his society, it seems doubtful that somehow the proletariat automatically acquires a special subjectivity able to transcend the bourgeois weltanschauung. Inasmuch as knowledge follows such interests, is it not even more likely that such thinking is itself evidence of only the objective situation and character of the proletariat? Scheler's response, then, extends a Marxist-like sociological analysis to the idea of the proletariat as privileged subject in history much as Marx himself had analyzed the ideology of the bourgeoisie. Indeed, from Schelers' perspective, both classes and their ancillary world-views are "victims" of the peculiar illusion of the self (whether social or individual) *as subject* and all else as object, an illusion which has its source in the transformation to bourgeois man.[267]

Personalism, paradoxically, undercuts the bourgeois notion of the self as subject and with equal force does not admit the cavalier objectification of that which is non-self. Being cannot be naively bifurcated along the lines of the subject and object divisions of bourgeois man—an insight demonstrated as much in the character of the person as social being as it is in the character of the person as intimate being. In appointing the proletariat to the privileged position of "subject," bourgeois Marxism follows the same mistaken path which bourgeois liberalism takes in elevating the pure individual to this position. One reduces subjectivity to an individual and the other to a class. But, for personalism, there is no privileged place wherein subjectivity inheres, no single locus of responsibility. Subjectivity and objectivity permeate the whole being of the person—both social and individual. Man's social being is but a perspectival view of the totality of the person; it cannot be absolutized as either subjectivity or objectivity.

Critique of Ideology

Among the more provocative elements of Max Scheler's philosophic enterprise is the position taken relative to the modern notion of critique, especially as expressed in the Kantian *Kritik* tradition. Although this study has dealt at length with the antipathic aspects of the position taken by Scheler, as for example in his apparent disdain for Husserl's transcendental turn and in his vituperative response to liberal rationalism, there also cannot be denied an evident and possibly unacknowledged influence of that critical tradition upon his same philosophic enterprise. Scheler, with many others of his generation of scholars, sees a thick strand of the tradition of *Kritik* interwoven with the fabric of Marxist thought. Nor surprisingly, both the outward antipathy and the tacit influence are present and made transparent in comparing Scheler's own personalist phenomenological analysis of ideology with Marxism's crititque of ideology.[268] The contrast with Scheler's personalist thesis is, again, most pronounced over and against those Marxist theories which remain locked within the aporial bourgeois dichotomy of self and non-self—or, as indicated, against those Marxist theories which stand most proximate to the tradition of *Kritik*. Such theories understand the Marxist notion of the material production of consciousness in a curiously restricted fashion. The objective patterns in the relations of production are perceived to give rise to complementary, parallel patterns of consciousness, as for example in the development of class consciousness in the bourgeoisie or the proletariat in the era of early capitalism. These patterns, or "ideologies," are seen to define broadly and determine man's understanding of self, world and others, serving too to enframe and structure those human practices which derive subsequently from such an understanding. In this manner, the conditions of one's material, social existence are equally the conditions of one's knowing and cognition. Moreover, the knowledge which follows from these conditions of knowing serves to perpetuate the conditions of one's social existence in a loop-like process. Intriguing as this theory is and despite whatever validity it deserves as an epistemology, it requires no special genius to wonder therefrom, how a Marxist theorist is able with confidence to ascribe any measure of certainty to his (or her) own analysis and theory? If, as is pertinent, the political theory of modern liberalism is to be spurned on account of the Marxist's "knowledge" that it reflects only the ideology of the bourgeoisie, on what more hallowed grounds can the Marxist claim immunity from ideology of another sort? How in any case is escape from the false consciousness of ideology possible?

In fact, it is here where the tentacle of the tradition of critical rationalism become evident in bourgeois Marxism. Not "grounds" exactly, but transcendental room is granted wherein the criteria of true consciousness might be rationally and critically ascertained. Just as with rational liberalism, reason is understood as able to enlighten consciousness. By critically examining the origins and history of ideologies under the rubric of the contradictions inhering in the relations of production, such theories contend that reason can and does transcend and emancipate false consciousness. Thus, one supposes, the bourgeois Marxist rests assured in the certainty of his or her analysis due to its basis in the critical utilization of reason. In this, further, lies the dominant interpretation of what aptly has come to be called the "critique" of ideology.

From Scheler's personalist vantage, however, the critical utilization of reason in bourgeois Marxism differs only in detail from the rationalist theories of bourgeois liberalism. Both manifest the far-reaching reinterpretation of reason which has its source in the anthropology of bourgeois man. In contrast, for Scheler reason is *never* transcendental. The processses of reason *follow* the perception of values. Founded thereon, critique is not a value free assessment of the criteria for true consciousness, true knowledge or so forth, but is steeped in the conditional value structure of actual men and women. Likewise, consciousness stands revealed as dependent upon this same conditional complex of values. In a debate with the *Kathedersozialist* Max Adler at Heidelberg in 1924, Scheler speaks to this point. Adler, betraying a neo-Kantian influence on his Marxism, contends that class ideology can be a transcended or overcome. Scheler finds such transcendence troublesome.

> A genuine Marxist, or a representative of the "absolute" class struggle, could *not* maintain this. I am in this regard even more "Marxist" than Adler in so far as I, too, have reduced all consciousness to *being* and all supreme laws and forms of reason to the processes of functionalization within the formal comprehension of being—but certainly not as Marx did. Rather, I have reduced them not only to material being but to the *whole* being of man.[269]

In other words, Scheler's objection to the turn of bourgeois Marxism toward critical idealism hinges on a perception that such a turn lacks ontological footing in the full reality of the person. Consciousness is *never* transcendental; it inevitably springs from and leads back to "not only material being, but to the *whole* being of man." Hence, any "critique" of false consciousness must arise from the totality of the person's reality, not from any transcendence of this reality nor from any narrow, privileged aspect of the totality.

Such a "critique" is Scheler's own concern. From an overview of the whole of his personalism, it is apparent that it stands as an effort to gather into comprehension (phenomenologically) the totality of the being of the person—partially, beyond doubt, in order to clarify the grounds wherein true consciousness might emerge. In so doing, upon such grounds, it must be presumed that all consciousness would not be false consciousness. A "critique" of ideology here is not only a possibilty, but an imperative. This intent lies beneath Scheler's sociology and anthropology of knowledge. By identifying the various conditions of consciousness, Scheler believes that these conditions can be controlled for, "suspended" and overcome. "Class prejudices, and also the formal laws of their formation, can *in principle, be overcome* by any member of a class—the more they are recognized in their sociological lawfulness."[270] Although often opaque to his own awareness, it seems that Scheler, too, shares a vision of enlightenment. Like the bourgeois Marxist critique of ideology, even like the neo-Kantians he vilifies, Scheler wishes to enlarge and enhance the realm of human creativity and responsibility by bringing to light and isolating the conditional, necessary and objective elements of human being and consciousness.

Similar as their goals may be, however, a fundamental difference exists between the critiques of ideology in Scheler's personalism and what has here been termed bourgeois Marxism. Scheler denies any recourse to a transcendental function for reason. All reasoning operates as value-seeking. Even the bourgeois Marxist's "knowledge" that there is access to a transcendental function in reason has its roots in the values of bourgeois man and is itself only a particular variety of *Herrschaftswissen*. Rather than derived from transcendental criticism, the personalist "critique" of ideology begins in a careful clarification and *affirmation* of the total reality of personal being—the reality as outlined in this study of Scheler's personalism. Specifically, such a "critique" must affirm the ontological footing of man's existentiality and anthropology, the "real factors" of human living, yet simultaneously must recognize personal responsibility and personal possibility relative to a range of values which stretch to the sublime and holy. In bringing to clarity his own objectivity via such "critique," the person is granted a recognition of his subjectivity; in discerning the full array of values, the person is granted a recognition of the possibilities inhering in the full measure of his responsibility.[271] Bourgeois Marxism in this interpretation, therefore, errs on two counts. The rationalist notion of critique which it adopts is unattainable *and* this notion itself is but another furtive manifestation of the character of bourgeois man.

PERSONALISM AND MARXISM

More than was the case with liberalism, the affinities evident between Marxism and Scheler's personalism suggest the possibility of a non-bourgeois, personalist reinterpretation of something that is still vaguely "Marxist." As just noted, Marxism and Scheler's personalism share a material realism, although Scheler obviously understands "material" and "real" in a broader sense than Marx would have allowed. Moreover, there is similarity in their respective understandings of historical society and both perceive cognition and knowledge in sociological and historical conditions. Functionally, it was outlined in the last chapter that Scheler's Christian socialism or "personalist" socialism would be little different in operation from some of the socialisms "with a human face" which some would call Marxist. Might it then be possible to consider a personalist Marxism in the same manner in which a personalist liberalism was considered earlier in this chapter?

The likely answer is "No." Despite the many parallels between Marxist thought and personalism, Marxism—understood as a theory which faithfully seeks to represent the thinking of Karl Marx—is a concept with boundaries which are more clear and definite than those of the ideal "liberalism." Marxism could not be Marxist if it were in full accord with Scheler's personalism. This is much more than the usual distinction between economic-scientific-orthodox Marxisms and humanist-philosophical-neo Marxisms. Scheler's analysis finds Marxism closely interlinked with the essential character of bourgeois man. Indeed, as these last pages have demonstrated, the philosophical and humanist varieties of Marxism, such as those of the early Lukacs, of the "critical school," of Sartre and so forth, distance themselves from personalism by their reliance on reason, critique or privileged subjectivity. In many respects, more orthodox Marxisms avoid these aspects of the bourgeois man and stand in closer proximity to Scheler's personalism. Yet, clearly, Marx himself would deny the intrinsic and independent reality of values and of spirit generally. For Scheler's personalism, such a rejection is inevitably reductionist—offering a deformed representation of what being a human person truly is.

If there is required some degree of rapprochement of personalism with Marxism, which is not clear, then it might be suggested that quarter for such may be found in the works of Maurice Merleau-Ponty. Merleau-Ponty's open-ended dialectic, his phenomenological approach to cognition, his broad understanding of the human condition are suggestive terrain from the vantage of personalism. Nonetheless, Merleau-Ponty's phenomenology veers in many respects too closely toward that of Edmund Husserl's, which itself shares an affinity with the bourgeois notions of rationality and critique that are so suspect in Scheler's thinking.

Conclusion
An Evaluation of Personalism
as Political Theory

T HIS STUDY LEAVES MUCH additional to be said regarding the possibility of Scheler's personalism as political theory. It has endeavored to focus only upon those aspects of Scheler's personalism most germane for the foundations of political theory, and largely has elected to concentrate upon only such aspects which engage most directly with the prominent issues and concerns of contemporary political theory and philosophy. Its effort has been to map the very suggestive terrain of the implications of personalism for political theory—to identify the general character of such theory while noting only therein the most obvious landmarks and perils. As a mapping exercise, its failures reflect the naivete which is requisite for unprejudiced explanation of ground which was previously unknown. Hence, there is apparent a certain inattention to troubling detail and, conversely, a certain narrow intensity of concentration regarding more intriguing insights and revelations.

Personalism as political theory, to summarize briefly, finds the be-all and end-all of politics to be the reality of the person. An on-going, real constellation of acts, the person subsists as essentially a practical being, constituted by acts but in some fashion transcendent in relation to these acts. As such, moreover, the character of the person shares the character of acts themselves. Importantly here, since acts are intentional vis-a-vis the world, acts being always *toward* or *for* something in the world, then person, too, is inseparable from an intentional existence with the world—especially, since the world is from the first given to experience as *values*. Additionally, by virtue of the transcendental relationship between the person as a constellation of acts and specific acts, there does not exist a causal relationship between values and acts, but a relationship which includes aspects of responsible choice arising from a recognition of a multitude of possible values. The character of politics in personalism as political theory

131

reflects this conception of the person. Politics, too, is constituted by acts which are intentionally joined with the perceived values of the world. It is a practical affair of personal acts, enframed within a given array of values in the experience of the world. Politics may not, on this account, rise above the given array of values belonging to its context in the world, but inasmuch as persons are responsible by virtue of the transcendental character of their relation to specific acts, so too politics is not a necessary construct of its context in the world. At its heart, the pattern of practices in politics issues from personal responsibility. Indeed, because the range of possible values extends to the sublime and holy, the "measure" of political practices may not be narrowly delimited to individual utility, social welfare, human need and so forth, but must be open to the greatest possible range of personal values.

"Person," as understood in this, encompasses both the intimate personality and the *Gesamtperson*. The intimate person must recognize the anthropological, sociological, and developmental origins of his individuality in corporation. Equally, full persons creatively stand atop mere individuality to transform it in a personal community. The political community, likewise, can be recognized as a special aspect of the sociality of the person. Just as the individual person has roots in an infant's unity with the experiential world of the mother and in a long developmental process is able to first identify and rejoice in its self, ideally, to finally overcome the self in order to responsibly join in the company of others, so too the polity may be seen to emerge through a sequence of transformations which point toward a possible culmination in a political community which celebrates the uniqueness and plurality of its citizens while foregoing the egocentric limits of merely a multiplicity of selves. In this possibilty a new manner of intersubjectivity is required, a "communion of persons." Remembering that the person is a constellation of acts, that these acts are purely execution, and that as pure execution they are beyond objectification, then persons in their essence are also beyond objectification. On this ground, the political relationships between persons, and between the intimate person and the *Gesamtperson*, cannot be relationships understood in terms of self versus non-self. Indeed, even the objectification which derives from treating others as equal to one's own self is untenable. Rather, the person must forego his own self to participate directly in the person of the other. Beyond a society of selves and non-selves, therefore, lies the possibility of a political community which welcomes and enhances the harmony which only an openness to the pluralism of personal diversity makes possible.

The politics seen between the lines of personalism as political theory is apparently one which shares a curious ambiguity with the politics familar to contemporary experience. Personalist politics takes the politics of such experience as its point of departure. It inquires into the origin of everyday politics, locating its roots (foundationally, if not historically) in man's anthropology, and traces its current character to the coming of bourgeois man. Personalism as political theory, however, finds the full reality of politics to be subsumed by neither its present context nor its past origins. The full reality of politics must consider its impending possibility. If Scheler's own estimation is to be accepted as indication, that impending possibility may lie more deeply in a transformation of the character of politics rather than its appearance. His own vision imagines personalist socialisms, and personalist democracies wherein the ineluctable uniqueness is not obscured by a recognition of the objective aspects of human existence or by an appreciation of the full breadth of the reality of human and personal sociality. In this, Scheler's enterprise shares the vision of political philosophy in the classical tradition and, with some reservations, that of the political theories of the Enlightenment tradition. By identifying the objective and necessary aspects of persons and the political order, that which is responsible, creative and highest in personal humanity is enhanced. Not prying the person from moorings in the context of existence, such enhancement would find "politics" to be more than beast-like reflection of the contours of existence and less than a somewhat divine visitation within existence.

In large part, the foregoing pages of this study have been "interpretive" in character. Elaborating certain elements of Max Scheler's personalism as political theory, contrasting these same elements against opposite elements of the paradigm of modern politics and, on occasion, more boldly tracing an outline of a personalist political theory itself as suggested by these elements, the study has been generally more elaborative than reflective. The reality of politics is such, however, that the *political* theorist cannot responsibly suffice with interpretation—or, at the very least, cannot responsibly suffice with mere interpretation. Responsible political theory, in other words, requires that personalism as political theory be weighed as more than another interpretation to be compiled with the many histories and surveys of political thinking and philosophy. So doing demands a touchstone of sorts against which the value of personalism as political theory might be assayed. In fairness to Scheler's own intent and work, that touchstone needs to be the full reality—both the existence and the possibility—of the *person*.[272] This means of evaluation, furthermore, is one which stands in close proximity to the understanding of praxis that is increasingly shared among diverse currents in political theory.

Unfortunately, a full evaluation of the political theory of personalism would require a study equal in length to the largely interpretive outline offered here. On the basis of these pages, however, certain difficulties have been brought to light which demand at least cursory mention in concluding this study—perhaps in part fulfilling the special obligations which must be borne by studies of political theory in this half of the century. These difficulties, variously noted and addressed by Scheler himself, are: *first*, the problem of transformation; and *second*, the problem of value perception.

In the passage of life from stage to stage, in the passage from life community to society, in the passage of the guiding image of man from the ''spirit of civilization'' to the hero, and in the emergence of the bourgeois man, Scheler is describing a *transformation* which he sees in light of a foundational order of reality.[272] Such passages mark an essential change in the character of the given reality and the process of transformation is evidently a central and, likely, crucial element in Scheler's fundamental understanding of things. Nonetheless, the consideration proffered of the character of transformation lacks a sensitive appreciation of many difficulties evident to contemporary thought and there is nowhere elaborated an analysis of the requisite conditions for such transformation. Early works such as *Ressentiment*, *The Nature of Sympathy* and *Formalism* conceive of the process in form reminiscent of the life philosophies. It is a two-fold, organic process, in other words, where a satiation or abundance of value experienced at the lower form leads towards a perception of the loftie values of the higher form. Further, where aspects of personal subjectivity are present, a transformation may then occur which is responsible and creative.[274] In later works, *Die Wissenformen*, *Man's Place* and so on the transformation process assumes a more objective character. Scheler, here, begins to speak of the process in developmental terminology, emphasizing the role of real factors and human conditions while deemphasizing the role of spirit and the subjective aspect of human affairs. For both the earlier and the later versions, however, the understanding of transformation is one of an essential change in the character of a given reality—whether human sociality, a guiding model or man himself.

Yet, in what ways does this essential change manifest itself? Need the transformation be a radical break with what was gone before, or is it a continuation or fulfillment of this past? For politics and political theory these are neither idle nor academic questions, yet Scheler's own response lacks required clarity. He speaks, in moments, of the "new" standing atop that which has been transformed, but such an assertion adds little light to what is generally a muddled ambiguity. A further refinement, patently, is appropriate.

Consider, then, the well-known exchange of correspondence between Hans-Georg Gadamer and Leo Strauss.[275] Having long perceived Gadamer as a checkpoint between himself and his *bête noir*, Martin Heidegger, Strauss writes in one instance with exasperation in response to Gadamer's explicitly hermeneutical turn, remarking that Gadamer, like Heidegger in his estimation, was directed now to plod the path celebrated in Spengler's curious title as—"the Decline of the West." Was Gadamer too preaching the "world night" of the end of philosophy and the end of political responsibility? In reply, Gadamer distances himself from both the morbid fascination with and the absolutizing of the Decline. Heidegger, he suggests (perhaps with unfairness), stares fixedly at the eastern horizon. Sure of the *Untergang* and the night beyond, Heidegger looks for the return. Gadamer, speaking of himself, "is turned, however, in an entirely different direction." "My point of departure," he notes, "is not the complete *forgetfulness of being*, the 'night of being' but rather—I say this against Heidegger as well as against Buber—*the unreality of such an assertion.*"[276] Neither decline nor progress, in this perspective, encompasses the reality of the present's relation with what has gone before. Indeed, the relation is in no sense vertical, but horizontal. It is not a relationship of determination, compulsion or domination, as much as it is dialectic—dialectic understood as a practical art which pursues not the destruction of deficient argument, but its "transformation." For personalism as political theory, then, there is room to sharpen aspects of Scheler's legacy. Transformation need not be a violent rejection of the transformed, nor a radical break with the present. Casually and loosely, personalism as political theory may pursue this more "practical" path toward the realization of its possibilities—surveying the horizon of possibilities for direction while avoiding the radicalness of ancient origins and millenial eschatons.

Whatever the placement and function of the process of transformation in Scheler's personalism, the role of values and their immediate perception is undoubtedly the mainspring of its theory of action and the foundation for its ethics and its analysis of knowledge

and ideology. The *problem of value perception*, on this account, is a difficulty which imperils the establishment of any political theory founded
upon this personalism. Scheler's masterwork on ethics, *Formalism in
Ethics and Non-Formal Ethics of Values*, is a subtle and complex argument maintaining that values are not simply subjective valuations but
true, objective ''value-facts'' which are sensible and independent of
human emotions and conditions. ''There is a type of experiencing,''
he writes, ''whose 'objects' are completely inacessible to reason;
reason is as blind to them as ears and hearing are blind to colors.''
Such experience, he continues,

> is a kind of experience that leads to *genuinely* objective objects
> and the eternal order among them, i.e., to *values* and the
> order of ranks among them. And the order and laws contained
> in this experience are as exact and evident as those of logic
> and mathematics; that is, there are evident interconnections
> and oppositions among values and value-attitudes and among
> the acts of preferring... [that] on the basis of these a genuine
> grounding of moral decisions and laws for such decisions is
> both possible and necessary.[277]

Upon this order of values, moreover, grounded as Scheler indicates,
stands the analysis of the values of the modern world, the conclusion
of which uncovers the profound perversion of the modern world lying deeply rooted in the heart of bourgeois man. It is the perception
of an array of values which reaches to the sublime and the holy by
which Scheler's personalism as political theory is able to observe that
the politics and society of the paradigm which begins with the coming
of the bourgeois is constrained to only the lowest of possible values,
those of mere utility and bestial welfare.

Despite the length and extent of the discussion of values and their
order, however, the ''revelation'' of the sensibility of values and their
eternal and objective order offered in Scheler's works depends over-
much upon moving prose and less than self-evident insight. Yet,
surely, the perception of values requires greater sufficiency and more
explicit demonstration—even abiding the sense of immediate insight
by which Scheler understands phenomenological *Anschauung*—then
is rendered in such presentation. Scheler's intent in his value theory
is to establish an unchanging and universal order, an order secure
from the flux of existential conditions, to which essentially
changeable men and women can appeal for moral and political
guidance. It is Kantianism, as he understands it, which looms before

him in his effort—a "second best" approach which requires a troublesome universality in reason, which deforms and abstracts the rich plurality of reality in categories and which foregoes the good itself for a "categorical imperative." Scheler demands real, value-based certainty, replacing reason with value perception and the imperative with an ontological order of values. Politically, following from this, that practice is best which realizes the highest in value.

The difficulty here rests in the distance which Scheler would draw between the essentially dynamic and "becoming" being of the person—the being of whom must adapt, responsibly or not, with his embeddedness in the context of existence—and the essentially static and eternal being of values and their order. He is once more returned to the duality of being, the act and object distinction, with which he begins his philosophy. How, then, is this dichotomy to be bridged? In what manner is the person to obtain moral or political guidance from the realm of values? This is the foundering point of Scheler's value perception, this separation in being between the being of values and the being of the person. On consideration, it would seem that there are two likely paths which personalism may pursue to resolve this difficulty, both of which involve a move away from the duality of being, both of which suggest intriguing linkages with currents in contemporary thought, and both of which are evident aspects of the frantic theorizing of Scheler's last years. The first path is a far-reaching extension of personalism's anthropology, a path which Scheler terms "meta-anthropology."[278] The second is a blurring and intermingling of act and object, spirit and life, man and world, and person and value, made possible by a postulated underlying unity in being that Scheler terms "the Ground of Being."[279]

The *first* path, the path of meta-anthropology, appears to be more closely congruent with the life-long direction of Scheler's personalism. The role of values in morality, politics and so forth, is retained by locating their existence and essence within the genesis and anthropology of the person himself. Since the early Scheler perceives the community, the ontogenesis of the person and a variety of other human processes as proceeding in accordance with an order of foundation that is conceived to mirror an objective and eternal order of values, is it not indeed possible that that order of values is more likely a reflection of an order in this same genesis and anthropology? In other words, rather than assigning to such values an independent and non-contingent existence external to man's own existence, might not these values and their order be themselves anthropological? Undoubtably, this is one of the directions toward which Scheler's own later philosophy was moving.

With this conception, the transcendental character of values as a problematic is altered. It becomes no longer a question of bridging a duality in being, no longer one of persons reaching beyond conditional experience in order to grasp objects of non-conditional character. Instead, values are discerned by inquiry into the dynamic character of the person, or in the foundational order by which the person is constituted. Such a conception is now quite common in the literature of contemporary social and political theory. It assumes a variety of forms: the linguistic quasi-transcendentals such as those of John Searle, Jürgen Habermas and Karl-Otto Apel, the classic psychological quasi-trascendentals such as those of Sigmund Freud and Jean Piaget; and, more circumspectly, the structural quasi-transcendentals of the structuralists and ethno-methodologists.[280] To complete the turn Scheler indicates toward "meta-anthropology," personalism as political theory might valuably benefit from the thinking undergirding these theories. But, there are also grounds for concern regarding the appropriateness of such a move for other aspects of personalism.

The now popular work of Jüergen Habermas is a case in point. Central to Habermas' endeavor is securing quasi-transcendental criteria by which social and political critique would be facilitated. In line with the direction such theories take, such criteria are quasi-transcendental because he locates them within human anthropology rather than granting them independent subsistence. In an early work, *Knowledge and Human Interests*, for example, Habermas borrows much from the last period of Scheler's writings and establishes these quasi-transcendentals as anthropologically rooted interests which constitute human cognition: a technical interest, a practical interest and a critical interest. These interests, especially the "critical" interest, assume a transcendental status for all responsible human choice and action.[281] With his later works, Habermas shifts the location of his transcendental from human interests to human speech, but its function does not change. Human communication itself, in his appraisal, implicitly suggests an ideal of what such communication ought to be—underforming, unconstrained, honest and so on. This "ideal speech situation," as it is called at one point, is proposed, in place of his earlier knowledge-constitutive interests, as a transcendental of sorts against which actual speech situations (as well as social and political situations) are to be judged and critiqued.[282]

Habermas' thesis suggests, at least as outlined here, a possible difficulty for resolving personalism's problem of value perception by means of the turn toward meta-anthropology. The difficulty is that many such approaches closely approximate the Kantian notion of critique from which much of Scheler's early personalism sought to escape. Habermas, Apel and so forth—just as Kant—find within mankind a special capacity or situation that serves to establish a screen or criterion by which reality is measured and categorized (be it an ideal speech situation as some similar anthropological universal). For Scheler and for the personalist political theory adapted from his thought, this is troublesome. As elaborated in this study, values for personalism are directly and immediately given in experience, not uncovered via critique. There is, therefore, a radically empirical sense of personalism which is perhaps jeopardized by the reduction of values to the sphere of anthropology. Moreover, does not such a reduction only again serve to emphasize the human subject and its special role in being—a notion which the later works of Scheler would largely reject? Indeed, is not anthropology itself the sort of reductionism which Scheler finds unacceptable? If the meta-anthropology of the last period of Scheler's thought is inclined in this direction, then much of Scheler's earlier thinking would likely stand in need of revision. Fortunately, as noted, there is a second path suggested by Scheler to resolve the problem of value perception.

The *second* path, that toward a ''Ground of Being,'' in part complements and in part radicalizes the meta-anthropological turn. For, where meta-anthropology finds ''objective'' values and their order to be lodged within the anthropology of the person, the turn toward a Ground of Being finds the person to share a common ground with all other being. The ontological order of values and values themselves, therefore, need not be utterly separate from the being of the person—divided by the difficult ontological rift. Instead, as an order in being itself—a being shared by the person—the order of such values might be understood as peculiarly present to the person much as would be his life, his world and other persons. When, for example, Scheler discerns an ''order of foundation,'' a pattern or sequence by which transformation may proceed, it is precisely an order in the Ground of Being to which he refers. The grounds for responsible per-

sonal action, following this, would lie in bringing to clarity, recognizing and acting in accord with the values and their order which are
present in the contextual "order of things."

This path is the path of the early works of Martin Heidegger, of
course. In *Being and Time*, Heidegger describes the particular
character of being human as *Dasein*—interpreted as that aspect of being through which being recognizes itself.[283] The understanding obviously changes the conception of what being human is all about. Being human is not *fundamentally* different than any other aspect of being. Even subjectivity is not particularly a human attribute as much as
it is one expression of being itself. Yet, at the same time, this conception of being human stands in complement with Scheler's realist
phenomenology and with the understanding of person as a constellation of acts.[284] Thus, the problem of value perception is greatly resolved
by eliminating the ontological distance between values and the person. Moreover, such an approach would appear to skirt the
epistemological difficulties evident in the meta-anthropological turn.

Yet, it must also be recognized that there is found a danger, a
political danger especially, in certain of the approaches to this unity in
a Ground of Being. In decentering human subjectivity, in locating
human being within the Ground of Being without *fundamental* differentiation between it and other ways of being, the risk is run of
coming to understand the person as we understand all other beings.
It is all too easy to imagine the political horrors which follow from
such a conception, wherein, for example, the justice afforded men
and women would be but an extension of the "justice" by which we
treat other beings of our experience. Here, one hopes, the Schelerian
concern with the dignity of the person, with personal responsibility
and creativity, would persevere despite an admission that person
shares a common plane of being with all creation. Perhaps were the
Schelerian interpretation of the Franciscan fraternity of man with
creation to be realized, the possibility this path lends to personalism
would be more readily perceived.

On either path, the meta-anthropological or toward a Ground of
Being, the direction which personalism as political theory must pursue remains one which is attuned to the full reality—existence and
promise—of the person.

Notes

1. Hans-Georg Gadamer, "What is Praxis?," in *Reason in the Age of Science*, trans. Frederick G. Lawrence, (Cambridge: MIT Press, 1981). See also Richard Bernstein's, *Praxis and Action: Contemporary Philosophies of Human Activity* (Philadelphia: University of Pennsylvanis Press, 1971).

2. Discussed in greater detail subsequently, it is worth here noting that the most intriguing possible link between Scheler's personalism and the praxis theories, is his understanding the person itself—i.e., its essence as a real and concrete unity of acts.

3. Max Scheler, "Philosopher's Outlook," in *Philosophical Perspectives*, trns. Oscar A. Haac (Boston: Beacon Press, 1958), p. 10.

4. See Scheler, "Versuche eine Philosophie des Lebens," in his *Gesammelte Werke*, Vol. 3: *Vom Umsturz der Werte*, ed. Maria Scheler and Manfred Frings (Bern: Francke, 195X), p. xxx. Cf. Friedrich Nietzsche,

   > This, indeed, is the most difficult thing: to close the open hand out of love and to preserve one's modesty as a giver.

   > "The Child with the Mirror"

   Thus Spoke Zarathustra, trans. R. J. Hollingdale (Middlesex: Penguin, 1969), p. 107.

5. Heidegger, "Andenken zu Max Scheler," in Paul Good, ed., *Max Scheler im Gegenwartsgeschehen der Philosophie* (Bern: Francke Verlag, 1975), p. 9.
   See also the parallels between Scheler's *Person* and Heidegger's *Dasein* as illustrated in Manfred Fring's excellent study, *Person and Dasein: Zur Frage der Ontologie des Wertseins* (The Hague: Nijhoff, 1969).

6. Martin Heidegger, "Andenken zu Max Scheler," in Paul Good, ed., *Gegenwartsgeschehen*, p. 9. Heidegger made this comment in Marburg, on May 21, 1928, at the beginning of a series of lectures at the university.

7. Ibid.

8. Thanks to Scheler's widow, Maria Scheler, and the work of Manfred Frings, the current editor of his *Nachlass*, essentially all of Scheler's manuscript material and various personal data has been transcribed and collected at the *Bayerische Staatsbibliothek* in Munich. See Eberhard Ave-Lallemant, *Die Nachläse der Münchner Phänomenologen in der Bayerischen Staatsbibliothek* (Wiesbaden: Harrassowitz, 1975).

9. The past ten years have seen a rekindling of interest in Scheler. In great part it would seem that this is due to the numerous English translation of Scheler's works which have recently become available (see the accompanying bibliography), but in part too, it seems that the focus of his thought is very much in accord with the thinking and works of a number of contemporary thinkers.

10. Much of this personal material is indebted to Raphael Staude's fine, if somewhat unsympathetic, biography, *Max Scheler: An Intellectual Portrait* (New York: Free Press, 1967), to Wilhelm Mader's more balanced consideration of Scheler's life and thought, *Max Scheler* (Reinbeck bei Hamburg: Rowohlt Taschenbuch, 1980), and to Fr. John M. Oestereicher's "Max Scheler: Critic of Modern Man," in *Walls are Crumbling: Seven Jewish Philosophers Discover Christ*, foreward by Jacques Maritain (New York: Devin-Adair, 1952).

11. Wilhelm Stern, "Autobiographical Sketch," in Vol. 1, *The History of Psychology in Autobiography* ed. Carl Murchison (Worcester, Mass.: Clark University Press, 1930), pp. 255-6. See also Staude, P. 9, and Mader, pp. 18-20.

12. Scheler, *Beiträge zur Festellung der Beziehungen zwischen den logischen und ethischen Prinzipien, Gesammelte Werk*, in Vol. 1: *Frühe Schriften*, ed. Maria Scheler and Manfred Frings (Bern: Francke, 1971).

13. Scheler, "Arbeit und Ethik," ibid.

14. *Die transendentale und die psychologische Methode*, ibid. Cf. Mader, p. 29-30.

15. Rather obliquely, this is noted by Scheler in his essay, "'Die deutsche Philosophie der Gegenwart," *Gesammelte Werke*, in Vol. 7: *Wesen und Formen der Sympathie* (Bern: Francke, 1973), p. 308. Edith Stein in her recollections of the Göttingen phenomenological circle cites instances when his claim in this regard were rather less than oblique. See Edith Stein, "Von den Studienjahren in Göttingen," in *Edith Steins Werke*, Vol. 7: *Aus dem Leben einer judischen Familie*, ed. L. Gelber (Freiburg: Herder, 1965), pp. 181-183.

16. Dietrich von Hildebrand, "Max Scheler als Persönlichkeit," in *Hochland*, Vol. 26 (September, 1928), pp. 413-18.

17. Scheler's marriage was falling apart and his wife reported details of an extra-marital affair to Munich's socialist newspaper. See Mader, pp. 37-41 and Staude, pp. 24-6.

18. Scheler, *Resentiment*, trns. William Holdheim (New York: Free Press of Glencoe, 1961); *The Nature of Sampathy*, trns. Peter Heath (London: Routledge & Kegan Paul, 1954); and *Formalism in Ethics and Non-Formal Ethics of Values: A New Attempt Toward the Foundation of an Ethical Personalism*, trns. Manfred Frings and Roger Funk (Evanston: Northwestern University Press, 1973).

19. Scheler, *Der Genius der Krieg und der Deutsche Krieg*, in *Gesammelte Werke*, Vol. 4: *Politische-Pädagogische Schriften*, ed. Manfred Frings (Munich: Francke, 1982). It might be noted, not as an apology, that Scheler was far from alone among German academics in 1914 in supporting the German war: Witness the propagandistic tracts of Werner Sombart, Ernst Troeltsch and Georg Simmel of the same period.

20. Scheler, *Krieg und Aufbau*, ibid.

21. Scheler, *On the Eternal in Man*, trns. Bernard Noble (London: SCM Press, 1960).

22. The exchange of letters between Scheler's Cologne friend, Peter Wust, and the editors of the Catholic journal *Hochland*, Otto Gruendler and Carl Muth, demonstrate the depth of Scheler's impact on Catholic intellectuals of the period and reveal much of Scheler's personal soulsearching. See Peter Wust's *Vorlesungen und Briefe*, ed. Alois Hunig, Vol. 10, of his *Gesammelte Werke*, ed. Wilhelm Vernekohl (Muenster: Verlag Regensberg, 1974). N. b. the letters from Gruendler to Wust, pp. 153–4 (7/14/22), pp. 218–23 (5/1/23) and Wust's Christmas letter to Muth, pp. 307–8 (12/20/23). See also Dietrich von Hildebrand's comments in "Max Scheler als Persönlichkeit."

23. Mader, p. 104–6, passim.

24. Scheler, *Gesammelte Werke*, Vol. 7: *Die Wissenformen und die Gesellschaft*, ed. Maria Scheler (Munich: Francke, 1960). See also *Problems of a Sociology of Knowledge*, trns. Manfred Frings (London: Routledge and Kegan Paul, 1980).

25. Scheler, *Man's Place in Nature*, trns. Hans Meyerhoff (New York: Noonday, 1961).

26. Scheler, *Problems of a Sociology of Knowledge*, trns. Manfred Frings (London: Routledge and Kegan Paul, 1980), p. 54.

27. Scheler, "Man and History," in *Philosophical Perspectives*, trns. Oscar Haac (Boston: Beacon, 1958), p. 65. The above translation is actually from Hans Meyerhoff's "Introduction" to his translation of Scheler's *Man's Place in Nature*, p. xii.

28. It has been generally agreed among Scheler scholars that his thought can roughly be divided into three periods, which might broadly be characterized as in terms of: a life philosophy period, a phenomenological period and a philosophical anthropology period. Nonetheless, the present work goes far to illustrate a pervasive con-

tinuity to Scheler's thought. Although Scheler's thinking undergoes many significant shifts, it needs to be noted that it never in any sense breaks with his previous thinking as much as it develops from it. Scheler remarks himself in the "Preface to the Third Edition" (1926) of his monumental ethical work, *Formalism in Ethics and Non-Formal Ethics of Values*, that the very ideas of his early works "represent some of the reasons and intellectual motives" (p.xxvi) for the later developments in his so-called "periods." To be sure, his religious thought *does* undergo profound reversal, but outside of theology, his philosophy is rather systematic and uniform from his Munich period through his death.

29. The two most vicious interpretations of Scheler in this vein are Marvin Farber's *Naturalism and Subjectivism* (Springfield, Ill.: Thomas, 1959), and Julius Kraft's book, *Von Husserl zu Heidegger; Kritik der phänomenologische Philosophie* (Franfurt a. M.: Oeffentliches Leben, 1957). Both writers are concerned to demonstrate that Scheler (and Heidegger) were proto-Nazis. Farber's is especially interesting; he lavishes praise on Edmund Husserl while attacking both Scheler and Heidegger for their supposed Nazi sympathies. Oddly, however, in his haste to discredit Scheler, Farber also claims that Scheler is a Marxist and an apologist for superstitious Catholicism and some sort of anti-Darwinist crank. Farber fails to offer substantiation for any of these charges, much less reveal how it might be possible for any one individual to be all these contradictory things. In actuality, Scheler is ruthless in his attacks on the Nazi movement, which in part accounts for their censure of his writings after their rise to power. Similarly, Mussolini's fascism is also ridiculed and racist political movements of all types draw his harshest criticism. There are elements of a sociobiology in Scheler's thinking, but in regard to race, his only remarks recommend interracial marriage as a solution to racial frictions. Scheler was closely acquainted with the works of Marx and with a number of academic Marxists, but his Marxism is only an occasional tool for him in his analysis of modernity. Although his influence is unmistakeable in the early Lukacs and Frankfurt critical theory, politically Scheler's affiliations move from aristocratic corporatism to Catholic centrism to left-liberalism.

30. Jose Ortega y Gesset, *Obras Completas*, 12 vols., 4: p. 510, as translated and quoted in Herbert Spiegelberg, *The Phenomenological Movement*, 2 vols. (The Hague: Nijhoff, 1960), 1: p. 228.

31. Scheler describes his pre-Husserlian inclinations in the direction of phenomenology in "Die Deutsche Philosophie der Gegenwart," p. 308.

32. See Scheler, "Versuche einer Philosophie des Lebens; Nietzsche-Dilthey-Bergson," in *Gesammelte Werke*, Vol. 3: *Vom Umsturz der Werte*, ed. Maria Scheler (Munich: Francke, 1955), pp. 311–39.

33. Gadamer, Hans-Georg, *Truth and Method*, trans. Sheed and Word Ltd. (New York: Crossroad, 1982), p. 214.
34. Although the important distinctions between these thinkers, especially in regard to their stance vis-à-vis the question of metaphysics, is being overlooked at this point, Scheler does not overlook the importance of the question. The possibility of metaphysics sharply divides these thinkers, just as will be seen it divides the phenomenologists. Scheler, in both traditions, finds his own stance precariously in between.
35. Ernst Troeltsch, *Der Historicismus und seine Probleme*, Vol. 3 of his *Gesammelte Werke* (Tübingen: Mohr, 1922); reprint ed., Raphael (Aalen: Scientia, 1967), p. 609, Also see Raphael Staude, p. 5.
36. Scheler, *Beziehungen zwischen den logischen und ethischen Prinzipien*, pp. 141–2, and "Man and History" in *Philosophical Perspectives*, pp. 74–5. The most sensitive consideration Scheler affords Nietzsche is in his essay "Versuche einer Philosophie des Lebens."
37. Scheler, *Ressentiment*, trns. William Holdheim, ed. Lewis Coser (New York: Schocken, 1972).
38. Ibid., p. 67.
39. The theme is discussed in various places in Scheler's works; see among others, his comparison of Kant's subject to Nietzsche's in his *Formalism and Non-Formalism*, pp. 515–6.
40. Scheler, "Versuche einer Philosophie des Lebens," p. 315.
41. Moritz Geiger, a colleague of Scheler in Munich, reveals in his eulogy on the occasion of Scheler's death, that Scheler was instrumental in arranging for an early translation and publication of Bergson's works in Germany. See Staude, p. 21, who cites Geiger's "Zu Max Schelers Tode," *Vossische Zeitung* (June 1, 1928).
42. The author apologizes for the violence which this cursory review does to Bergson's subtle criticism of reason and his concept of intuition. Read Bergson's *Creative Evolution*, trns. Arthur Mitchell (Westport, Conn.: Greenwook, 1975; reprint ed., 1944).
43. Scheler, "Phenomenology and the Theory of Cognition," in *Selected Philosophical Essays*, trns. David Lachtermann (Evanston: Northwestern University Press, 1973), pp. 190–1. See also "Versuche einer Philosophie des Lebens," 336–8.
44. Scheler, "Versuche einer Philosophie des Lebens," p. 333. This theme is treated in more detail in his long essay "Erkenntnis und Arbeit," in *Gesammelte Werke*, Vol. 8: *Die Wissenformen und die Gesellschaft*, ed. Maria Scheler (Munich: Franche, 1963), pp. 246–9.
45. Scheler, "Phenomenology and the Theory of Cognition," pp. 163–4. See also the section on Dilthey in "Versuche einer Philosophie des Lebens," where Scheler is lavish in his praise of the thinker.
46. It is surprisingly easy to view this distinction, posited by Dilthey, as the starting point of much of Scheler's own philosophy. Consider his

foregoing critique of Bergson's monistic life philosophy, his division of being into being-as-act (cultural?) and being-as-object (natural?), his oft-berated seeming duality between spirit and life, and his own division of cognition and science into catergories which seem only little more refined than Dilthey's. The history of ideas is a tricky business, however, and ultimately is of limited value in appraising the significance of a given idea or writer. Moreover, as will become clear, the sharp dichotomies of Dilthey are very much softened in Scheler, and a stress on the unity of these divisions in the body of living man becomes fundamental. The key to this unity in man, is that unlike Dilthey—who follows Kant in denying the accessibility of the human spirit in its interiority to "knowledge"—Scheler contends that not only the objective contours of human spirit, but the subjective intentions of human spirit are "knowable." See "Erkenntnis und Arbeit," p. 205.

47. As with Bergson, the reader's understanding is begged for this extremely cursory treatment of Dilthey. Consult Rudolf A. Makkreel's *Dilthey: Philosopher of the Human Studies* (Princeton: Princeton University Press, 1975), for a more full consideration of these topics.

48. Scheler, "Idealism and Realism," in *Selected Philosophical Essays*, p. 324.

49. In other words, Dilthey, as is his purpose, only attempts to perceive the "outward" structures of history and culture. He does not endeavor to probe beneath this "objective" level in order to experience the subjective intentions of persons.

50. As an example, see his "Forms of Knowledge and Culture," in *Philosophical Perspectives*.

51. Scheler, "Die Deutsche Philosophie der Gegenwart," p. 274.

52. Scheler, "Die tranzendentale und die psychologische Methode," p. 335. Also see "Die Deutsche Philosophie der Gegenwart," p. 274-5.

53. *Jahrbuch für Philosophie und phänomenologische Forschung*, vol. 1 (1913), p. v. This translation is borrowed from Herbert Heinrich Meyer, "A Critical Study of May Scheler's Philosophical Anthropology in its Relation to his Phenomenology" (Ph.D. dissertation, Boston University Graduate School, 1972), p. 16.

54. The situation of Husserl's thought versus psychologism, as presented above, greatly benefitted Dallas Willard, "The Paradox of Logical Psychologism: Husserl's Way Out," *American Philosophical Quarterly*, 9:1 (January 1972), pp.94-100.

55. See Husserl, *Logical Investigations*, 2 vols., trns. J. N. Findlay (New York: Humanities Press, 1970), 1: pp. 350-62.

56. Ibid., pp. 312-26 and 329-30.

57. See Edmund Husserl, *Ideas: General Introduction to Pure Phenomenology*, trns. Boyce Gibson (London: Allen & Unwin, 1931), pp. 54-6 and 125-6. Roman Ingarden's *On the Motives which Led Husserl to*

Transcendental Idealism, trns. A. Hannibalsson (The Hague: Martinus Nijhoff, 1975), much more thoroughly considers this transition in Husserl's thought and proved helpful in preparing this material. See also, ''Husserl and the Problem of Idealism,'' by Theodor W. Adorno in *Journal of Philosophy* 37 (1940), pp. 5–18.

58. Husserl, *Ideas*, pp. 113–4.
59. Ibid., pp. 257–65.
60. Scheler, ''Die Deutsche Philosophie der Gegenwart,'' p. 308.
61. See Spiegelberg, pp. 228–31.
62. See Georg Misch, *Lebensphilosophie und Phänomenologie* (Leipzig, 1931; reprint ed. Stuttgart: Teubner, 1967), for an excellent treatment of what life philosophy and metaphysics would entail for phenomenology. Unfortunately his treatment of Scheler is incorporated into his discussion of Martin Heidegger.
63. Husserl, ''Philosophy as Rigorous Sciences,'' in *Phenomenology and the Crisis of Philosophy*, trns. Quentin Lauer (New York: Harper & Row, 1965).
64. Scheler, ''Phenomenology and the Theory of Cognition,'' p. 137.
65. The quoted essay, for example, dates from 1913. Scheler at this time probably had some awareness of Husserl's growing idealism, but his *Ideas* is not cited in the text and likely had not as yet been published. Although there is a difference of purpose suggested between the early Husserl and Scheler at this time, there appears to be no substantive disagreement as to the understanding of phenomenology. Jörg Willer argues that Scheler had premonitions of Husserl's formal tendencies from the beginning; see ''Der Bezug auf Husserl im Frühwerk Schelers,'' *Kantstudien*, 72:2 pp. 175–85.
66. Scheler, ''Phenomenology and the Theory of Cognition,'' pp. 138–9.
67. Ibid., p. 138–9.
68. Scheler, ''Die Deutsche Philosophie der Gegenwart,'' p. 309.
69. Scheler, ''Phenomenology and the Theory of Cognition,'' p. 140. See also Scheler's late piece, ''Idealism-Realism,'' which is also translated in Lachtermann.
70. By not following Husserl into transcendental idealism, Scheler incurs Husserl's rejection of his thought. The breach which ensues leads to a general fragmentation of the phenomenological movement. In response to the idealism of the later Husserl, Scheler remarks to Helmuth Plessner in the late 1920's that ''the word phenomenology ought never more be used,'' for with Husserl ''it is doing nothing more than what philosophy has always done.'' Husserl less kindly, refers to Scheler's thought as sham, or ''fool's gold.'' See Plessner's *Husserl in Gottingen*, Gottinger Universitatsreden, N. 24 (Gottingen: Vandehoeck & Ruprecht, 1959), p. 21; and Spiegelberg quoting Husserl in private conversation, in Speigelberg, p. 230.

71. Scheler, "Die Deutsche Philosophie der Gegenwart," p. 313.
72. Scheler, "Philosophische Weltanschauung," in *Gesammelte Werke* Vol. 10: *Späte Schriften*, ed. Manfred Frings (Munich: Francke Verlag, 1976), p. 76. See the somewhat free translation of this esay in *Philosophical Perspectives*, trns. Oscar Haac (Boston: Beacon Press, 1958), p. 2.
73. Scheler, "Phenomenology and the Theory of Cognition," *Selected Philosophical Essays*, p. 159. Cf. Manfred Frings, *Max Scheler, A Concise Introduction to the World of a Great Thinker* (Pittsburgh: Duquesne University Press, 1965), p. 179.
74. Scheler, "Idealism-Realism," p. 312.
75. *Supra*, pp. 36–8.
76. Scheler, "Idealism-Realism" p. 305.
77. Scheler, "Idealism-Realism," p. 318. Cf. *Non-Formalism*, pp. 135-6. "Ontology" is used here in the broad sense—not in the Heideggerian sense which sharply distinguishes between "ontic" and "ontological." Being itself is not Scheler's central concern, though his discussion of it in the terms of the "ground of Being" is very evocative of Heidegger to the contemporary reader. Scheler's foremost concern, however, is with the unique being of being man; this he terms "Person" and Heidegger terms "*Dasein*."
78. Scheler, "Erkenntnis und Arbeit," p. 360.
79. Ibid., p. 365. See also *Non-Formalism*, p. 135. Martin Heidegger has a very persuasive critique of the general thesis of resistance as the primal experience of reality in his early period; cf. *Being and Time*, trns. Jonathan Macquarrie and Edward Robinson (London: SCM Press, 1962), p. 210ff and p. 290ff.
80. Scheler, "Idealism-Realism," p. 295.
81. Scheler, "Erkenntnis und Arbeit," p. 363.
82. See Ludwig Landgrebe, *Major Problems in Contemporary European Philosophy*, trns. Kurt Reinhardt (New York: Ungar, 1966), pp. 36-39, and Manfred Frings, *Person und Dasein* (The Hague: Martinus Nijhoff, 1969), pp. 88-97.
83. Scheler, *Formalism*, pp. 133–7; also see *On the Eternal in Man*, trns. Bernard Noble (London: SCM, 1960), pp. 83-6.
84. Scheler, *Man's Place in Nature*, trns. Hans Meyerhoff (New York: Noonday, 1961).
85. Scheler, "Idealism-Realism," pp. 315–6.
86. Scheler, *Man's Place*, pp. 51–4.
87. Scheler, "Idealism-Realism," p. 317.
88. Scheler, *Die Stellung des Menschen im Kosmos*, in *Gesammelte Werke*, Vol. 9: *Späte Schriften*, ed. Manfred Frings (Bern: Francke, 1976), p. 9. See also *Man's Place*, p. 3.

89. Scheler, "Man in the Era of Adjustment," in *Philosophical Perspectives*, p. 102. See also the excellent explication of the concept of man in Scheler's last period in Francis N. Dunlop, "Scheler's Idea of Man," *Aletheia*, 2 (1981), pp. 220–33.
90. Scheler, *Formalism*, p. 29; see also p. 370–92.
91. See, among several sources, his early work *Ressentiment*, trns. William Holdheim, ed. with introduction by Lewis Coser (Glencoe: Free Press, 1961) and his later monograph *Problems of a Sociology of Knowledge*, trns. Manfred Frings (London: Routledge and Kegan Paul, 1980). Of the Bourgeois, more will be said subsequently.
92. Scheler, *Man's Place*, pp. 31–5. Scheler's thinking here seems much influenced by his acquaintance with Wilhelm Dilthey. For an intriguing comparison, see Michel Foucault's essay "The Subject and Power" in *Michel Foucault: Beyond Structuralism and Hermeneutics*, 2nd ed., by Hubert Dreyfus and Paul Rabinow (Chicago: University of Chicago Press, 1983).
93. Scheler, *Formalism*, p. 374.
94. Apparently aware of this maze of subtleties regarding the relationship between person and world, Scheler occasionally refers to being-as-object *at its most basic level* as experiences of undistinguished "pockets of resistance." Hence, these are not then epistemological objects except *a fortiori* through objectification by persons. See "Idealism-Realism," *passim*.
95. Scheler, *Formalism* pp. 76–7. See also the subsequent section in ibid., "Person and the 'Ego' of Transcendental Apperception," p. 374ff, and his essay "The Idols of Self-Knowledge," in Lachtermann, pp. 17–30. Cf. Jean-Paul Sartre, *The Transcendence of the Ego*, trns. with introduction by Forrest Williams and Robert Kirkpatrick (New York: Noonday, 1957), where Sartre explores a similar theme. Although Sartre does not refer to Scheler's work, he and Scheler both take Kant's noumenal subject and phenomenology as the initial starting point for their discussion and conclude with a rejection of the possibility of the transcendental ego.
96. Scheler, "Erkenntnis und Arbeit," pp. 203–7.
97. Scheler, *Formalism*, p. 374. The possibility of reflection in his thought is one which needs to be addressed in the literature. Scheler would certainly oppose any sort of rationalist critique, but what other manner of reflection does he propose?
98. Ibid., p. 383. For the sake of clarity, a bit of license was taken with these quotes. These remarks and much of the subsequent material in this section support those interpretations which perceive a strong Fichtean influence in Scheler's philosophy, derived perhaps via Eucken and Trendelenberg. See Reinhold J. Haskamp, *Spekulativer und*

Phänomenologischer Personalismus: Einflüsse J. G. Fichtes und Rudolf Euckens auf Max Schelers Philosophie der Person (Freiburg: Verlag Karl Alber, 1966). Nonetheless, it should be noted that Scheler is generally critical of Fichte's thought as a whole owing to its idealism.

99.   Ibid., p. 390 and p. 482.
100. Actually, these areas are selected as representative of number of similar topics in Scheler's thinking where act, person, spirit and so forth are depicted as constrained or expressed only through objective, existential reality.
101. See *Formalism*, pp. 130–6.
102. Ibid., pp. 142– and pp. 393–6.
103. Scheler, *The Nature of Sympathy*, trns. Peter Heath with introduction by Werner Stark (Hamden, Conn.: Shoe String, reprint edition, 1970); see Chapter 6, *passim*.
104. Ibid.
105. Ibid., pp. 244–52.
106. Scheler, *Man's Place*, pp. 8–34.
107. Ibid., pp. 13–4. See the previous discussion of the concept of resistance, *supra*, pp. 39–41.
108. Scheler, *Man's Place*, pp. 14–9.
109. Ibid., p. 22. Terminology here is borrowed from Alfred Schutz's "Scheler's Theory of Intersubjectivity and the Alter Ego," in his *Collected Papers*, Vol. 1, ed. Paul Arthur Schlipp (The Hague: Martinus Nijhoff, 1962), p. 151.
110. Scheler, *Man's Place*, pp. 29–34. Scheler refers specifically to Koehler's work with apes in regard to this level. See Wolfgang Koehler, *The Mentality of Apes*, Trns. Ella Winter (London: Kegan Paul, 1925).
111. Ibid., p. 36.
112. Cf. Sigmund Freud's psychoanalytic thesis of the human psyche and its development, especially the relation of the id to the ego and superego. See Sigmund Freud, *The Ego and the Id*, in Vol. 19 of *The Complete Psychological Works of Sigmund Freud*, trns. James Strachey, et al. (London: Hogarth, 1947). Parents will attest, moreover, that in childhood development, the infant demonstrates increasing capacity both for identifying and manipulating objects in their environment and for becoming cognizant of the self. The contemporary reader may also perceive an interesting anticipation of Jean Piaget's theory of human psychological development which is paralleled in Scheler's brief treatment of the ontogenesis of the personality. See Piaget's classic, *The Child's Conception of the World* (New York: Basic Books, 1968).
113. Scheler, *The Nature of Sympathy*.
114. Scheler, *Sympathy*, p. 246.
115. Scheler, *Formalism*, p. 526. See also his *Problem of a Sociology of Knowledge*, trns. Manfred Frings with introduction by Kenneth Stik-

kers (London: Routledge and Kegan Paul, 1980), p. 48. Cf. Toennies, *Community and Society*, trns. Charles P. Loomis (New York: Harper & Row, 1963).

116. Scheler, *Formalism*, pp. 526-8.
117. Ibid., pp. 529-33.
118. Note the striking similarity to Hegel's treatment of the relationship between the individual and community. Cf. Hegel's *Philosophy of Right*, trns. T. M. Knox (Oxford: Clarendon, 1965), pp. 148-60.
119. Scheler, *Formalism* p. 533.
120. Ibid., p. 522.
121. Scheler, *Formalism*, p. 387.
122. Ibid., p. 371.
123. Ibid., p. 372.
124. Ronald Perrin, "Max Scheler's Concept of the Person: Towards a Radical Humanism," (Unpublished doctoral dissertation, University of California, San Diego, 1971). Perrin's Dissertation was directed by Herbert Marcuse.
125. Social scientists might note that the doing of social science hangs in the balance of this question. How is a human science possible when the person of any human is precluded from objectification and, thus, direct cognitive knowing?
126. Scheler, *Man's Place*, p. 47.
127. Scheler, *Sympathy*, pp. 96-102.
128. It might be noted that Scheler asserts that this hierarchy is only an order of foundation and, thus, is non-causal although the higher stages rest upon the lower. The translation of the various stages of the sympathy hierarchy follows that of Peter Heath, the translator of *Sympathy*. Although Heath's terms are somewhat strained, their usage has been generally accepted among English readers of Scheler.
129. Scheler, *Sympathy*, p. 97.
130. Ibid., p. 98.
131. Ibid., p. 99. The quote is from Goethe's "Einlass" to *Buch des Pardies*.
132. Scheler, *Ressentiment*, p. 121. See the modest retraction of this statement in *Sympathy*, p. 99.
133. Scheler, *Sympathy*, p. 101.
134. Scheler, *Formalism*, p. 100-1; see also "Ordo Amoris," translated in Lachtermann. Scheler's most detailed elaboration of his ethics is in his *Formalism*.
135. Scheler, *Formalism*, p. 538-9.
136. Scheler repeatedly identifies himself with the likes of Simmel and Jaspers in regard to the need for *Verstehen* in the human sciences. See "Die Deutsche Philosophie der Gegenwart," p. 305-6.
137. Ibid., p. 393-4. Ths begs the question of personal freedom, which will be considered subsequently; see "Zur Phänmonologie und

Metaphysik der Freiheit,'' in *Gesammelte Werke*, Vol. 10: *Schriften aus dem Nachlass I*, ed. Maria Scheler (Bern: Francke Verlag, 1957).

138. Scheler, *On the Eternal*, p. 273.
139. Scheler, *Sympathy*, pp. 77–95.
140. Scheler, *Ressentiment*, p. 172.
141. Scheler, ''Der Bourgeois,'' P. 351.
142. Scheler, *Sympathy*, pp. 82–95.
143. Scheler, *Sympathy*, p. 89. Scheler also noted with approval that this non-hierarchic approach is the basis for the Franciscan social ministry; ibid., p. 91.
144. Scheler appears to reconsider a number of the troubling implications of the Franciscan and similar conceptions toward the end of his life. See the collections of manuscripts, ''Manuskripte zu den Metaszienzien'' and ''Manuskripte zu Lehre vom Grunde alle Dinge'' in his *Gesammelte Werke*, Vol. 11: *Schriften aus dem Nachlass II*, ed. Manfred Frings (Bern: Francke, 1979). Even in these late papers, however, Scheler does not consider directly the question of man's proper attitude toward nature.
145. See Schlelr's ''The Forms of Knowledge and Culture,'' in *Philosophical Perspectives* and ''Manuskripte zu Metaszienzien'' in *Nachlass II* in reference to such a new science.
146. Scheler, ''Über Ursprung und Wert des kapitalistischen Geschichtsauffassung,'' in the unpublished collection of manuscripts, ''Zur Situation der Zeit,'' CC.V.9, p. 51, in Scheler's archive at the Bayerische Staatsbibliothek. The author was kindly given permission by Manfred Frings, editor of Scheler's collected works, to review this portion of Scheler's unpublished manuscripts and notes. Much of the following discussion is derived from this and other pieces from the ''Situation der Zeit'' materials.
147. Scheler, *Sociology of Knowledge*, p. 39.
148. Scheler, ''Dekadenzprobleme: Zu Spenger,'' in the unpublished manuscripts of ''Zur Situtation der Zeit,'' pp. 25-30. Cf. Scheler, *Problems of a Sociology of Knowledge*, trns. Manfred Frings (London: Routledge and Kegan Paul, 1980) pp. 151-3.
149. Scheler, *Problems*, pp. 153-4.
150. Scheler, ''Man and History,'' in *Philosophical Perspectives*, p. 46.
151. Scheler, ''Dekadenzprobleme,'' p. 9.
152. In his *Sociology of Knowledge*, Scheler discusses in some detail this thesis that subjectivity must manifest itself in the real and ideal objects of one's existence in the world—i.e., the objects of nature and history.
153. Scheler, ''Man and History,'' pp. 92-3.
154. This discussion is indebted to Richard Rorty's *Philosophy and the Mirror of Nature* (Princeton: Princeton University Press, 1979) and to Leo Strauss' *What is Political Philosophy?* (Chicago: University of Chicago Press, 1961).

155. In the *Critique of Pure Reason*, Kant does take the radical step of severing essential knowledge from man, requiring philosophy *a priori* to focus on man. In this manner, Kant begins the anthropological turn in philosophy which Scheler inherits. Yet, Kant is unable to appreciate the full historical character of man himself and, thus, transcendental reason and critique becomes *de facto* an absolute standard.

156. This historical understanding of the person is by no means a late conception in Scheler's thought, for even in works as early as *Ressentiment* he dismisses any basis for a "fixed" human nature.

157. The Nietzschean term "genealogy" wold seem to be particularly apt for describing Scheler's notion of "order of foundation." Both ideas stree the non-causal character of a sequence of events behind a given historical phenomenon. In other words, both stree the relativity of history itself and the immersion of subjectivity in history. Moreover, Scheler was *very* well acquainted with Nietzsche's intent behind his choice of terms in this matter, as is witnessed in *Ressentiment*. Yet, Scheler opts not to utilize the terminology, settling instead for his own cumbersome "order of foundation." If some reason is sought for Scheler's choice, it may lie in his insistence that the order of values central to his ethics is seen as "objective" in its being. See, *Sociology of Knowledge*, pp. 39–40.

158. Scheler, "Dekadenzprobleme," p. 12.

159. This caveat is intended to outline the boundaries of this study. It concerns itself witht he political theory of the personalism elaborated in Scheler's writing—a personalism which is founded on a realist, ontological phenomenology and intricately linked with a similarly founded philosophical anthropology. Intriguing as Scheler's political inclinations may be, their basis in his philosophy and their influence on his philosophy are foci more appropriate to the study of the history of ideas. The fine works by Staude and Mader on Scheler, moreover, adequately explore such interconnections; and, reference must be made to Walter Laqueur's *Weimar: A Cultural History* (New York: Putnam, 1974) and to H. Stuart Hughes' *Consciousness and Society: The Reorientation of European Social Thoughts, 1890–1930* (New York: Knopf, 1958) for studies which outline the general tableau of the intellectual atmosphere and culture of Scheler's historical setting.

160. Ibid.

161. It needs to be noted that the Marxist notion of class interest is still self-interest according to Scheler. Hence, Marxism is viewed as merely a somewhat different manifestation, along with bourgeois liberalism and backward-looking conservativism, of a single political paradigm—one which sees politics in terms of self-interest and material welfare.

162. Scheler, of course, never specifically outlines such a schema.

163. Scheler, "Vorbilder und Fuhrer," p. 260.

164. Ibid., p. 261.
165. Cf. the neo-Marxist notion of false consceousness and the critique of ideology; see Marx, *The German Ideology*, and Georg Lukacs, *History and Class Consciousness*. Other notions might also be considered here such as Mannheim's thesis in *Ideology and Utopia*, regarding the role of the free intellectuals, and Thomas Kuhn's understanding of paradigm and historical change in his *Structure of Scientific Revolution*.
166. Scheler, "Vorbilder und Führer," p. 267.
167. Ibid., p. 263.
168. Ibid., p. 269.
169. Neither in his sociology of knowledge nor here in "Vorbilder u. Führer" does Scheler make clear the ontological status of ideas, models and so forth. This is a fundamental inadequacy in his thinking, which pierces to the very root of his philosophy. In the "Idealism-Realism" essay of his later years, he seeks to grant outright the objective reality of ideas on the basis that they offer "resistance" to efforts of "suspension" or negation. One wonders, following this, how such ideas differ from non-noetic reality? The author would like to read into such passages a gradual move by Scheler away from his ontological dualism. This in not the present study's central concern, but one does see an obvious shift in his later thought from a comprehension of noetic reality as autonomous and essentially distinct in itself to a position which understands noetic reality as inseparable from the narrowly expressible only through historical and experiential reality. See, for example, his essay "Spinoza," in *Philosophical Perspectives*. At any rate, unlike Husserl who was able to surmount the problem of the reality of ideas by reduction of all reality to phenomenological intentionality, Scheler's dilemma results from a distinction between being-as-act and being-as-object. Perhaps a dialectical substructure-superstructure "unity in contradiction" such as M. Merleau-Ponty's would resolve Scheler's dilemma, but Scheler's insistence on the powerlessness of noetic reality would preclude such an option.
170. Ibid., p. 268.
171. Scheler, in "Vorbilder und Führer," does not describe the typology of these guiding-models in regard to their foundational order with the degree of detail given here. Moreover, he examines the typology in terms of a waning of personal responsibility and dignity from the top (the saint) to the bottom (the artist of enjoyment). The present study considers the order in obverse fashion or reasons of symmetry with previous sections. Note, also, the contrasts and similarities of Scheler's sequence of transformations according to an "order of foundation" with Hegel's celebrated *Aufhebung* and the dialectic of spirit.
172. Scheler, "Vorbilder und," Führer," p. 313.

173. Note that Scheler very much distances himself from Kant's, Schopenhauer's and the colloquial usage of the word "genius." The genius is not a clever calcultor nor a technical or scientific wizard.

174. This concept does not contradict the sharp criticism which Scheler has previously directed against the "international." As he states, the "cosmo-political realm is naturally distinct from the 'international.'" Indeed, he continues, "it stands as far above the 'national' as the 'international' stands below." ("Vorbilder und Führer," p. 289) Apparently he would locate the "international" within the model of the leading spirit of civilization.

175. Scheler, "Vorbilder und Führer," p. 290. Refer also to Fred R. Dallmayr's very sensitive consideration of these issues in his *Twilight of Subjectivity: Contributions to a Post-Individualist Theory of Politics* (Amherst: University of Massachusetts Press, 1981).

176. In the highest form, Scheler here intends the person of God as the other with which the saint begins—but he by no means limits it to this highest person. Perhaps he has in mind something like the well-known prayer of Francis of Assisi which begins "Lord, make me an instrument of your peace..." Here there is no negation of personal subjectivity, but the subjectivity of the other—in this case, God's—precedes and is joined to one's own. Although Scheler's terminology indicates his own linkage of these concepts with certain religious aspects, he nowhere identifies such notions directly with religious beliefs or experience. Indeed, his personalism, he claims at one point, ultimately proved to be the source of his break with Catholicism and deist religion in general.

177. This participation in the being of the other person is discussed in previous sections; see Chapter 2, "Person and Other."

178. "Vorbilder und Führer," p. 281-2.

179. Witness, for example, the ironic and now fashionable jaundiced eye by which many modern Marxists view Marx's own prediction of the communist society. It is fascinating to assess the parallels and contrasts between Marx and Scheler on this score. In the *German Ideology* and elsewhere, Marx takes great pains to assert that communism is not an ideal to which society must conform, but a real dynamism in material history itself. Avoiding the problems of Scheler's apparent duality, Marx's "ideal" is not an ideal, it is a necessary but still emerging "real." The difficulties with this, struggled with by writers a diverse as Lukacs and Lenin, is the role of human creativity and responsibility in the arena of such necessity. Scheler, as explored in the work of the Frankfurt School thinker, Kurt Lenk, struggles for a middle ground between Marxist historical materialism and idealism in this regard. Hence, while maintaining a duality (overlooking other hints in his late

works), the realm of spirit—the Ideal—is presented as entirely powerless. Only to the extent that ideals can find some accord with the
dynamics of material reality can they acquire efficacy.

180. Among other sources see Howard Becker's review of Scheler's lecture
at the war college, "Befuddled Germany: A Glimpse of Max Scheler,"
American Sociological Review 8 (Spring 1943): pp. 209–21. Scheler,
Gedanken zu Politik und Moral, ed. Manfred Frings, (Bern: Francke
Verlag, 1973). Scheler, "The Idea of Peace and Pacificism," trns. Manfred Frings, *British Society for Phenomenology Journal*, 7 (October 1976)
pp. 154–66 and 8 (January 1977) pp. 36–50.

181. Scheler, *Gedanken*, p. 12.

182. Ibid., p. 15.

183. Ibid., p. 17.

184. This notion of resistance as the primary experience of subjectivity is
treated with more detail in the first chapter of this study. See the section on the Revival of Metaphysics, Anti-Epistemology and
Phenomenology. Also, see Scheler's essay "Idealism-Realism.

185. Scheler, *Gedanken*, p. 7.

186. Scheler, *Problems*, pp. 37-8.

187. Scheler, "Peace and Pacifism."

188. "*Christlicher Sozialismus als Antikapitalismus*" (1919), which was intended to be a part of a larger study entitled "The Essence and
developmental Laws of Capitalism: A way to Christian Socialism,"
has recently been printed in *GW V.4: Politisch-Pädagogische Schriften*,
edited by Manfred Frings (Munich: Francke, 1982). "*Chancen und
Mächte des Aufstiegs und Niedergangs*" (1923?) has yet to appear in
print; in Scheler's archive it is numbered CC. V. 21, and is grouped
with similar materials under the heading *Zur Situtation der
Zeit*—"Towards the Situtation of the Times."

189. Scheler, *Chancen*, p. 13.

190. Ibid., p. 15. The text goes on to note that Mussolini and the new
Spanish dictator will be but the first swallows of a coming flock.
Ironically, Scheler also speaks of Hitler's growing movement in this
essay. Remember, this was probably written in only 1923!

191. Scheler, *Sozialismus*, p. 672.

192. Ibid., p. 673.

192. No allusion to the notion of "paradigm" as popularized in Thomas
Kuhn's sense of paradigm shift in scientific revolutions is intended in
this context. Paradigm is used here to encompass various Schelerian
terms such as *Verfassung, Begriff* and so forth, because it does not in-
voke the epistemological overtones associated with words like "conception." Scheler's "paradigms" involve constellations or patterns of
values which precede any "thinking." There are modest affinities between the thesis of Scheler and Kuhn. Yet, in distinction, Scheler's
transformations are of man and the things which bear values, whereas

Kuhn's are radical conceptual changes relative to man's perspective on the natural world. See Kuhn's *The Structure of Scientific Revolutions* (Chicago: University of Chicago Press, 1962).

193.   Scheler, "Der Bourgeois," in *Gesammelte Werke*, Vol. 3: *Vom Umsturz der Werte*. See also *Ressentiment*, "Die Zukunft des Kapitalismus" and the second part of *Problems of a Sociology of Knowledge*.

194.   Refer to Chapter 2 for a discussion of the origin of personal subjectivity. Also, see "Zur Idee des Menschen" in *Gesammelte Werke*, Vol. 3: *Vom Umsturz der Werte* and "Man in the Era of Adjustment." Note accordingly that the idea of self-responsible evolution pictures man as possessing at a least moment of freedom in history. Even, however, in the radical sense of such free evolution, freedom is constrained and conditioned by history for Scheler: cf. "Man and History."

195.   As will become clear subsequently, Scheler is not here urging a romantic return to the medieval world-view or community structure. The concepts of self, other and community were equally as incomplete in that period, if only in different ways. The similarity between Scheler's thesis and the sociologies of Weber and Sombart may stem from his study year at Heidelberg during Weber's tenure there and from his close acquaintance with Sombart.

196.   *Ressentiment*, p. 158-9.

197.   Liberalism will be generally defined in context; however, its usage in this study conforms to the usual definition long associated with: formal, individually held, *a priori* rights; limited, participatory government; procedural justice; contractually-based political duties and obligations; etc. Scheler's most direct remarks on liberalism are perhaps found in in his otherwise unremarkable essay on the population growth rate in post-war Germany, "Bevölkerungsprobleme als Weltanschauungsfragen," especially the section 'Liberal Weltanschauung,' in *Gesammelte Werke*, Vol. 6: *Schriften zur Soziologie und Weltanschauungslehre*, ed. Maria Scheler (Bern: Francke, 1963).

198.   Although offering a liberal political theory himself, John Rawls's work, *A Theory of Justice* (Cambridge: Belknap, 1976), offers a brief but synoptic overview of the formal aspects of liberal political thought.

199.   Scheler, *Formalism in Ethics and Non-Formal Ethics of Values*. See especially his section "Formalism and Apriorism," pp. 45–110, and his section "Formalism and Person," pp. 370–595.

200.   Ibid., pp. 5–6 N. b. Scheler agrees with Kant that "goods" are relative to the life experiences of men. Scheler claims, however, that Kant errs by assuming that goods and values are identical. Values and their order for Scheler, as noted previously, are the objective and real basis for ethics because they, unlike goods, are not relative to men's experiences.

201.   See the consideration given Scheler's ethics in the first chapter of this study, *supra*, pp. 42–43.

202. Quotoations in this passage are taken from *Formalism*, pp. 371-2.
203. Scheler, however, goes beyond the usual community-individualism division toward a more Weberian notion of the succession of societal forms. Ibid., pp. 526-35 and *supra*, pp. 101-116.
204. Ibid., p. 529.
205. See, among several sources, Scheler's remarks concerning Aristotle's ''political animal'' in ibid., p. 524.
206. CF. Scheler's *Gedanken zu Moral und Politik*, edited by Manfred Frings (Bern: Francke, 1973), pp. 5-6; his *Formalism*, p. 525; and his essay ''Man in the Era of Adjustment'' in *Philosophical Perspectives, passim*.
207. Refer to Chapter II and the discussion of the ontogenesis of the person, pp. 94-101.
208. Refer to the Chapter II discussion of the phylogenesis of the person, pp. 101-116.
209. Refer to *Formalism*, pp. 533 ff.
210. Ibid., pp. 531-3.
211. It is tempting to refer to this distinction as one between early and later liberalism, or between classical liberalism and utilitarianism. In his work, *Ressentiment*, trns. Willian Holdheim (New York: Free Press, 1961), Scheler comes close to making such a conclusion, However, since Scheler does refrain from making such a division, utilitarianism and classical liberalism are treated under the generic term ''bourgeois liberalism'' in this essay.
212. *Formalism*, p. 352-3. Note also the inherent notion of material progress which is characteristic of liberalism.
213. Scheler does, in fact, argue that utility, pleasure and advantage are all merely different aspects of the same phenomenon. See *Ressentiment*, p. 152ff.
214. Scheler in passages such as this seems to be clearly referring to the like of Bentham. Bentham plainly treats all pleasures as equal and additive. One wonders, however, how well Scheler was acquainted with the works of J. S. Mill who proposed that there were qualitative differences between pleasure and that pleasures were not additive at the highest levels where they could only be truly appreciated by superior men. Also, consider that progress here would be conceived only as a quantitative, continued aggregation of more and more things.
215. J. S. Mill is an example among several. See the introductory chapter to his *On Liberty* (Indianapolis: Bobbs-Merrill, 1958).
216. *Formalism*, pp. 350-1.
217. In *Formalism*, Scheler claims that the more primary factors upon which needs are based would be the vital, natural impulses of life. As we shall see subsequently, however, these are also unacceptable for other reasons as the cornerstones of civilization and politics.
218. Ibid., p. 351-2.

219. Ibid., p. 349.

220. Scheler does not agree with Nietzsche that Christianity is the result of *ressentiment*. Rather, he believes the *ressentiment* emerges with bourgeois man and subsequently has perverted all institutions—including Christianity—of the modern age.

221. See *Erkenntnis und Arbeit*, in Scheler's *Gesammelte Werke*, Vol. 8: *Die Wissenformen und die Gesellschaft*, edited by Marie Scheler (Bern: Francke, 1960), pp. 212-39.

222. *Ressentiment*, p. 154.

223. *Formalism*, p. 154. Scheler occasionally organizes values in four modes instead of five.

224. *Gedanken zu Moral und Politik*, p. 5.

225. *Gedanken*, pp. 16-20.

226. Scheler, *Sociology of Knowledge*, p. 124.

227. Scheler, *Formalism*, p. 275.

228. Cf. Kant's preface to *Foundations of the Metaphysics of Morals*, trans. L. W. Beck (Indianapolis: Bobbs-Merrill, 1959), p. 5ff.

229. In this vein, see John Rawl's *A Theory of Justice* (Cambridge: Belknap, 1976); see especially his thesis of the separation of the reasoning man from the chaos of reality by way of the veil of ignorance. In other respects, however, it is impossible to wholly classify Rawls in the rationalist liberal camp. Too often he also interjects elements of utility liberalism into his thesis.

230. Even imagining an artificial intelligence which could reason, one can scarcely believe the rationalists would allocate human choice to a machine. Here the heart would murmur within them it would seem.

231. *Formalism*, p. 275.

232. Ibid., p. 271.

233. *Problems of a Sociology Knowledge*, p. 40-1. Note that Scheler is here rejecting two different versions of rationalism. He rejects a rationalism of human reasoning and a rationalism based on an objective and universal reason.

234. See Scheler's *Man's Place in Nature*, trns. Hans Mayerhoff (New York: Noonday, 1961), pp. 69-70, where he discusses the nature of man as *becoming* human—i.e., actively participating in the unfolding of being's self awareness.

235. See the latter portion of thte first chapter of this study or refer to *Erkenntnis und Arbeit*, p. 201-2 and pp. 231-3 and Scheler's *On the Eternal in Man*, trns. Bernard Noble (London: SCM Press, 1960), pp. 198-213.

236. *On the Eternal Man*, p. 202.

237. Ibid., pp. 206-7.

238. *Erkenntnis und Arbeit*, pp. 197-200.

239. Ibid., pp. 203-5. See also "Liebe und Erkenntnis" in his *Gesammelte Werke*, Vol. 6: *Schriften zur Soziologie und Weltanschauungslehre*, ed. Maria Scheler (Bern: Francke, 1963).

240. Scheler, "Ordo Amoris" in *Selected Philosophical Essays*, trns. David Lachtermann (Evanston: Northwestern University Press, 1973), pp. 110–11. Cf. also Jürgen Habermas' notion of knowledge constitutive interests in his *Knowledge and Human Interests*, trns. Jeremy Shapiro (Boston: Beacon Press, 1968).
241. Refer to his article, "Die Deutsche Philosophie der Gegenwart."
242. Refer to the second foreword to his *Formalism*.
243. See his essay "Die Jugendbewegungen."
244. Many of the materials including in the collection of his unpublished papers, *Zur Situation der Zeit*, are frightening in their insights into the growing popularity of Adolf Hitler and the National Socialists. In regard to communism, it might be noted that Scheler first welcomes the Russian Revolution as a freeing of the Russian people from the barbarism of the feudalism of Czar and land, and as a freeing of the Eastern spirit from the shackles of orthodoxy. By the pivotal mid-Twenties, however, his enthusiasm for the new regime waned as new shackles were seen to replace orthodoxy and even the works of ancient philosophers were placed under censorship.
245. Appealing as these etymology games may be, there remains a certain nominalist illusion which must be guarded against. The author is dubious that the contemporary usage of the term "legitimacy" carries the implications of Divine law, natural law, cosmic or ontological order as were invoked by its roots.
246. Scheler is aware of various currents in Marxism and many interpretations of Marx's works. By the large, however, it is what today has become referred to as "orthodox" Marxism with which he is most familiar. Too, many of the more philosophical of Marx's writings were generally unknown before 1930. It may be that his acquaintance with Marxist thinking reflects his familiarity with Werner Sombart and/or with his study year at Heidelberg during the height of Max Weber's scholarship.
247. By way of illustration, some mention of Scheler's relationship with Soviet communism is in order. In the early 1920's his view of the Soviet regime as largely positive. At this time he sees the revolution as freeing the Russian people from a feudal servitude to Czar and land, and as freeing the Russian spirit from the dogmatism of orthodoxy. Indeed, it is roughly at this time, according to Mader (p. 123), that he accepts an invitation from Trotsky to present a series of lectures at the reorganized university at Moscow. Only financial problems on the Soviet end later precluded the trip. By the later 1920's, however, Soviet communism is seen only negatively. Calling it Czarism reborn, he notes with sadness the new orthodoxy imposed by censorship and the extremely bourgeois character of the new regime. See *Problems*, p. 167.

248. As with the previous vignettes in this chapter, here too the study paints with a broad brush what truly deserves much greater attention to detail.

249. Relevant passages from Marx's writings might be referred to for comparison with the above bourgeois Marxist interpretation. See the Preface to his *Contribution to the Critique of Political Economy*, his section "Critique of the Hegelian Dialectic and Philosophy as a Whole" which appears in *The Economic and Philosophical Manuscripts of 1844*, his "Theses on Feuerbach," the first section of *The German Ideology*, his Introduction to *The Grundrisse*, and his Afterword to the second edition of *Capital*. Exceptions to this interpretation can be found in Georg Lukacs' *History and Class Consciousness* and in Maurice Merleau-Ponty's *Adventures of the Dialectic*, trns. Joseph Bien (Evanstron: Northwestern University Press, 1973).

250. For relevant works, see (in no particular order) the section on "Value Shifts in Modern Morality" in *Ressentiment*, "Der Bourgeois," "Die Zukunft des Kapitalismus," "Man and History," the section "Christian Love and the Twentieth Century" in *On the Eternal*, and the sections "Cultural Sociology" and "Material Problems" in *Problems of a Sociology of Knowledge*.

251. Scheler, *Problems*, p. 118.

252. Ibid., p. 134.

253. Ibid., p. 125.

254. This is a common theme. For Scheler, knowledge is guided by interests; it is not a neutral operation—a point, by the way, which has been borrowed by some writers of the Frankfurt School; see Jürgen Habermas, *Knowledge and Human Interests*. In Scheler's theory, types of knowledge accord with the types of value-objects in a given person's complex of values. Refer to the section "Material Problems" in *Problems*, "Erkenntnis und Arbeit," "Liebe und Erkenntnis" and *supra*, pp. 55–57.

255. See the discussion of liberal formalism and rationalism, *supra*, Chapter Four.

256. Pascal, Blaise, *Pensees*, as cited in Loren Eiseley's *The Firmament of Time* (New York: Knopf, 1963), p. 159.

257. "Der Geist und die ideelen Grundlagen der Demokratie der grossen Nationen," in *Gesammelte Werke*, Vol. 6: *Schriften zur Soziologie und Weltanschauungslehre*, ed. Maria Scheler (Bern: Francke, 1963), p. 174.

258. Scheler's discussion of the dialectic is cursory and nowhere systematic. One must wonder, furthermore, if Scheler has adequately reflected on the proximity of his own thinking to dialectics. What, in fact, occurs in the various transformations discussed in his philosophy if it is not the renowned *Aufhebung* of dialectics?

259. Scheler, *Problems*, p. 171.

260. Scheler, *Gedanken*, p. 23.
261. Scheler; among several sources, refer to his essay, "Dekadenz-problem—zu Spengler," pp. 57–60.
262. Relevant materials in Marx's writings include: "On the Jewish Question," "Critique of the Hegelian Dialectic and Philosophy as a Whole," the Introdocution to *The Grundrisse* and the *Manifesto of the Communist Party.*
263. *Supra*, Chapter Two.
264. Scheler, *Problems*, p. 38. This is Frings' translation, although the word *Geist* is changed here to "spirit" instead of "mind."
265. See *Formalism*, pp. 533–5.
266. This may be overstating the point. In passages of *On the Eternal in Man* and *Problems*, it is hinted that, again like Mannheim, philosophers or intellectuals might be special in this regard. See *Problems*, p. 168 and cf. Karl Mannheim, *Ideology and Utopia*, pp. 209–12.
267. See "Erkenntnis und Arbeit," pp. 380–2.
268. Relevant works of Marx would be the first portions of the *The German Ideology*, the Preface to *Contribution to the Critique of Political Economy*, and his essay "Critique of the Hegelian Dialectic and Philosophy as a Whole."
269. Scheler, *Problems*, p. 147. The translation is Frings', and it illustrates the problems of translating Scheler. The German has a tone which is missed in English. "Der echte Marxist und Vertreter des 'absoluten' Klassenkampfes dürfte dies ja *nicht* tun. Ich selbst bin darin fast mehr 'Marxist' als Adler, insofern als auch ich alles Bewusstsein auf das *Sein*, alle obersten Vernunftgrunsätze und -formen auf Funktionalisierung erfasster Seinsformen zurückführe—allerdings nicht wie Marx auf das nur materielle Sein, sondern auf das *ganze* Sein des Menschen." *Probleme*, p. 145.
270. Scheler, *Problems*, p. 170.
271. The author takes a broad view of Scheler's personalism in this point, one which overlooks a significant but unclear element in his argument which would fog this interpretation. Scheler argues [*Problems*, pp. 167–70, *On the Eternal*, pp. 98–101, and *Philosophical Perspecitves*, pp. 1–12] that there is a certain type of knowing which serves to overcome ideology. He identifies this variously as "philosophical" or "slavational" knowing. To some extent, this knowing is the same grasping of the totality of the human person which here is designated simply as "critique." Unfortunately, Scheler also at moments brings this type of knowing dangerously near to the idea of transcendental knowledge which he rejects in rationalism and rationalist bourgeois Marxism.
272. Were Scheler's thought empiricist, it might be concluded that a weighing of the validity of the theory would revolve around explaining the experienced facts of political practices. Were it idealist,

likewise, this might be accomplished by comparing it with some ideal of the political order. Were it critical, perhaps some analysis of the methods of the theory would be in order based upon certain universally recognized criteria. But good scholarship does not lie behind this sort of "fairness." One may valuably argue, for example, that Plato's *Republic* is not a practical blueprint for city organization, or that David Easton's *A Systems Analysis of Political Life* fails to account for the full nature of man in politics by focusing too narrowly on external political behavior. Such evaluation is eminently "fair" in the best sense. The fairness of evaluating Scheler's personalism as political theory against the reality of the person ideally involves the latter notion of fairness—a substantive notion, not a procedural one.

273. His usage of terminology to describe the passage from one essential character to another is not standardized. On occasion the word "transformation" is used, but more often the process is only described without designation.

274. See *Formalism*, p. 344–46.

275. Refer to the translation of much of ths correspondence in the *Independent Journal of Philosophy*, 2 (1978): 5–12.

276. Ibid., p. 8. The concern of Strauss, by the way, coincides with Gadamer's publication of *Truth and Method* (New York: Crossroad, 1982).

277. Scheler, *Formalism*, p. 255. See also "Ordo Amoris."

278. Scheler, "Philosopher's Outlook," p. 11.

279. Scheler, *Man's Place*, p. 88.

280. This is a broad statement, obviously ignoring the important distinctions between these theories. See the Bibliography for reference to these writers' relevant works.

281. Habermas, *Knowledge and Human Interests*, trns. J. Shapiro (Boston: Beacon, 1972).

282. Habermas, "Toward a Theory of Communicative Comptence," *Inquiry* 13 (1970), pp. 359–76.

283. Heidegger, *Being and Time*.

284. See Frings, *Person and Dasein*, for discussion of relationship between Scheler's person and Heidegger's *Dasein*.

Bibliography

PRIMARY WORKS

Scheler, Max Ferdinand. "An *a priori* Hierarchy of Value-Modalities. Trans. Daniel O'Connor. In *Readings in Existential Phenomenology*. Edited by Nathaniel Lawrence and Daniel O'Connor. Englewood Cliffs, N.J.: Prentice-Hall, 1967.
———. "Anmerkungen über den soziologischen Ursprung der Hochkulturen und den Ursprung der Wissenschaft." In *Gesammelte Werke GW* Vol. 8: *Die Wissenformen und die Gesellschaft*. Edited by Maria Scheler. Munich: Francke, 1960.
———. "Arbeit und Ethik." In *GW* Vol. 1: *Frühe Schriften*. Edited by Manfred Frings and Maria Scheler. Munich: Francke, 1971.
———. "Arbeit und Weltanschauung." In *GW* Vol. 6: *Schriften zur Soziologie und Weltanschauungslehre*. Edited by Marie Scheler. Munich: Francke, 1963.
———. "Bevölkerungsprobleme als Weltanschauungsfragen." In ibid.
———. "Der Bourgeois." In *GW* Vo. 3: *Vom Umsturz der Werte*. Edited by Maria Scheler. Bern: Francke, 1955.
———. "Christentum und Gesellschaft." In *GW* Vol. 6.
———. "Christliche Demokratie." IN *GW* Vol. 4: *Politisch-Pädagogische Schriften*. Edited by Manfred Frings. Munich: Francke, 1982.
———. "Christlicher Sozialismus als Antikapitalismus." Ibid.
———. "Die Deutsche Philosophie der Gegenwart." In *GW* Vol. 7: *Wesen und Formen der Sympathie*. Edited by Manfred Frings. Bern: Francke, 1973.
———. "Erkenntnis und Arbeit." In *GW* Vol. 8.
———. *Formalism in Ethics and Non-Formal Ethics of Values: A New Attempt Toward the Foundation of an Ethical Personalism*. Translated by Manfred Frings and Roger Funk. Evanston: Northwestern University Press, 1973.
———. "Der Friede unter den Konfessionen." Ibid.
———. "Die Frage nach dem 'Ursprung' der nationalen Gruppenformen." In *GW* Vol. 6.

———. "Future of Man." Translated by Howard Becker. *The Monthly Criterion.* 7 (February, 1928): 100-19.

———. *Gedanken zu Moral und Politik.* Edited by Manfred Frings. Bern: Francke, 1973.

———. "Der Geist und die ideelen Grundlagen der Demokratien der grossen Nationen." In *GW* Vol. 6.

———. *Der Genius des Krieges.* In *GW* Vol. 4. pp. 209-19.

———. "Humility." Translated by Barbara Fiand. *Aletheia* 2 (1981): pp. 209-19.

———. "The Idea of Peace and Pacifism." Translated by Manfred Frings. *Journal of the British Society for Phenomenology* 7 (October 1976): pp. 154-66; and in 8 (January 1977): pp. 36-50.

———. "Der Krieg als Gesamterlebnis." In *GW* Vol. 4.

———. "Liebe und Erkenntnis." In *GW* Vol. 6.

———. *Man's Place in Nature.* Translated by Hans Meyerhoff. New York: Noonday Press, 1961.

———. "The Meaning of Suffering." Translated by Daniel Liederbach, S. J. In *Max Scheler (1874-1928) Centennial Essays.* Edited by Manfred Frings. The Hague: Nijhoff, 1974.

———. Munich, West Germany. Handschriftabteilung der Bayerische Staatsbibliothek. Max Schelers Archiv.

"Causalfaktoren." CC. V. 15 (1921).

"Chancen und Mächte des Aufstiegs und Niedergangs." CC. V. 21 (1924).

"Christliche Demokratie." CC. V. 7 (1919).

"Christlicher Sozialismus." CC. V. 11 (1919).

"Heldenverehrung." CC. V. 18 (c. 1922).

"Philosophie und Nation." CC. V. 2 (1917).

"Politische Geschichtsauffassung." CC. V. 16 (c. 1921)

"Rasse als primär Realfaktor." CC. V. 17 (1921).

" Stammtafel des kapitalistischen Geistes." CC. V. 5 (1917).

"Über die Jugendbewegung." CC. V. 22 (1923).

"Über die Ursprung und Wert der kapitalistischen Geschichtsauffassung." CC. V. 9 (c. 1917).

"Über" Geist und Ethos der Nationen." CC. V. 1 (c. 1919).

"Was ist christlicher Sozialismus?" CC. V. 12 (1919).

"Zum Nationalistaat." CC. V. 3 (c. 1917).

"Zu Spengler, Dekadenzproblem." CC. V. 20 (1922).

———. "Nation und Weltanschauung." In *GW* Vol. 6.

———. *The Nature of Sympathy.* Translated by Peter Heath. London: Routledge and Kegan Paul, 1954.

———. *On the Eternal in Man.* Translated by Bernard Nobel. London: SCM Press, 1960.

———. "On the Tragic." Translated by Bernard Stambler. In *Cross Currents* 4 (1954): pp. 178–91.

———. *Philosophical Perspectives*. Translated by Oscar Haac. Boston: Beacon Press, 1958.

———. "Politik und Kulter auf dem Boden der neuen Ordnung." In *GW* Vol. 4.

———. "Pragmatist, Idealist und der Weise." In *GW* Vol. 8.

———. *Problems of a Sociology of Knowledge*. Translated by Manfred Frings. London: Routledge and Kegan Paul, 1980.

———. "Problems with a Sociology of Knowledge." Translated by Ernest Ranly. In *Philosophy Today* 12 (Spring 1968): pp. 42–70.

———. "Prophetischer oder marxistischer Sozialismus?" In *GW* Vol. 6.

———. "Reality and Resistance: On *Being and Time*, 'Section 43'." Translated By Thomas Sheehan. In *Listening* 12 (Fall 1977): pp. 61–73.

———. "Recht, Staat und Gesellschaft." In *GW* Vol. 4.

———. *Ressentiment*. Translated by William Holdheim with Introduction by Lewis Coser. New York: Free Press of Cgencoe, 1961.

———. *Selected Philosophical Essays*. Translated by David Lachtermann. Evanston, Illinois: Northwestern University Press, 1973. The collection includes "The Theory of Three Facts," "Ordo Amoris," "Phenomenology and the Theory of Cognition" and "Realism-Idealism."

———. "1989 und 1914." In *GW* Vol. 4.

———. "The Sociology of Knowledge: Formal Problems." Translated by Rainer Koehne. In *The Sociology of Knowledge: a Reader*. Edited by J. Curtiss and J. Petras. New York: Praeger Publishers, 1970.

———. "Soziologie des Wissens und Erkenntnistheorie." In *GW* Vol. 8.

———. "Towards a Stratification of the Emotional Life." Translated by Daniel O'Connor. In *Readings in Existential Phenomenology*. Edited by Nathaniel Lawrence and Daniel O'Connor. Englewood Cliffs, New Jersey: Prentice Hall, 1967.

———. "Über die Nationalideen der grossen Nationen." In *GW* Vol. 6.

———. "Über die positivistische Geschichtsphilosophie des Wissens." in ibid.

———. Versuche einer Philosophie des Lebens." In *GW* Vol. 3.: *Vom Umsturz der Werte*. Edited by Maris Scheler. Bern: Francke Verlag, 1955.

———. "Von kommenden Dingen." In *GW* Vol. 4.

———. "Vordilder und Führer." In *GW* Vol. 10.: *Schriften aus dem Nachlass: Band I*. Edited by Maria Scheler. Bern: Francke Verlag, 1957.

———. "Die Zukunft des Kapitalismus.;; In *GW* Vol. 3.

———. "Zur Idee des Menschen." In *GW* Vol. 3.

———. "Zur Phänomenologie und Metaphysik der Freiheit." In *GW* Vol. 10.

———. "Zur Rehabilitierung der Tugend." In *GW* Vol. 3.

———. "Zur soziologistischen und materialistischen Auffassung des Erlösungswissens." In *GW* Vol. 8.

SECONDARY WORKS

Abel, Theodore. *Systematic Sociology in Germany: A Critical Analysis.* New York: Octagon Books, 1929.

Adorno, Theodor. *Against Epistemology: A Metacritique.* Translated by Willis Domingo. Cambridge, Mass.: MIT Press, 1983.

———. "Husserl and the Problem of Idealism." *Journal of Philosophy* 37 (Winter 1940): 5–18.

Alexander, Ian W. *Berqson, Philosopher of Reflection.* London: Bowes, 1957.

Apel, Karl-Otto. *Transformation der Philosophie.* 2 vols. Frankfurt a. M.: Suhrkamp Verlag, 1973.

Ave-Lallemant, Eberhard. *Die Nachlässe der Münchener Phänomenologen in der Bayerischen Staatsbibliothek.* Wiesbaden: Otto Harrassowitz, 1975.

———. "Die phänomenologische Reduktion in der Philosophie Max Schelers." "In Paul Good, Gegenwartsqeschehen.

Barth, Hans. "Max Scheler." In *Neue Schweizer Rundschau* 1 (1933–34): pp. 242–53.

Baumgart, David. "Some Merits and Defects of Contemporary German Ethics." *Philosophy* 13 (April 1938): pp. 183–95.

Baumgartner, Alois. "Max Scheler und der deutsche Sozialkatholizismus (1916–1921)." In Jahrbuch für christliche Sozialwissenschaften 20 (1979: pp. 39–57.

Barnes, Harry and Becker, Howard. *Contemporary Social Theory.* New York: Appleton-Century, 1940.

Becker, Howard. "Befuddled Germany—A Glimpse of Max Scheler." In *American Sociological Review* 8 (spring 1943): 209–11.

Becker, Howard and Dahlke, H. O. "Max Scheler's Sociology of Knowledge." In *Philosophy and Phenomenological Research* 2 (1941–2): pp. 310–22.

Bendersky, Joseph W. *Carl Schmitt: Theorist for the Reich.* Princeton, New Jersey: Princeton University Press, 1983.

Berger, Peter and Luckmann, Thomas. *The Social Construction of Reality, A Treatise in the Sociology of Knowledge.* New York: Doubleday, 1962.

Bergson, Henri. *Creative Evolution.* Translated by Arthur Mitchell. Westport, Conn.: Greenwood, 1975 (reprint of 1944 edition).

Bernstein, Richard J. *Praxis and Action: Contemporary Philosophies of Human Activity.* Philadelphia: University of Pennsylvania Press, 1971.

Bochenski, I. M. *Contemporary European Philosophy.* Translated by D. Nicholl and K. Aschenbrenner. Berkeley: University of California Press, 1956.

Booth, Meyrick. *Rudolf Eucken: His Philosophy and Influence.* New York: Scribner's, 1913.

Buber, Martin. *Das Problem des Menschen.* Heidelberg: Schneider, 1948.

――――. "The Philosophical Anthropology of Max Scheler." Translated by R. G. Smith. *Philosophy and Phenomenological Research* 1 (1946): pp. 207-11.

Cartwright, David. "Scheler's Criticism's [of Schopenhauer]." *Schopenhauer Jahr* 62 (1981): pp. 144-52.

Cassirer, Ernst. "'Spirit' and 'Life' in Contemporary Philosophy." Translated by Brettel and Paul Schlepp. In *The Philosophy of Ernst Cassirer*. Evanston: Library of Living Philosophers, 1949: pp. 855-88.

Clark, M. E. "Phenomenological Systems of Ethics." *Philosophy* 7 (1932): pp. 414-430 and 8 (1934): pp. 52-65.

Cohen, Carl. "The Road to Conversion." In *LBI Yearbook* 4 (1961): pp. 259-79.

Dallmayr, Fred R. *Twilight of Subjecticity: Contributions to a Post-Individualist Theory of Politics*. Amherst: University of Massachusetts Press, 1981.

Denninger, Erhard. *Rechtsperson und Solidarität*. Frankfurt A. M.: Alfred Metzner Verlag, 1967.

Deeken, Alphons, S. J. *Process and Permanence in Ethics: Max Scheler's Moral Philosophy*. New York: Paulist Press, 1974.

Dilthey, Wilhelm. *Meaning in History*. Translated by H. P. Rickman. London: Allen and Unwin, 1961.

――――. *Selected Writings*. Translated and edited by H. P. Rickman. Cambridege: Cambridge University, 1976.

Driesch, Hans. *Lebenserinnerungen*. Munich: Ernst Reinhardt Verlag, 1951.

Dunlop, Francis. "Scheler's Idea of Man: Phenomenology versus Metaphysics in the Late Works." *Aletheia* 2 (1981): pp. 220-34.

――――. "Scheler's Theory of Punishment." In *Journal of the British Society for Phenomenology* 9 N. 3 (October 1978): pp. 164-74.

Emad, Parvis. "Max Scheler's Notion of the Process of Philosophy." In *Southern Journal of Philosophy* 10 (Spring 1972): pp. 7-16.

――――. "The Great Themes of Scheler." In *Philosophy Today* 12 (Spring 1968): pp. 4-12.

Eucken, Rudolf. *The Individual and Society*. Translated by W. R. V. Brode. London: Unwin, 1923.

Farber, Marvin. "Max Scheler on the Place of Man in the Cosmos." *Philosophy and Phenomenological Research* 14 (March 1954): pp. 231-50.

――――. *Naturalism and Subjectivism*. Springfield, Ill.: Thomas, 1959.

――――. *Phenomenology and Existence: Towards a Philosophy within Nature*. New York: Harper and Row, 1967.

Fetscher, Irving. "Max Schelers Auffassung von Krieg and Frieden." In Paul Good, *Gegenwartsgeschehen*.

Fiand, Barbara. "An Appreciation of Max Scheler's Essay on Humility, Introduction and Commentary." *Aletheia* 2 (1981): pp. 200-9.

Flavell, J. H. *The Developmental Psychology of Jean Piaget*. Princeton: Princeton University Press, 1963.

Fleischmann, Karl. "Max Scheler und der Pazifismus." *Schweizerische Rundschau* 32 (1932-33): pp. 373-6.

Foucault, Michel. *The Archaeology of Knowledge*. Translated by A. M. Sheridan Smith. New York: Pantheon, 1972.

————. *Power/knowledge: Selected Interviews and Other Writings, 1972-1977*. Edited by Colin Gordon. Translated by Colin Gordon et al. New York: Pantheon, 1980.

Freud, Sigmund. *The Ego and the Id*. Vol. 19 of *The Complete Works of Sigmund Freud*. Translated by James Strachey, et al. London: Hogarth, 1947.

————. "Civilization and its Discontents." In *Complete Works* Vol. 20.

————. "Future of an Illusion." In *Complete Works* Vol. 19.

Frings, Manfred. *Max Scheler: A Concise Introducton to the World of a Great Thinker*. Pittsburgh: Duquesne University Press, 1965.

————. "Husserl and Scheler—Two Views on Intersubjecticity." In *The Journal of the British Society Phenomenology* 9 N. 3 (October 1978): pp. 143-9.

————. "Max Scheler: Rarely Seen Complexities in Phenomenology." In *Phenomenology in Perspective*. Edited by F. J. Smith. Kent, Ohio: Kent University Press, 1961.

————. "Max Scheler's Theory of Social Economy with Special Attention to its Ethical Implications." *Review of Social Economy* 23 (September 1965): 127-42.

————. "Non-Formal Ethics of Our Time." In *Philosophy Today* 9 (Summer 1965): pp. 85-93.

————. "Heidegger and Scheler." In *Philosophy Today* 12 (Spring 1968): pp. 27-39.

————. "Max Scheler: A Descriptive Analysis of the Concept of Ultimate Reality." *Ultimate Reality and Meaning* 3 (Spring 1980) pp. 135-43, 1980.

————. "Nothingness and Being. A Schelerian Comment on Heidegger." In *Radical Phenomenology*. Edited by John Sallis. Atlantic Highlands: Humanities Press, 1978.

————. *Person und Dasein: Zur Frage der Ontologie des Wertseins*. The Hague: Nijhoff, 1969.

————. "Towards the Constitution of the Unity of the Person." In *Linguistic Analysis and Phenomenology*. Edited by William Mays and S. C. Brown. Lewisburg: Bucknell University Press, 1972.

————. "Zur Idee des Friedens bei Kant und Max Scheler." In *Kantstudien* 66 (1975): pp. 85-101.

Funk, Roger, L. "Thought, Values, and Action." In *Centennial Essays*.

Friedrich, Carl J. "Phenomenology and Political Science." In Vol. 2 *Phenomenology and the Social Sciences*. Edited by Maurice Natanson. Evanston: Northwestern University Press, 1973.

Gadamer, Hans-Goerg. "Max-Scheler—der Verschwender." In Paul Good, *Gegenwartsgeschehen*.

————. *Philosophical Hermeneutics*. Translated and edited by David E. Linge. Berkeley: University of California Press, 1966.

————. *Philosophische Lehrijahre: Eine Rückschau*. Frankfurt a. M.: Klostermann, 1977.

————. *Truth and Method*. Translated by Sheed and Word Ltd. New York: Crossroad Publishing, 1982.

————. Various untitled reviews of forthcoming volumes of Scheler's *Gesammelte Werke*. *Philosophische Rundschau* 2 (1954): p. 237, 4 (1956): p. 248, 6 (1958): p. 158, 8 (1960): p. 312, 27 (1980): p. 299.

Gehlen, Arnold. "Ruckblick auf die Anthropologie Max Schelers." In Paul Good, *Gegenwartsqeschehen*.

————. "Über die Geburt der Freiheit aus der Entfremdung." *Archiv für Rechts- und Sozialphilosophie* 40 (1952–53) pp. 338–53.

Geiger, Moritz. "Zu Max Schelers Tode." In *Vossische Zeitung* June 1, 1928.

Germino, Dante. *Beyond Ideology: The Revival of Political Theory*. New York: Harper and Row, 1967.

Gibson, Boyce. *Rudolf Eucken's Philosophy of Life*. London: Adam and Charles Black, 1912.

Good, Paul. "Anschauung und Sprache. Vom Anspruch der Phänomenologie auf asymbolische Erkenntnis." In *Max Scheler im Gegenwartsgeschehen der Philosophie*. pp. 111–26. Edited by Paul Good. Bern: Francke Verlag, 1975.

Gusfield, Joseph R. "Mass Society and Extremist Politics." In *American Sociological Review* 27 (Feb. 1962): pp. 19–30.

Guthrie, Hunter. "Max Scheler's Epistemology of Emotions." In *Modern Schoolman* 16 (1939): pp. 51–4.

Habermas, Jürgen. *Knowledge and Human Interests*. Translated by Jeremy J. Shapiro. Boston: Beacon Press, 1972.

————. *Theory and Practice*. Translated by John Viertel. Boston: Beacon Press, 1973.

Hall, Calvin S. *A Primer of Freudian Psychology*. New York: World, 1954.

Hannah, Thomas, ed. *The Bergsonian Heritage*. New York: Columbia University Press, 1962.

Hartmann, Nicolai. "Max Scheler." *Kantstudien* 33 (1928): p. xiv.

Hartmann, Wilfried. *Max Scheler: Bibliographie*. Stuttgart: Friedrich Fromman Verlag, 1963.

————. "Scheler's Theory of the Person." *Philosophy Today* 12 (Spring 1968): pp. 246–61.

Haskamp, Reinhold J. *Spekulativer und phänomenologischer Personalismus*. Freiburg: Verlag Karl Alber, 1966.

Heath, Peter, "The Idea of a Phenomenological Ethics." In *Phenomenology and Understanding*. Edited by Edo Pivcevic. London: Cambridge University Press, 1975.

Hegel, Georg Wilhelm Friedrich. *The Phenomenology of Spirit*. Translated by A.V. Miller. Oxford: Clarendon Press, 1977.
———. *The Philosophy of Right*. Translated by T. M. Knox. Oxford: Clarendon, 1965.
Heidegger, Martin. "Andenken an Max Scheler." In Paul Good, *Gegenwartsgeschehen*.
———. *Being and Time*. Translated by John Macquarrie and Edward Robinson. London: SCM Press, 1962.
———. *The Essence of Reasons*. Translated by Terence Malick. Evanston, Illinois: Northwestern University Press, 1969.
———. *Heidegger: Basic Writings*. Edited by David Farrell Krell and Translated by David Krell et al. New York: Harper and Row, 1977.
Hildebrand, Dietrich von. "Max Scheler als Persoenlichkeit." In *Hochland* 27 (1928-9): pp. 70–80.
Hintze, Otto. "Max Schelers Ansichten über Geist und Gesellschaft." In *Gesammelte Abhandlungen*, Band 2: *Soziologie und Geschichte*. Göttingen: Vandenhoeck und Ruprecht, 1964.
Hirst, Paul Q. *Social Evolution and Social Categories*. New York: Holmes and Meier, 1976.
Hocke, Gustav Rene. "Scheler als Sokrates." *Die Zeit*. 36 (August 30, 1974): p. 16.
Honigsheim, Paul. "Max Scheler als Sozialphilosoph." *Kölner Vierteljahrsheft für Soziologie und Sozialwissenschaft* 8 N. 3 (1929): pp. 293–45.
Horkheimer, Max. "Bermerkungen zur philosophischen Anthopologie." *Zeitschrift für Sozialforschung* 4 N. 1 (1935): pp. 1–25.
———. "Ideologie und Wertgebung." In *Ideologie—Wessenschaft—Gesellschaft*. Edited by Hans-Joachim Lieber. Darmstadt: Minerva, 1976.
Hufnagel, Erwin. "Aspekte der Schelerschen Personlehre." *Kant-Studien* 65 (1974): pp. 436-56.
Hughes, H. Stuart. *Consciousness and Society: The Reorientation of European Social Thought, 1890-1930*. New York: Knopf, 1958.
Husserl, Edmund. *The Crisis of European Sciences and Transcendental Phenomenology*. Translated by David Carr. Evanston, Illinois: Northwestern University Press, 1970.
———. *Cartesian Meditations: An Introduction to Phenomenology*. Translated by Dorian Cairns. the Hague: Nijhoff, 1973.
———. *The Idea of Phenomenology*. Translated by W. P. Alston and G. Nakhnikian. The Hague: Nijhoff, 1966.
———. *Ideas: General Introduction to Pure Phenomenology*. Translated by W. R. Boyce Gibson. New York: Macmillan, 1931.
———. *Logical Investigations*. 2 vols. Translated by J. N. Findlay. New York: Humanities Press, 1970.
———. "Philosophy as Rigorous Science." In *Phenomenology and the Crisis of Philosophy*. Translated by Quentin Lauer. New York: Harper and Row, 1965.

Ingarden, Roman. *On the Motives which Led Husserl to Transcendental Idealism.* Translated by A. Hannibalsson. The Hague: Nijhoff, 1975.

Jaspers, Karl. *Man in the Modern Age.* [Die geistige Situation der Zeit.] Translated by Eden and Cedar Paul. London: Routledge and Kegan Paul, 1951.

de Jonge, Alex. *The Weimar Chronicle: Prelude to Hitler.* New York: Paddington, 1978.

Kant, Immanuel. *Critique of Practical Reason.* Translated by Lewis White Beck. Indianapolis: Bobbs-Merrill, 1956.

———. *Critique of Pure Reason.* Tranlated by N. K. Smith. New York: Humanities, 1929.

———. *Foundations of the Metaphysics of Morals.* Translated by Lewis White Beck. Indianapolis: Bobbs-Merrill, 1959.

Kanthack, Katharina. *Max Scheler: Zur Krisis der Ehrfurcht.* Berlin: Minerva Verlag, 1963.

Keller, Wilhelm. "Philosophische Anthropologie—Psychologie—Transzendenz." In *Neue Anthropologie.* Edited by Hans-Georg Gadamer and Paul Vogler. Stuttgart: Georg Thieme Verlag, 1975.

Kelly, Eugene. *Max Scheler.* Boston: Twayne Publishers, 1977.

Klumpp, Eberhard. "Der Begriff der Person und das Problem des Personalismus bei Max Scheler." Doctoral dissertation in philosophy. Tübingen, 1951.

Kohn, Hans. "Political Theory and the History of Ideas." *Journal of the History of Ideas* 25 N. 2 (1964): pp. 303–7.

Koster, Hans Dieter. "Max Schelers Beitrag zur Rechts- und Stattsphilosophie." Doctoral dissertation in philosophy. Hamburg, 1950.

Kraft, Julius. *Von Husserl Zu Heidegger: Kritik des phänomenologischen Philosophie.* Frankfurt a. M.: Öffentliches Leben, 1957.

Kuhn, Helmut. "Max Scheler als Faust." In Paul Good, *Gegenwartsgeschehen.*

———. "Politik als Wissenschaft." In *Politik und Wissenschaft.* Edited by Hans Maier, Klaus Ritter and Ulrich Matz. Munich: Beck, 1971.

Landgrebe, Ludwig. "Geschichtsphilosophische Perspektiven bei Scheler und Husserl." In Paul Good, *Gegenwartsgeschehen.*

———. *Major Problems in Contemporary European Philosophy.* Translated by Kurt Reinhardt. New York: Ungar, 1966.

———. "Phenomenology and Metaphysics." *Philosophy and Phenomenological Research* 16 (March 1967): pp. 197–205.

Landmann, Michael. *Philosophical Anthropology.* Translated by David J. Parent. Philadelphia: Westminster Press, 1974.

Laqueur, Walter. *Young Germany.* New York: Basic Books, 1962.

———. *Weimar: A Cultural History.* New York: Pantheon, 1974.

Lauer, Quentin. "The Phenomenological Ethics of Max Scheler." In *International Philosophical Quarterly* 1 (1961): pp. 273–300.

———. *Phenomenology: Its Genesis and Prospect.* New York: Harper and Row, 1965.

Lenk, Kurt. *Von der Ohnmacht des Geistes: Darstellung der Spätphilosophie Max Schelers*. Tübingen: Hopfer-Verlag, 1959.

————. "Schopenhauer und Scheler." In *Schopenhauer-Jahrbuch* 37 (1956): pp. 55–66.

————. "Soziologie und Ideologiekritik: Bemerkungen zur Marxismusdiskussion in der deutschen Soziologie von Simmel bis Mannheim." In *Kölner Zeitschrift für Soziologie und Sozialpsychologie*. 13 (1961): pp. 227–38.

Lieber, Hans-Joachim. "Bemerkung zur Wissenssoziologie Max Schelers." In Paul Good, *Gegenwartsqeschehen*.

Leiss, W. "Max Scheler's concept of *Herrschaftswissen*." In *Philosophical Forum*. 2 (Spring 1971): pp. 316–31.

Lotz, Johannes Bapt., S. J. "Person und Ontologie." In *Scholastik* 37 (1963): pp. 335–60.

Loewith, Karl. *From Hegel to Nietzsche*. Translated by David E. Green. New York: Holt, 1964.

————. "Max Scheler und das Problem einer philosophischen Anthropologie." In *Theologische Rundschau* 7 (Winter 1935): pp. 349–72.

Luebbe, Hermann. *Politische Philosophie in Deutschland: Studien zu Ihrer Geschichte*. Basel: Benno Schwabe Verlag, 1963.

Lukacs, Georg. *History and Class Consciousness*. Translated by Rodney Livingston. Cambridge, Mass.: MIT, 1971.

Luther, Arthur. "The Articulated Unity of Being in Scheler's Phenomenology." In *Max Scheler (1874–1928) Centennial Essays*. Edited by Manfred Frings. The Hague: Nihjoff, 1974.

————. "Scheler's Interpretation of Being as Loving." In *Philosophy Today* 14 (Fall 1970): pp. 217–28.

Luetzler, Heinrich. "Ein Genie—Max Scheler." In his *Persönlichkeiten*. Freiburg: Herder, 1978.

————. *Der Philosoph Max Scheler*. (pamphlet) Bonn: Bouvier, 1947.

Mader, Wilhelm. *Max Scheler*. Reinbeck bei Hamburg: Rowohlt Taschenbuch Verlag, 1980.

Makkreel, Rudolf A. *Dilthey: Philosopher of the Human Studies*. Princeton: Princeton University Press, 1975.

Mannheim, Karl. *Essays on the Sociology of Knowledge*. Edited by Paul Kecskemeti. London: Routledge & Kegan Paul, 1952.

————. *Ideology and Utopia: An Introduction to the Sociology of Knowledge*. Translated by L. Wirth and E. Shils. New York: Harcourt Brace Jovanich, 1938.

————. *Man and Society in an Age of Reconstruction*. London: Routledge & Kegan Paul, 1940.

Marcel, Gabriel. *Creative Fidelity*. Translated by Robert Rosthal. New York: Crossroad, 1982.

————. *Man Against Mass Society*. Translated by G. S. Fraser. Chicago: Regery, 1962.

————. *Problematic Man.* Translated by Brian Thompson. New York: Berder & Herder, 1967.

Marcuse, Herbert. "Contribution to a Phenomenology of Historical Materialism." *Telos* 4 (Autumn, 1969): pp. 37–68.

————. *Eros and Civilization: A Philosophical Inquiry into Freud.* New York: Vintage, 1962.

————. *Reason and Revolution: Hegel and the Rise of Social Theory.* Boston: Beacon Press, 1960.

Marx Karl and Engels, Friedrich. *The Marx-Engels Reader.* Edited by Robert C. Tucker. New York: Norton, 1978.

Meja, Volker. "The Sociology of Knowledge and the Critique of Ideology." *Cultural Hermeneutics* 3 (May, 1975): pp. 51–75.

Merleau-Ponty, Maurice. *Adventures of the Dialectic.* Translated by Joseph Bien. Evanston: Northwestern University Press, 1973.

————. "Christianity and Ressentiment." In the *Review of Existential Psychology and Psychiatry* 9 (Winter, 1968): pp. 1–22.

————. *Phenomenology, Language and Sociology: Selected Essays of Maurice Merleau-Ponty.* Edited by John O'Neill. London: Heinemann, 1974.

Meyer, Herbert. "A Critical Study of Max Scheler's Philosophical Anthropology in Relation to his Phenomenology." Doctoral dissertation in philosophy at Boston University, 1972.

Misch, Georg. *Lebensphilosophie und Phänomenologie: eine Auseinandersetzung der Diltheyschen Richtung mit Heidegger und Husserl.* (Reprint of 1929 edition.) Stuttgart: Teubner, 1967.

Masse, George L. *The Crisis of German Ideology.* New York: Brosset & Dunlap, 1964.

Mounier, Emmanuel. *Personalism.* Translated by P. Mairer. Notre Dame, Indiana: University of Notre Dame Press, 1952.

Mueller, Max. "Person und Funktion." In *Philosophisches Jahrbuch* 69 (1962): pp. 371–404.

Nietzsche, Friedrich. *Beyond Good and Evil.* Translated by Marianne Cowan. Chicago: Gateway, 1955.

————. *Thus Spake Zarathustra.* Translated by R. J. Hollingdale. New York: Penguin, 1961.

————. *Twilight of the Idols and the Anti-Christ.* Translated by R. J. Hollingdale. New York: Penguin, 1961.

————. *The Will to Power.* Translated by Walter Kaufmann and R. J. Hollingdale. New York: Vintage, 1968.

Nota, John, S. J. "Max Scheler's Philosophy of History." In the *Proceedings of the XIV International Congress of Philosophy: Vienna September, 1968.* Vienna: Herder, 1969.

Oesterreicher, John. "Max Scheler: Critic of Modern Man." In *Five in Search of Wisdom.* Notre Dame, Indiana: University of Notre Dame Press, 1962.

Orth, Ernst Wolfgang. "Husserl, Scheler, Heidegger. Eine Einführung in das Problem der philosophischen Komparistik." In *Husserl, Scheler,*

Heidegger in der Sicht neuer Quellen. Edited by Ernst Wolfgang Orth. Freiburg: Karl Alber—Phänomenologische Forschungen, 1978.

Perrin, Ronald. "Max Scheler's Concept of the Person: Towards a Radical Humanism." Doctoral dissertation in philosophy at the University of California, San Diego, 1971.

Pintor-Ramos, Antonio. "Max Scheler en el pensamiento hispanico." In *Revista de Occidente Agosto* (Spring 1974): pp. 40–61.

Plessner, Helmuth. "Erinnerungen an Max Scheler." In Paul Good *Gegenwartsgeschehen.*

———. *Husserl in Göttingen.* Göttinger Universitätsreden xxiv. Göttingen: Vandenhoeck & Ruprecht, 1959.

Ranly, Ernst. "Ethics in Community." In th *Proceedings of the American Catholic Philosophical Association* (1968): pp. 152–8.

———. *Scheler's Phenomenology of Community.* The Hague: Nijhoff, 1966.

Reinach, Adolf. *Was ist Phänomenologie?* Munich: Kösel-Verlag, 1951.

Ricoeur, Paul. "Phenomenology of Freedom." In *Phenomenology and Philosophical Understanding.* Cambridge: Cambridge University Press, 1975.

Ringer, Fritz. *The Decline of the German Mandarins: The German Academic Community, 1890–1933.* Cambridge: Harvard University Press, 1969.

Roazen, Paul. *Freud: Political and Social Thought.* New York: Vintage, 1970.

Rombach, Heinrich. "Die Erfahrung der Freiheit: Phänomenologie und Metaphysik in Widerstreit und Versöhnung." In Paul Good *Gegenwartsgeschehen.*

Rothacker, Erich. *Schelers Durchbruch in die Wirklichkeit.* Bonn: Kistler, 1949.

Schaeffers, Bernhard. "Christentum und Sozialismus: Ein Briefwechsel Zwischen Max Scheler und Johann Plenge." In *Soziale Welt* (1966 Vol. 17): pp. 66–78.

Schlipp, Paul Arthur. "The 'Doctrine of Illusion' and 'Error' in Scheler's Phenomenology." *Journal of Philosophy* (Fall 1927): pp. 624–33.

———. "Max Scheler." *Journal of Philosophy* 35 (1929): pp. 574–88.

———. "The 'Formal Problems' of Scheler's Sociology of Knowledge." *Philosophy Review* 36 (1927): pp. 101–20.

Schmitt, Carl. *The Concept of the Political.* Translated by George Schwab with Comments by Leo Strauss. New Brunswick, New Jersey: Rutgers University Press, 1976.

———. *Politische Romantik.* Munich: Dunker & Humbolt, 1919.

Schneck, Stephen F. "Towards a Schelerian Politics: The Concept of Community in the Works of Max Scheler." Master's thesis in Government at the Unversity of Notre Dame, 1980.

Schoeps, Hans Joachim. "Die Stellung des Menschen im Kosmos." In Paul Good, *Gegenwartsgeschehen.*

Schuster, George N. "Introductory Statement to a Symposium on the Significance of Max Scheler for Philosophy and Social Science." *Philosophy*

and Phenomenological Research 2 (1942): pp. 1–8.
Schutz, Alfred. "Max Scheler's Epistemology and Ethics." *The Review of Metaphysics* 11 (1957): pp. 304–14 and 12 (1958): pp. 486–501.
———. "Max Scheler's Philosophy." In *The Collected Papers of Alfred Schutz: Volume 3.* Edited by Maurice Natanson. The Hague: Nijhoff, 1962.
———. "The Problem of Social Reality." Ibid. Volume 1.
———. "Scheler's Theory of Intersubjectivity and the General Thesis of the Alter Ego." Ibid.
Sheehan, Thomas. "Introduction to Scheler on Heidegger." *Listening* 12 (Fall 1977): pp. 61–73.
Smith, F. J. "Being and Subjectivity: Heidegger and Husserl." In *Phenomenology in Perspective.* Edited by F. J. Smith. The Hague: Nijhoff, 1970.
———. "Peace and Pacifism." In *Max Scheler (1874–1928) Centennial Essays.* Edited by Manfred Frings. The Hague: Nijhoff, 1974.
———. "Scheler's Critique of Husserl's Theory of the World of the Natural Standpoint." *Modern Schoolman* 55 (May 1978): pp. 387–96.
Spengler, Oswald. *The Decline of the West.* 2 vols. Translated by Charles Francis Atchinson. New York: Knopf, 1932.
Spiegelberg, Herbert. *The Phenomenological Movement.* Two vols. The Hague: Nijhoff, 1971.
Stark, Werner. *The Sociology of Knowledge.* London: Routledge and Kegan Paul, 1958.
Staude, John R. *Max Scheler: An Intellectual Portrait.* New York: Free Press, 1967.
Stein, Edith. "Von den Studienjahren in Göttingen." In *Edith Steins Werke. Band VII: Aus dem Leben einer judischen Familie.* Edited by L. Gelber, et al. Freiburg: Herder, 1965.
Stern, Fritz. *The Politics of Cultural Despair.* Berkeley: University of California Press, 1961
Strasser, Erich. *Phenomenology of Feeling.* Pittsburgh: Duquesne Press, 1977.
Strauss, Leo. *The City and Man.* Chicago: University of Chicago Press, 1969.
———. *What is Political Philosophy?* Chicago: University of Chicago Press, 1961.
Tallon, Andrew. "Love in the Heart Tradition." In *Phenomenology and the Understanding of Human Destiny.* Edited by Stephen Skousgaard. Washington: American University Press, 1981.
Theunissen, Michael. *Der Andere.* Berlin: Walter de Gruyter, 1965.
———. "Wetterstum und Stille. Über die Weltdeutung Schelers und ihr Verhältnis zum Seinsdenken." In Paul Good, *Gegenwartsgeschehen.*
Toennies, Ferdinand. *Comunity and Society.* Translated by Charles P. Loomis. New York: Harper and Row, 1963.
Turski, G. K. "Some Considerations on Intersubjectivity and Language." *Gnosis* 1 (Spring 1979): pp. 29–44.
Tymieniecka, Anna-Teresa. *Phenomenology and Science n Contemporary European Thought.* New York: Farrar, Straus & Cadahy, 1962.

Vacek, Edward. "Max Scheler's Anthropology." *Philosophy Today* 23 (Spring 1979): pp. 238–48.

Voegelin, Eric. *Anamnesis*. Translated by Gerhart Niemeyer. Notre Dame, Ind.: University of Notre Dame Press, 1978.

——. *From Enlightenment to Revolution*. Edited by John H. Hallowell. Durham, N. Carolina: Duke University Press, 1975.

Von Wiese, Benno. *Ich erzähle mein Leben*. Frankfurt a. M.: Insel, 1982.

Von Wiese, Leopold. "Max Scheler: Einige persönliche Erinnerungen." *Kölner Vierteljahrshefte für Sozialwissenschaften* 7 (Fall 1928).

Weber, Max. *The Protestant Ethic and the Spirit of Capitalism*. Translated by Talcott Parsons. New York: Scribner's, 1958.

——. *The Methodology of the Social Sciences*. Translated by E. Schils and H. Finch. New York: Free Press, 1949.

Willard, Dallas. "The Paradox of Logical Psychologism: Husserl's Way Out." *American Philosophical Quarterly* 9 (January 1972): pp. 94–100.

Willer, Joerg. "Der Bezug auf Husserl im Frühwerk Schelers." *Kantstudien* 72 (Spring 1981): pp. 175–85.

Wojtyla, Karol (Pope John Paul II). *The Acting Person*. Translated by Adrzej Potocki. Dordrecht: Riedel, 1979.

——. *Toward a Philosophy of Praxis: An Anthology*. Edited by Alfred Bloch and George Czuczka. New York: Crossroad, 1981.

Wust, Peter. "Am Grabe Max Schelers." *Kölnische Volkzeitung*. June 16, 1928.

——. "Gestalten und Gedanken." In his *Gesammelte Werke: Band V*. Edited by Wilhelm Vernekohl, et al. Muenster: Verlag Regensburg, 1967.

——. Various letters concerning Scheler to editors, Academics and so forth, in his *Gesammelte Werke, Band X: Vorlesungen und Briefe*.

Zaner, Richard M. *The Concept of Self: A Phenomenological Inquiry Using Medicine as a Clue*. Athens, Ohio: Ohio University Press, 1981.

——. *The Way of Phenomenology: Criticism as a Philosophical Debate*. Indianapolis: Pegasus, 1970.

Name Index

179

Subject Index

188 *Subject Index*

the other as subject 60–61
person as subject 49–51
Subject/object dichotomy 22, 25, 27, 31, 34, 36, 48, 50, 51, 117, 119
Subjectivism 4, 27
Sublimation 52
Sympathy 10, 62–64

T

Technology 107
Teleology 53, 95
Theory/practice dichotomy 108
Transcendence 23, 29, 35, 131, 138–139
Transcendental ego 28–29, 36, 48, 50
Transformation 53, 54–57, 59–60, 61, 76, 84, 102, 121, 123, 132, 134–135
    in genesis of person 53, 114, 115, 121, 132
    in modal levels of life 54–57
    of politics 61, 76, 84, 132
    problem of 134–135
    of sociality 59–60, 102, 123, 132

U

Understanding 62
Universality 109–110
Utility values [Modal level of value, see table p. 55.] 80, 96–97, 98, 106–108, 114, 115, 116, 118, 132

V

Values (real values) 8, 10, 17, 42, 51, 52, 69, 71, 74, 78–79, 87, 94, 96–97, 99, 103–108, 118, 120, 128, 131–132, 138–139
    and acts 51–52, 107, 131
    and cognition 42–43, 112–113
    and ethics 64–65, 107
    inversion of 106–107, 118

order of 71, 107 [See table of modal levels, p. 55.]
    and politics 85–86, 96–97, 99, 103–107, 131–132
    positive values 103, 104–106
    negative values 103–106
Value perception 134, 135–140
Vegetative life [Modal level of Life, see table p. 55.] 54
Verstehen 62, 66. *See also* Understanding
    Dilthey's understanding of 20
Vicarious feeling 63. Modal level of sympathy, *see* table p. 55.
Virtu 81
Virtue 107
Vital values 81, 86–87, 107–108. Modal level of value, *see* table p. 55
    and politics 87–87.
Volntarism 3, 112

W

Wandervögel 114
War 10, 11, 75
Weimar Republic 7, 13, 14, 97, 114, 115
Weltanschauung 21–22
Wesensanschauung (essential insight) [See also Ideation.] 20, 42–43
    as deactualizing process 43
Will 41, 110, 112
World 51–52, 66–74
    as constellation of objects 66
    as history 79–74
    as medium for person 52, 66
    as nature 66–69
World War I 9, 10, 11, 13, 90, 91
    as catharsis for cultural rebirth 91

Y

Youth movement 114